AN 1864 DIRECTORY AND GUIDE

TO NEVADA'S

AURORA

EMBRACING A GENERAL DIRECTORY OF BUSINESSES,
RESIDENTS, MINES, STAMP MILLS, TOLL ROADS, ETC.,
INCLUDING AN ACCOUNT OF THE GRAND CELEBRATION
OF JULY 4, 1864, AND A BRIEF HISTORY OF THE

WIDE WEST MINE

COMPILED FROM THE MOST AUTHENTIC SOURCES BY

Clifford Alpheus Shaw

To my sister Cathy
For caring

Copyright © 2009 by Clifford Alpheus Shaw
All Rights Reserved

ISBN 1442138211
EAN-13 978-1442138216

This book is a revised and expanded edition of the author's *Boom Town Directory and Ghost Town Guide to Nevada's Aurora* published in 2006.

The cover and book content design are by the author. All photographs are by the author unless otherwise noted. The cover's black and white photo overlay of 1890 Aurora is courtesy of the Nevada State Museum, Carson City, Nevada Department of Cultural Affairs.

The author would like to thank the Nevada Historical Society in Reno for their assistance and support; Mary McKeough for sharing her photographs and recollections about Aurora; Bob Stewart for sharing his knowledge about Aurora; Fred Frampton for his help in developing the Residents of Aurora list; and Jack Scott for his support of the author's volunteer work at Bridgeport which resulted in many of the photographs used in this book. For a brief description of the author, see page 227.

CONTENTS

LIST OF MAPS..v

PREFACE...vii

INTRODUCTION..1

FLUSH TIMES..3
    MAP LOCATION INDEX..11
    AURORA TIMELINE 1860 TO 1960..........................13

DIRECTORY..15
    THE GRAND CELEBRATION OF JULY 4, 1864......59

DULL TIMES...153

RESIDENTS OF AURORA 1861-1864....................163

NOTES..204

BIBLIOGRAPHY...205

NEWSPAPER ARTICLES ABOUT AURORA........209

DIRECTORY INDEX...225

MAPS

BRADY'S MAP OF AURORA & ESMERALDA 1862……….4

STREET AND BUILDING LOCATION MAP 1864…………10

TOWNS AND ROADS NEAR AURORA 1864…………….106

TOWNS AND ROADS NEAR AURORA TODAY………...107

LOCATION OF THE WIDE WEST VEIN…………….…..144

SANBORN & PERRIS MAP OF AURORA 1890…………..154

AERIAL PHOTOGRAPH OF AURORA 1940……………..160

Frashers Fotos, Pomona, California

PREFACE

My fascination with the ghost town of Aurora, Nevada, began when I first saw the photograph on the left sixteen years ago. I was visiting Bodie State Historic Park and a park ranger asked me if I wanted to see some old photographs of the ghost town of Aurora. When he showed me this haunting image of three men standing in front of a brick saloon I was suddenly taken aback. Who were these people and how could such an imposing brick structure as this just vanish? I later learned the three men—Andy Anderson, Gus Peterson and Fried Walker—were miners posing for the renowned postcard photographer Burton Frasher (1888-1955) in front of Aurora's Merchants' Exchange Saloon on Antelope Street during 1927.

As I looked at them they looked back at me and I thought I heard one of them say: "Hundreds were born here, thousands lived and worked here, and hundreds are buried here—don't let them forget." I had already visited the abandoned town site a few times and I remember thinking that since there were no standing buildings left, Aurora could not have been that large or important. Because nearby Bodie, California, had many buildings left to see, Bodie must have been far more interesting and important in its day than Aurora.

However, after a decade and a half of extensive research on the history of Aurora I can now say my first impression was wrong. As the old saying goes—"You can't judge a book by its cover." Even without her buildings, Aurora is one of the most colorful and historically important old town sites in the American West. One must imagine Aurora as it once was in its former glory to understand and appreciate the old town, which is precisely why I wrote this book.

INTRODUCTION

Underneath a thick cover of sagebrush, many miles from civilization, lay the shattered and buried remains of one of Nevada's earliest and most important mining towns. Looking out over the deserted landscape today, it's hard to imagine that during the Civil War, Aurora was home to over five thousand people. During the town's sixty-year existence from 1860 to 1920, hundreds were born, thousands lived and prospered, and hundreds were buried in a place now lost and forgotten. Where once stood a thousand buildings of wood, stone, and brick, not a single structure remains standing today. As one visitor commented, Aurora was the "most gone town" he had ever seen.

An 1864 Directory and Guide to Nevada's Aurora

Gone as it is today, try and image the Herculean effort it took to transform this largely unexplored wilderness into a booming, full-blown city brimming with everything you see listed in this book's directory. All this stuff, all these people, had to be hauled in by wagons from all corners of California and Nevada over treacherous mountain passes on roads built especially for Aurora. And most amazing of all, these resourceful pioneers managed to accomplish all this in only three years!

This book attempts to convey the enormity of what Aurorans once achieved by including descriptions of the town's former businesses, organizations, and buildings listed alphabetically much like a modern phone directory. In an effort to recreate the sense of excitement and optimism that once existed, many first-hand accounts written by visiting newspaper correspondents have been included.

Aurora's "remains" are located along remote dirt roads about seventeen miles east of Bridgeport, California, in Mineral County, Nevada (see map on page 107). Although portions of the town are located on private property, most of Aurora's remaining historic ruins are located on National Forest lands administered by the Humboldt-Toiyabe National Forest. Aurora's historic importance was recognized in 1974 when the entire town site was placed on the National Register of Historic Places. Federal law prohibits the removal of any historic artifact.

FLUSH TIMES

The explosive surge from frontier wilderness to frontier city made Aurora a household word to most Californians in the early 1860s. It all started during the late summer of 1860 when three prospectors gazed in amazement at gleaming white walls of gold-laden quartz veins protruding some thirty feet above the ground. The Esmeralda Mining District was born and only a few years later Aurora was one of the largest and most important cities east of the Sierra Nevada Mountains.

The town's phenomenal growth attracted newspaper correspondents from all over the west (see the Annotated List of Newspaper Articles about Aurora from 1860 to 1864 starting on page 209). Since the citizens and government of California believed Aurora was located within their state, descriptions of the town's rapid growth frequently appeared in most of the state's leading newspapers:

> *Our population has doubtless doubled within the last two months, and for the most part the increase has been made up of sturdy miners, mechanics and merchants, with a sprinkling to be seen of lawyers, sporting men, etc. A walk through our streets in the evening reminds one forcibly of the early days of California.* (San Francisco *Alta California,* May 29, 1863)

An 1864 Directory and Guide to Nevada's Aurora

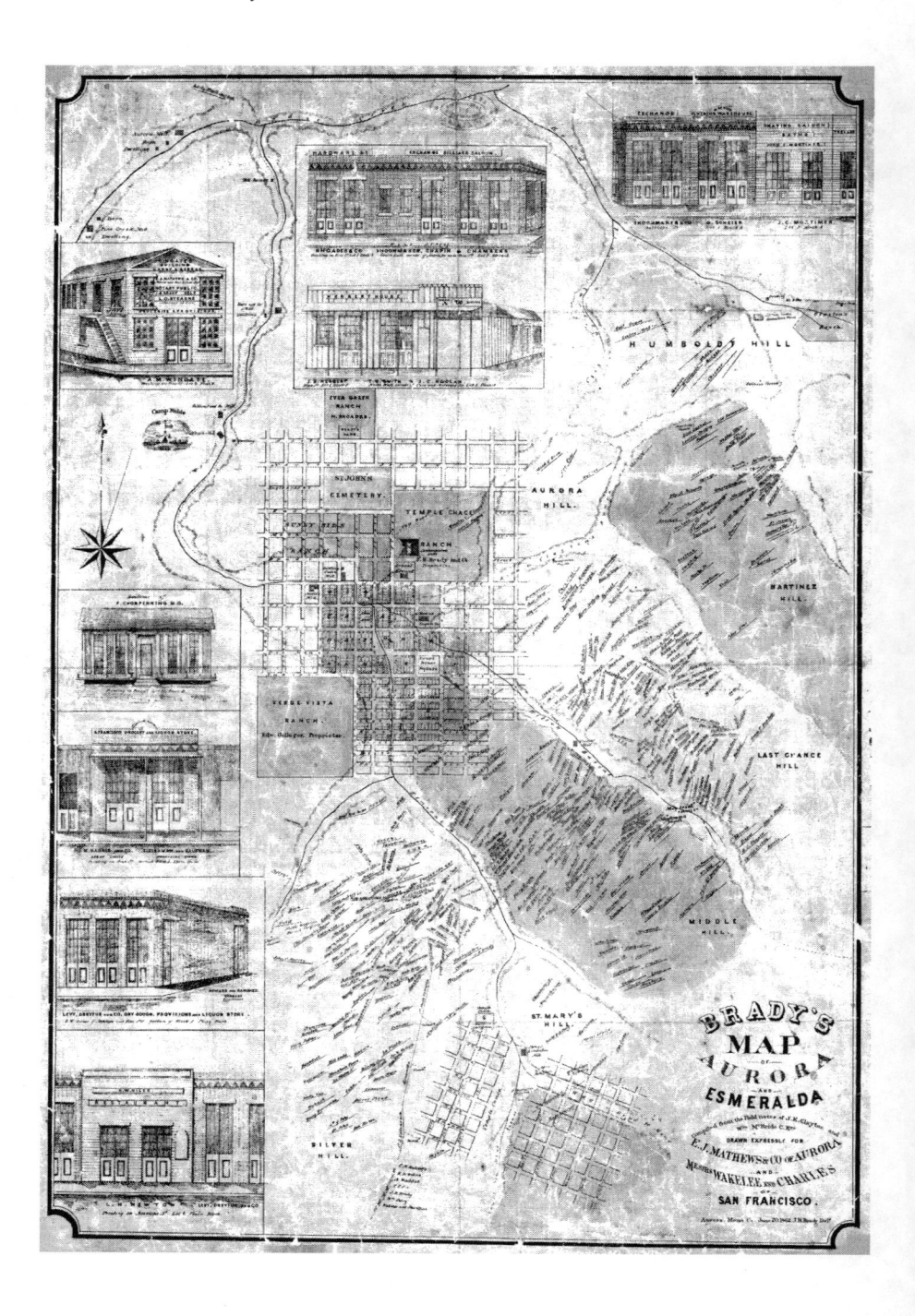

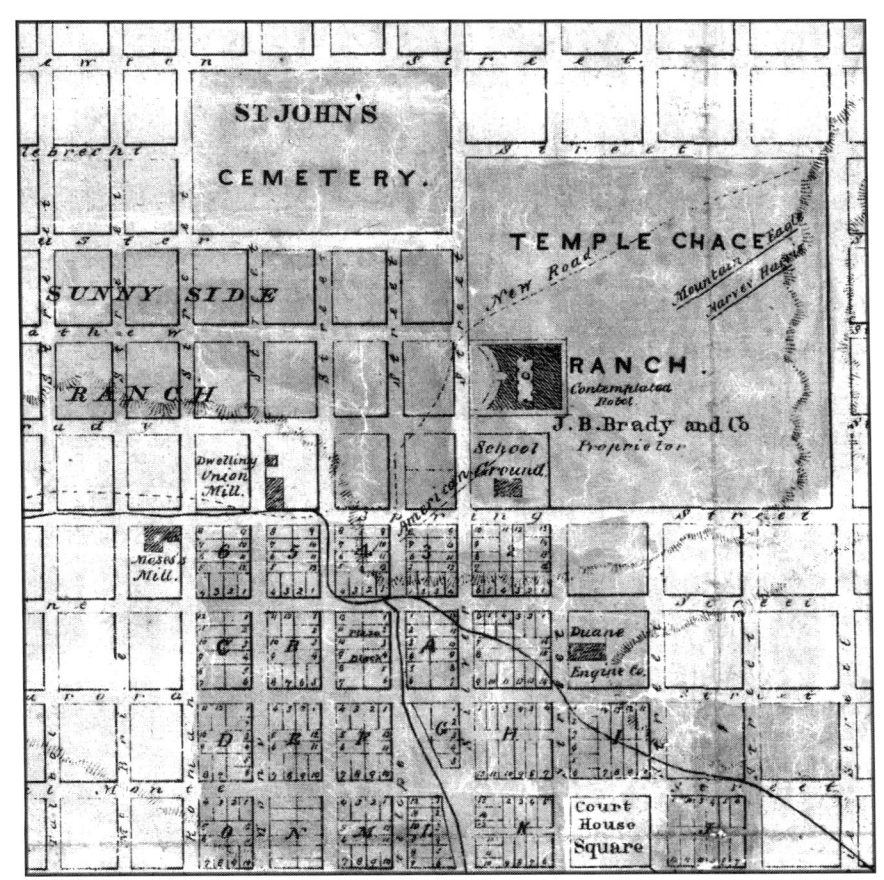

Above is a detail of downtown Aurora from "Brady's Map of Aurora and Esmeralda" shown on the left. Originally printed in color during June 1862, the map was derived from the field notes of J. E. Clayton and Wm. McBride (see page 139). Aurora's two major thoroughfares—Pine and Antelope Streets—are located immediately to the north (up) and west (left) respectively of lot block "A" in the center of the above image. The "Contemplated Hotel" in Temple Chace Park was never built, and the "School Ground" near the proposed hotel was later located west of "Court House Square." (Nevada in Maps online image collection from the Mary B. Ansari Map Library, DeLaMare Library, University of Nevada, Reno. The original map is from the Nevada Historical Society.)

In an article entitled "Flush Times of a Mining Town" a correspondent calling himself "A Forty-Niner" described Aurora's atmosphere:

> *The stranger, entering this place for the first time, is favorably reminded, by the stir and activity that everywhere prevail, of the good times of '49 and '50. We have here, moreover, other characteristics of those "flush times"—rough and ready business habits, plenty of money in circulation among all classes, frequent mining excitements occasioned by "rich strikes" and new leads: and, what is not so desirable, any quantity of gambling hells and whisky shops, with the usual allurements of the olden time in frontier mining camps.*(San Francisco *Daily Evening Bulletin,* May 26, 1863)

Another visitor noted that houses seemed to pop-up overnight:

> *Aurora is increasing in prosperity every day, and approaching with rapid strides the importance of its mountain sister, Virginia. I arrived here some two months ago, and since that time nearly 100 houses have sprung up, as if by enchantment— sometime three or four in a night! I have never seen a mining camp whose population has increased so rapidly as that of Aurora.* (San Francisco *Daily Evening Bulletin,* July 31, 1863)

Because timber was in short supply, and the raw materials needed to make bricks were plentiful and nearby, brick buildings were springing up all over town:

> *Aurora is only thirty months old and has a population of between three and four thousand. There are seven hundred and sixty-one buildings within the city limits, sixty-four of the number being brick (ten of which are of two and three story).*(Sacramento *Daily Union,* August 6, 1863)

Flush Times

Aurora reached the peak of her prosperity and development just after the great Civil War battles of Gettysburg and Vicksburg in the summer of 1863. Booming Aurora, and her close rival Virginia City, reveled in these "flush times." The following description of Virginia City from Mark Twain's *Roughing It* captures the sense of adventure and excitement both cities felt simultaneously:

> *The sidewalks swarmed with people—to such an extent, indeed, that it was generally no easy matter to stem the human tide. The streets themselves were just as crowded with quartz wagons, freight teams, and other vehicles. The procession was endless. So great was the pack that buggies frequently had to wait half an hour for an opportunity to cross the principal street. Joy sat on every countenance, and there was a glad, almost fierce, intensity in every eye, that told of the money—getting schemes that were seething in every brain and the high hope that held sway in every heart. Money was as plenty as dust; every individual considered himself wealthy, and a melancholy countenance was nowhere to be seen...The 'flush times' were in magnificent flower!*

Although the town's population had already begun to decline, Aurora's business and building development peaked during the fall of 1863. The following summary of how Aurora looked at this exciting point in time comes from a California newspaper article:

> *The present population is about 3,500, and increasing daily. The town contains about 700 houses, 47 of which are brick, one-half of that number are of two and three stories–many of them are not only substantial, but really beautiful, and would do credit even to San Francisco. The business of the town is divided as follows: 30 provision stores, 42 drinking saloons, 3 drug stores, 10 dry goods stores, 3 hardware stores, 4 tin*

shops, 12 blacksmith shops, 1 express office, post office, 4 meat markets, 7 tobacco and cigar stands, 4 livery stables, 3 baker shops, 5 boot and shoe maker shops, 3 barber shops, 4 confectioners, 2 boot-blacks, 3 saddler and harness makers, 5 gambling saloons, 4 hotels, 7 restaurants, 1 dentist, 1 daguerrean room, 3 breweries, 17 lawyers, 15 physicians, 2 assayers, 1 Masonic and 1 Odd Fellow's Association, 2 fire companies, and 1 brass band of 13 pieces. (Sonora *American Flag,* October 25, 1863)

The article went on to state that Aurora's population included 250-300 women, 80-100 children, 50 Chinese, and 10-12 African Americans. About 700 men were employed in 68 incorporated tunnel companies and mining shafts. There were nine ore-crushing stamp mills in operation and two huge stamp mills, the Del Monte costing $150,000, and the Antelope costing $100,000, currently under construction. The current gold and silver bullion production was about $110,000 per month.

The following historic photograph, map, and directory are presented to give today's visitor to Aurora a sense of what it must have been like to visit this booming city during these "flush times." The town's more interesting and important buildings and businesses have been noted on the following photograph and map, and are indexed to entries in the directory. The symbol **[R]** next to a listing in the directory indicates that ruins, typically the remains of a building foundation or piles of bricks and lumber, exist at that particular site today.

The photograph of Aurora on the next page was taken from the prominent rock outcrop known as Lover's Leap about 1890, and is courtesy of the Nevada State Museum, Carson City. Because most of Aurora's buildings had either been moved to other mining camps like Bodie, or were destroyed by fire by the time this photograph was taken, less than one quarter of the buildings that existed during the mid 1860s are present in this image. Last Chance Hill was the site of Aurora's two leading mines—the Wide West and the Real del Monte.

Flush Times

An 1864 Directory and Guide to Nevada's Aurora

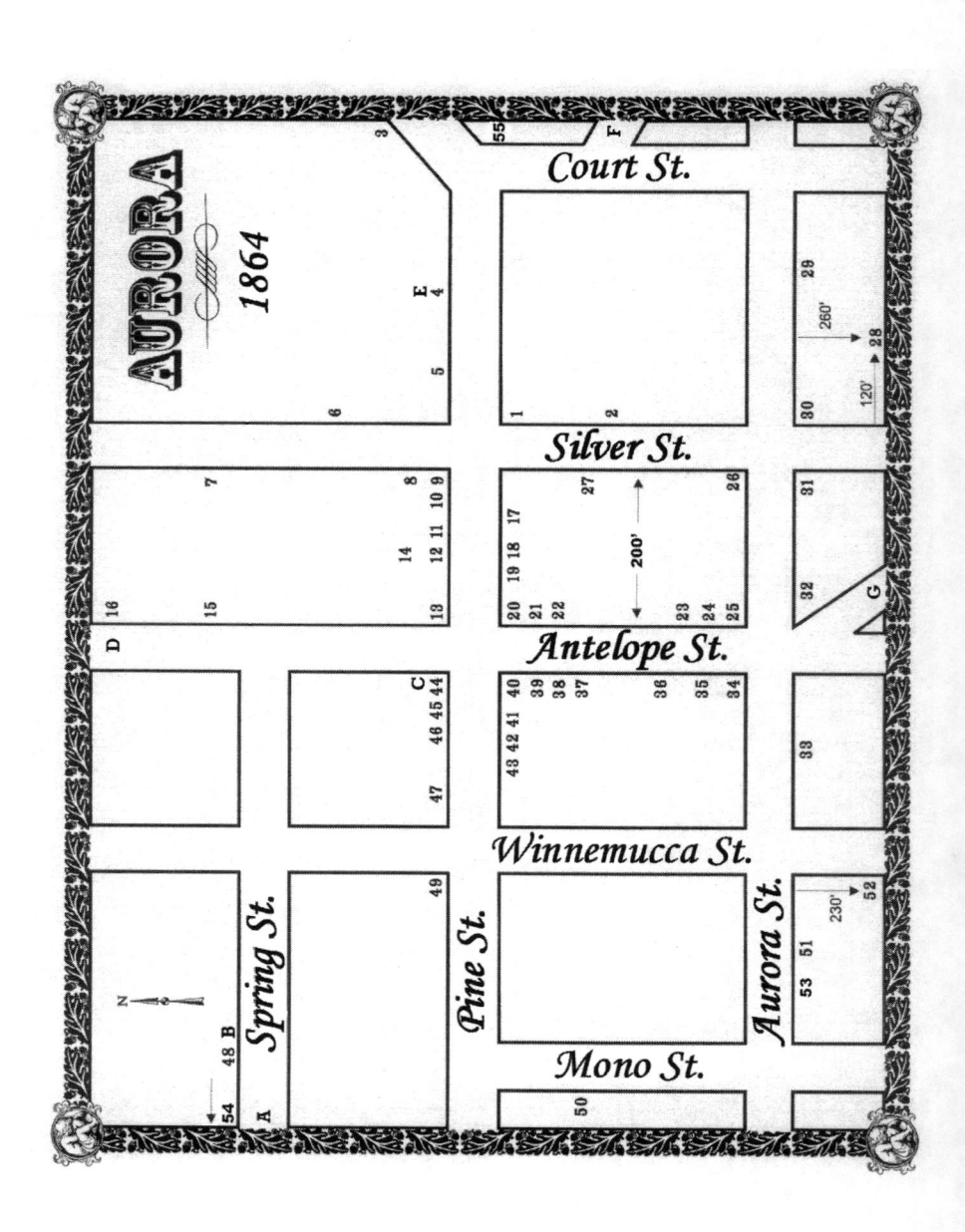

Flush Times

MAP LOCATION INDEX

A- Road down Esmeralda Gulch to Del Monte Canyon and Bodie
B- Existing wood head-frame from old stamp mill circa early 1900s
C- Existing concrete wall once part of old power substation
D- Road to Fletcher, Hawthorne, Bridgeport, or Carson City
E- Existing rock walls once part of Bradford's Brick Store
F- Wide West Street to Owens River/Benton Road
G- Road to Esmeralda Camp and Mono Lake
1- Courthouse
2- Pioneer Bakery; Dr. Mastny, Dentist
3- Mark Twain's Cabin on Pine
4- Bradford's Brick Store (City Meat Mrkt); Reed's Photo Gallery
5- Cooper and Graves Blacksmith Shop; Randolph's Blacksmith
6- Aurora Daily Times
7- Armory Hall
8- Van Wych and Winchester Assay Office
9- Dreyfus and Lauer's Store
10- Molineux Hardware Store
11- Wingate Hall
12- John Neidy's Brick Building; Danniz Saloon
13- Bechtel Notary; Gem Saloon; Levison and Co's Saloon
14- Mono County Jail
15- Centre Meat Market Store
16- Cardinell's Dance Hall
17- Wells Fargo Office; Garesche Banker; Schwartz's Books
18- Green's Drug Store; Mortimer & Huff Barbers
19- Rhodes & Co.'s Hardware Store
20- Exchange Saloon
21- Schier's Store
22- Teel & Wand's Saloon
23- Kimball & Canfield's Store; Fraternal Organizations
24- Kennedy & Porter's Saloon; Harrison's Jewelry Store

An 1864 Directory and Guide to Nevada's Aurora

25- Fire Department; Tremont Hotel
26- San Francisco House; Hefs & Demming's Saloon
27- Wm. T. Gough, Attorney; Petit and Parry Building Contractors
28- Public Schoolhouse
29- Methodist Church
30- St. Charles Hotel
31- Geneley's Store
32- Fashion Stable
33- Esmeralda Daily Union
34- Esmeralda Exchange Saloon; Woodcliff's Stationery Store
35- Carter & Crocker's Store
36- Pioneer Drug Store; San Francisco Saloon; Dr. Collins/Reims
37- Barnum Hotel; Washington Baths
38- Post Office; Pioneer Book Store; Armstrong Stock Broker
39- Barnum Restaurant
40- Levy & Co.'s Aurora Emporium Store
41- Sanchez & Howard Bankers
42- Fleishman & Kaufman's Store
43- Exchange Stable
44- Caro, Galland & Co.'s Store; Excelsior Book Store
45- Herbert House Hotel
46- Union Stable
47- American Hotel; Dublin City Store
48- Union Foundry and Blacksmith Shop
49- Merchants' Exchange Hotel, Saloon and Restaurant
50- Levy & Co.'s Residence
51- Sanchez's Residence
52- Baptist Church
53- Fried Walker's Residence circa 1940s
54- To Mark Twain's Cabins on Spring St.
55- Superintendent's House

AURORA TIMELINE 1860 to 1960

August 25, 1860- J. M. Braly, E. R. Hicks, and J. M. Cory establish the first mining claims at Esmeralda Camp near the future site of Aurora and then travel to nearby Monoville to announce their find.

August 30, 1860- Braly, Hicks, Cory and about 30 miners travel from Monoville to Esmeralda Camp and form the Esmeralda Mining District, which was thought to be located in either the Utah Territory or California.

October 8, 1860- The first on-site report from Aurora written September 27, 1860, appears on the front page of San Francisco's *Alta California*.

March 2, 1861- Nevada Territory created.

March 24, 1861- Mono County, California, created with Aurora designated as the county seat.

April 4, 1861- Article about Esmeralda appears in the *New York Times*.

June 1, 1861- First elections held for Mono County officials.

June, 1861- The Pioneer Mill, Aurora's first stamp mill, begins crushing ore.

November 25, 1861- Esmeralda County created by Nevada Territory with Aurora designated as the county seat.

April, 1862- Samuel Clemens (Mark Twain) begins his six month residency in Aurora.

May 10, 1862- First edition of Aurora's *Esmeralda Star* published.

An 1864 Directory and Guide to Nevada's Aurora

September 11, 1862- Speculation in Aurora's mining stocks grows rapidly with the formation of the San Francisco Stock and Exchange Board.

June 23, 1863- In the belief that Aurora is in Nevada, Nevada's Territorial Governor appoints Esmeralda County officials.

July, 1863- Aurora's peak population of 5,000 is reported.

September 2, 1863- Dual elections held for both Mono and Esmeralda County at Aurora.

September 16, 1863- The Kidder and Ives boundary survey team reaches Aurora and declares the city to be in Nevada.

February 2, 1864- Aurora's vigilante group known as the "Citizen's Safety Committee" was formed with 600 members. Seven days later, four members of the Daly Gang were hung near Armory Hall.

October 30, 1864- Nevada becomes a state.

January 6, 1866- Aurora's first major fire burns all the buildings along Antelope Street. Aurora's population down to about 800.

1900- Aurora's population down to 75.

1914- Population grows to 350 with the revival of Aurora's mines.

1919- Post office closes and Aurora becomes a ghost town.

1946- Destruction of Aurora's brick buildings begins in earnest.

February 20, 1955- Aurora's last resident Fried Walker dies at nearby Hawthorne, Nevada.

1960- Aurora's brick buildings vanish forever.

DIRECTORY

ARMORIES AND MILITIA COMPANIES

With Civil War passions running high among Aurora's northern and southern sympathizers, and the threat of Indian attacks looming, a militia force named the Esmeralda Rifles was formed in April 1862. The unit's activities included training, drilling, parading, providing assistance to Aurora's civil authorities in maintaining law and order, and controlling secessionist-related activities during the restless days of the Civil War.

> *On the arrival of the government arms sent by Gov. Nye, a military company was organized, called the Esmeralda Rifles, under the command of captain Teel. Fifty-one members signed the roll; they will act as home guards.* (San Francisco *Daily Evening Bulletin,* April 16, 1862)

The Esmeralda Rifles began building their armory on a hill north of Pine Street in the fall of 1862:

An 1864 Directory and Guide to Nevada's Aurora

> *The Esmeralda Rifles have bought a fine lot in a prominent location in town, and are to erect immediately a good substantial hall for an armory and drill room. The hall is to be of wood, spacious, one story high, and finished in such a style as to serve the purpose of any dramatic company or troupe who may favor us with a visit, and also be a suitable place for public meetings, balls, and conventions.* (Sacramento *Daily Bee*, October 10, 1862)

Completed in November 1862, Armory Hall **(7)** was the earliest and most important public facility in Aurora up until the completion of Wingate Hall and Preble & Devoe's Hall in the fall of 1863. The spacious 30 x 60 ft. wooden building was also used for a wide variety of public social and civil events:

> *The immediate occasion for the ball was the dedication of their new and commodious military hall, just completed, which was most neatly and appropriately decorated for the occasion with national flags, emblems, large mirrors, paintings, the arms and accoutrements belonging to the company, etc., including the swords so recently presented to the company by your worthy citizen, J. W. Tucker; the whole being tastefully and even artistically, trimmed and interspersed with wreaths and festoons of evergreens. But the crowning glory of the occasion was the ladies, God bless them! (some fifty in number), with their bright eyes, cheerful countenances, rich, tasteful, and elegant dresses, neatly trimmed and ornamented with the red, white, and blue.* (San Francisco *Alta California*, December 14, 1862)

> *As evidence of the importance of a large public room in this place, the armory hall is used by the district court in the morning; at 2 o'clock p.m. a large funeral was attended from the room, and in the evening a gay and festive promenade concert and ball was held in it for the benefit of the common*

Directory

school fund, which was largely attended and a decided success. (Sacramento *Daily Union*, October 21, 1863)

The Rifles were reorganized into a cavalry unit called the Esmeralda Rangers during August 1863. In response to an unrelenting crime wave, a vigilante group calling themselves the "Citizen's Safety Committee" took charge of the arms of the Esmeralda Rangers and used Armory Hall for their headquarters during February 1864. Four members of the infamous Daly gang were hung from gallows erected only a hundred feet northeast of the hall.

Concerned about the security of their arms after the vigilante violence, the Rangers moved their weapons from Armory Hall to the basement of John Neidy's brick building on Pine Street **(12)** in May 1864:

Yesterday we visited the new Armory of the Esmeralda Rangers, which is a very handsome apartment in the basement of Mr. John Neida's [Neidy's] *brick building, on Pine street. A row of little closets has been fitted up along the walls, one for each member of the company, in which the uniforms and accoutrements are kept. Each closet has written upon it the name of the person whose uniform it contains, and whenever the company gets through with their public exercises and parades, each member proceeds to the Armory and deposits his suit and arms in his own box, instead of carrying them home with him, as has been the custom.* (Aurora *Esmeralda Daily Union,* May 7, 1864)

Even after the Rangers removed their weapons, and newer and larger meeting halls were opened, Armory Hall was still the favorite location for important public gatherings such as Aurora's 1864 Independence Day "Grand Celebration" in 1864 (see page 59).

An 1864 Directory and Guide to Nevada's Aurora

Panoramic view east (left) to south (right) from the hill where Armory Hall once stood. Last Chance Hill is in the distance on the left, and downtown Aurora once stood from the center to Antelope Street on the far right. This site was selected by the Esmeralda Rifles because it provided a 360° view ideal for protecting the town from would be attackers.

In May 1863, the sixty-three member Hooker Light Infantry was formed with Jacob Hess as Captain. Like the Rifles, the Hooker Light Infantry was created to assist the civil authorities in maintaining law and order in and around Aurora. The unit changed its name to the Aurora City Guard and was led by Captain John Palmer during 1864. The Guard had their own armory in a brick building on the corner of Silver and Aurora **(31)**.

The two units often marched and drilled together as reported in the following newspaper articles:

> *RETURN OF THE MILITARY TO AURORA.—On the evening of the 3rd the Esmeralda Rangers, Capt. Teal; and Hooker Light Infantry, Capt. Hess; arrived from Camp Gilmore* [located three miles south of Stockton]. *They were escorted by a number of citizens on horseback, preceded by the Aurora Brass Band. The "Union Gun"— the same that the copperheads recently attempted to destroy—which had been placed on the top of Last Chance Hill, was the first to announce the approach of our gallant volunteers. As they marched down Pine street to the flag staff, they were greeted upon all sides with loud and prolonged cheering by their loyal brethren, whom it is but just been designated as the "Home*

Directory

Panoramic view south (left) to west (right) from Armory Hall. Antelope Street is on the left and Spring Street and Lover's Leap is on the right.

Guard." Patriotic saloon-keepers threw open their doors, and for two or three hours there was a good time generally. One of the most interesting and pleasing features of the occasion was the assembling of our noble troops round the flag-staff, [see page 52] and there, under the ample folds of our large and magnificent Star Spangled Banner, a hundred voices in soul inspiring strains, made the welkin ring with that loyal song "The Battle Cry of Freedom." The song was new to us, and was enthusiastically cheered by all, save a few copperheads whose hang-dog faces were observed peering round brick corners and from behind whisky barrels. After marching and countermarching through the principle streets, the companies were dismissed. (Sonora *American Flag*, October 15, 1863)

MILITARY— The Esmeralda Rangers, Captain Teel, and Aurora City Guard, Captain Palmer; were both out on drill yesterday afternoon. After practicing for an hour in their respective exercises, the Rangers accompanied the Guards, by invitation, to their Armory, corner of Silver and Aurora streets, and joined in a good, social time over foaming buckets of lager. (Aurora *Esmeralda Daily Union*, April 18, 1864)

The fate of Armory Hall is unknown. By the late 1880s, Armory Hall was no longer mentioned in any Aurora newspapers as a place used for meetings and the building does not appear on the 1890 photograph on page 9. There are no know photographs of Armory Hall and except for a few square nails and bits of broken glass, there is noting left to see today of Aurora's first public meeting hall.

ASSAY OFFICES

ASSAY OFFICE.

VAN WYCK & CO.

Silver Street, Aurora, Cal.

GOLD AND SILVER BULLION,

Melted and Assayed. Assays made from Quartz, Ores, &c.

☞ We guarantee the correctness of our Assays, and solicit tl e patronage of Miners and dealers in Bullion.

⁎ Returns made in Bars the day of deposit
apr4nl

Pioneer Assay Office - owned by Krauss and Reese.

Van Wyck & Winchester (8)

ATTORNEYS AND BROKERS

When miners claimed a gold-bearing quartz vein, they were entitled to follow that vein even if it ran under or through another miners claim. Because mining district laws regarding this matter were typically ambiguous and open to many interpretations, the conflicts that inevitably occurred were either settled with a gun or in a local court of law. The former solution benefited the undertaker, the latter attracted droves of attorneys who reveled in an "orgy of litigation."

Nowhere was this "orgy" more visible than a legal case involving two of Aurora's most famous mines—the Pond and Real

Del Monte. This case, one of the most prominent 19th century legal cases in Nevada history, was resolved in January 1864 after costing the companies millions (in today's dollars) in attorney's fees:

> *The jury in the case of the Pond and Del Monte, finally, after two days session, came to the conclusion to "agree to disagree." They came into court and so reported, and were discharged. So the whole trial must be repeated again, unless the parties come to some understanding, and make a compromise. It is said that this suit has cost the litigants upwards of $200,000. We should not be at all surprised to see both mines fall into the hands of the lawyers in the long run, if the contest is continued.* (Carson *Daily Independent*, December 19, 1863; as summarized in Angel's *History of Nevada*)

In addition to litigation, property transactions involving mining stocks and real estate were also much in demand. Town lots in particular were a hot commodity in early 1863:

> *Cash is being paid for every article bought or sold. Lots for building purposes that could not be sold for $500, now bring readily from $2,500 to $3,000.* (San Francisco *Alta California,* April 29, 1863)

Armstrong, J. A. (38) - dealer in mining stocks.

Bechtel, F. K. (13) - attorney, notary public, conveyancer, and commissioner of deeds for California.

Boring W. H., & Hayden - attorneys on Silver. Boring also served as the Justice of the Peace.

Bradford, J. B. - notary in "Bradford's Building" on Pine.

Brown, L. A. - stockbroker

An 1864 Directory and Guide to Nevada's Aurora

Genella, Joseph (36) - real estate, mining stock and money broker.

Gough, Wm. T. (27) - attorney in the building formerly occupied by the Mono County Recorder.

Haskell, D. H. - attorney and notary public.

Kendall, Quint, and Hardy - attorneys in wood house on lot owned by Mrs. Gallager on the east side of Silver, north of Pine.

Mathews, E. J. - partner with Wheeler, H. C. of San Francisco, owned the Esmeralda Mining Agency specializing in buying and selling real estate and mining claims.

Merideth, W. C. - notary public, conveyancer, commissioner of deeds for California, mortgages, power of attorney, and "other legal papers carefully drawn."

Mesick, A., and Van Vories, W. - attorneys on Silver.

Morse, A. C. (7) - attorney and notary.

Pawling, T., & Sims, C. - attorneys on the lot owned by A.M. Wingate **(27)**.

Phelps, R. - attorney on Esmeralda.

Richardson, J. H. - notary public, conveyancer of real estate, and mining stock agent (with E. J. Mathews) on Pine.

Seawell, W. - attorney on Pine.

Schwob, A. - commission office on north side of Pine.

Winchester, W. - mining stockbroker.

BAKERIES

Denslinger (or Denelenger), Jacob - bake shop on the east side of Antelope north of Pine adjoining Bechtel's property.

Marchant, John - bakery south of Fashion Stable which offered "Milk, Fresh Bread, Pies, and Cakes" as well as "Boston Brown Bread and Beans every Sunday Morning."

Pioneer Bakery (2) - owned by C. Prince on Silver.

PIONEER BAKERY.

THE PRORRIETOR would inform his old friends and patrons that he has moved from his old stand on Pine street to Silver street near opposite the County Clerk's office, where he is prepared to furnish Rye, Graham, Milk, and every kind of the finest quality of

Bread, Cakes and Pies.

BANKERS

Sanchez, Ramon, & Howard, J. L. (41) - office at the west end of Levy & Co's brick store.

HOWARD & SANCHEZ, BANKERS,
AURORA, MONO COUNTY, CALIFORNIA.

BUY AND SELL EXCHANGE on San Francisco; Purchase Gold and Silver Bullion; make advance on same for assay or deposit in the U.S. Mint; make collections on most favorable terms.

Garesche, F. G. (17) – dealer in gold and silver bullion with an office in the Wells Fargo building.

BARBER SHOPS AND BATHS

Banister, J. - barbershop on southwest corner of Pine and Silver.

Mortimer & Huff (18) - listed as "colored barbers" above Green's Drug Store on Pine in the 1864 Tax Assessors Role.

Washington Baths,

AND SHAVING SALOON,

Antelope street, next door to the Post Office,

AURORA.

WARM. COLD and SHOWER BATHS, from six A. M. till ten P. M.
Shaving and Hair Cutting by experienced artists.
JAS. JAMESON,
JOHN L. PEBELIE,
Proprietors.

Washington Baths and Shaving Saloon (37) - Jameson and Prebelie proprietors.

BLACKSMITH SHOPS

Cooper and Graves (5)

Denby, J. B. - on southwest corner of Court and Pine.

Houseley - on lot owned by Towels & Co. on the southwest corner of Winnemucca and Spring.

Humphrey's - owned by Brown and Weston on Esmeralda St. "above Fashion Stables."

Morrison & Minear - paid "particular attention to horse and ox shoeing" in their shop on the corner of Court and Wide West Streets. According to their newspaper add: "If you want your oxen or horses 'IRON CLAD' or anything else done in the blacksmith line" go by all means to Morrison & Minear.

Randolf, E. - stone shop just east of Cooper and Graves.

Directory

Union Foundry, Blacksmith Shop, and Stamp Mill (48) [R] - a 35 x 60 ft. foundry and stamp mill with a blacksmith, boiler making, and machine shop owned by G. W. Coffee. The remains of a stamp mill from the early 1900s are still standing just east of the foundry site.

Although small, the stamp mill portion of this impressive industrial facility was "perfect:"

A miner by the name of Coffee erected a mill in Aurora in 1863. He later added a small quartz mill, which while but a miniature was perfect in its equipment, it had two four stamp batteries; weight of stamps 200 pounds each; four amalgamating pans, two eight feet in diameter, two five feet — usual proportion. (Bishop *Inyo Register*, November 11, 1915)

A foundry in Aurora is somewhat hard to believe but it did actually operate:

ESMERALDA CASTINGS— Last evening we happened in at the Union Foundry just as the workmen were making a blast. Some wood was first put into the melting furnace, then some coal, and after the coal commenced burning well, some iron; then iron and coal were put in alternately till there were about 2,500 pounds of iron in the furnace when the

---

NOTICE!

Union Foundry!

Machine, Blacksmith & Boiler Works

THE undersigned takes pleasure in announcing to Mill owners and others, that having all the necessary machinery completed in his establishment, he is now prepared to do ALL KINDS of

Casting, Blacksmithing, Boiler-Making and Repairing;

— ALSO —

Turning and Fitting for Saw and other Mills.

All kinds of repairing punctually attended to. Also, connected with the establishment is a

PLANING MACHINE!

for Dressing and Matching Flooring, Sticking Mouldings together with Circular Saws, Jigg or Scroll Saw, and everything suitable for Matching and Dressing Flooring, Siding, Battens, Scroll Brackets, &c., at the shortest notice and on reasonable terms.

Matched Flooring, Siding and Battens,
Constantly on hand and for sale.

G. W COFFEE, Proprietor.
Aurora, August 19, 1863.

25

blower was turned on and in about ten minutes the melted metal began to run. The largest piece cast was a retort weighing about 800 pounds. A large number of car wheels, stamp shoes, dies, and other small pieces of quartz-mill machinery were cast. The proprietor, Mr. G. W. Coffee, has patented a new stamp shoe. (Aurora *Esmeralda Daily Union,* May 5, 1864)

BREWERIES

City Brewery [R] - 24 x 32 ft. brick building located on the north side of Spring St. west of town owned by J. Blasauf. The building was located on the former site of one of Mark Twain's cabins (see page 101).

ESMERALDA BREWERY,
F. STEHLER Proprietor,
Brews The finest
Lager Beer
Of any Brewery on the Pacific Coast. He uses the best of Barley for his Malt, and the purest Mountain Water in the Sierra Nevada Range, and as an evidence that it is good, every keg is exhausted before being returned to the Brewery.

Esmeralda Brewery [R] - brick building owned by F.Staehler (or spelled Stehler) located at Esmeralda Camp about two miles south of Aurora along the old road to Mono Lake. The brewery operated into the 1870s and served the needs for both Aurora and nearby Bodie.

A rock-lined well (left) that once provided "the purest Mountain Water in the Sierra Nevada Range" is located in a meadow just above the brewery's ruins. The well now provides water to the area's abundant wildlife including wild horses on rare occasions.

26

Directory

BRICKYARDS

Because lumber was scarce and expensive, and the ingredients needed to make brick were abundant and relatively cheap, Aurorans turned to brick as their favorite building material. Even when wood became more plentiful, the town continued its brick making ways in an attempt to emphasize Aurora's permanence and importance. Aurora was somewhat unique compared to other Nevada mining camps because most of the town's more important commercial buildings, residences, and stamp mills were made entirely of locally manufactured brick:

> *The manufacture of brick has commenced in good earnest. Already three yards are at work on Esmeralda Gulch, below Union Mill, and have several thousands of brick molded; also two yards on Cottonwood ravine, and one on Willow Gulch in active operation.* (San Francisco *Alta California,* May 26, 1863)

> *To convey to your mind some idea of the vast amount of improvements that have been going on, I will state, that there have been during the past summer; and there are now, five large brickyards in actual operation, turning out from 600,000 to 800,000 each. And yet there is no brick to be purchased at any of the yards.* (San Francisco *Alta California,* September 4, 1863)

Barbiens [R] - east side of Cottonwood gulch.

Esmeralda [R] - owned by Clark and McDonald, just west of town on the south side of Spring Street west of the Moses Mill.

Hoems [R] - just west of town on the south side of Spring Street owned by A M Wingate.

Miller's [R] - just west of town on the south side of Spring Street between Hoems and Esmeralda brickyards.

Preble & Co's [R] - in Cottonwood Gulch south of Barbiens' brickyard.

Brickyard ruins up Cottonwood Canyon south of Aurora.

BROTHELS

Aurora's numerous prostitutes and brothels were typically not the subject of newspaper articles in the 1860s. But their presence was undeniable as noted by William Brewer in the summer of 1863:

> *Here* [at Aurora's saloons], *too, are women— for nowhere else does one see prostitutes as he sees them in a new mining camp. All combine* [gambling, drinking and prostitutes] *to excite and ruin.*

Aurora's infamous Daly Gang reportedly lived near some of Aurora's more prominent prostitutes including Ellen "Nellie" Sears, Eliza Dennison, Mary Smith, Adelaide "Kit" Carson, Anna Haskill, and Elizabeth Williams. According to one report, these women "generally confined their professional work to their own rooms." A lot and wooden building owned by "Miss Mary Smith (Manny) formerly occupied by Big Lizy" was located on the hill just above Bradford's Store **(4)**. According to one particularly reliable report, brothels were located everywhere in town:

> *We* [Esmeralda County Grand Jury] *would especially call the attention of the proper authorities to a nuisance now infecting nearly every part of the city, to wit, the numerous disgusting Chinese brothels that exist on most of our public streets, to the great detriment of public morals and danger of property, and recommend that some action be immediately taken that will effectually abate the evil.* (Aurora *Esmeralda Daily Union,* March 31, 1864)

CAMP NOBLE

Conflicts between cattlemen and the Owens Valley Indians over missing cattle led to an Indian uprising in the spring of 1862. Some Aurorans feared these hostilities might reach Aurora:

> *Great excitement is raging furiously through our town. "Have you got a revolver or rifle to spare?" "Can you lend me your horse?" "Yes, four* [Indians] *were killed* [in Owens Valley]*, three white wounded." I have a horse, but no saddle." "Not wounded much?" "Only a scratch by an arrow."* (San Francisco *Daily Evening Bulletin,* March 26, 1862)

In an effort to quell the disturbances, Nevada Territorial Governor James Nye sent a contingent of soldiers from Ft. Churchill to Owens Valley. On their way south, the soldiers stopped at Aurora sometime during late March of 1862. They left Aurora in early April:

> *The soldiers from Ft. Churchill under Lieut. Noble, left Aurora for the Owen's river country last Friday* [April 4th]. (San Francisco *Alta California*, April 16, 1862)

Before Lt Noble troops arrived on the scene, a bloody battled ensued between the Indians and a contingent of armed Aurorans who had traveled to Owens River to help the cattlemen. N. F. Scott, Mono County's first sheriff, was killed in the battle. On his return from the hostilities, Lt. Noble again camped at Aurora toward the end of April:

> *The wretched and disgraceful business of fighting the Indians having terminated, we have for results nine whites killed, the Indians emboldened, and all communication with the Tulare country cut off just when it is most important that it should be kept open...Lieut. Noble is encamped with his company near this place* [Aurora]. (San Francisco *Daily Evening Bulletin*, May 6, 1862)

Lieutenant Noble was not the only group of soldiers to camp at Aurora. On May 11th, Captain Edwin Rowe left Fort Churchill with orders to establish a camp at Aurora and then proceed south to Owens Valley to settle the Indian uprising once and for all. He arrived in Aurora on May 14th and proceeded to establish what would become known as "Camp Noble." The camp was broken up in August just before the soldiers returned to Fort Churchill.

Although all signs of Camp Noble have completely vanished, the former site is located about a mile west of Aurora next to the Napa Stamp Mill along the road to Bodie.

CARPENTERS AND BUILDERS

Kelly & Vernon – architects and carpenters in an office on Aurora Street next to the Esmeralda Exchange Saloon and across the street from the *Esmeralda Daily Union* newspaper printing shop.

Mosher & Jewett - painting and paper hanging.

Petit & Parry - on the lot owned by A.M. Wingate **(27).**

> **A. P. PETIT, ARCHITECT.**
> Plans, Elevations, Details, and Specifications for Stores, Warehouses, Mills and Residences; Estimates of Cost furnished at reasonable rates and with dispatch. Will superintend the construction of the same with satisfaction and promptness.
>
> **PETIT & PARRY, CONTRACTORS AND BUILDERS,**
> Will contract to erect Buildings of Brick, Stone or Wood, furnishing all materials, and complete the same with satisfaction, upon prices to suit the times.
> A. P. PETIT.   JOHN PARRY.

Price, John - architect and builder office on the corner of Antelope and Juniper.

White, J. E. - carpenter and builder at Cardinell's Hall, North Antelope.

Williams & Waters - carpenter shop on Silver.

CEMETERY

The Mono County Board of Supervisors condemned a five acre tract of land on the hill just north of Aurora for a cemetery in 1861. Originally called the St. John's Cemetery, the site also served the burial needs of the surrounding area:

> *It is often said that Aurora is an unhealthful place, but such is not the case. There has been an average of two thousand people here for two years and a half; and there are but sixty-five graves in the place. A large percentage of those who have died here were victims of 'sage brush whisky' and quack doctors. Many have been killed, accidentally and otherwise, and quite a number who died elsewhere are buried here.* (Sacramento *Daily Union*, August 6, 1863)

> *I will state the inhabitants have been on the increase, until now they reach the number of three thousand five hundred. Out of this population, during a period of thirty-five months, there have been only seventy interred in the new and old cemetery—fifty-three by natural death, and the other seventeen by the hand of violence, or other-wise.* (San Francisco *Alta California*, September 4, 1863)

There are two separate cemetery sites at Aurora. The main area of headstones is located within and around a fenced area maintained by the citizens of nearby Hawthorne. A second smaller area of headstones is located a few hundred yards north of the main area along a dirt road. If you visit the cemetery, it is worth noting that the vast majority of headstones are for people who died in the 1870s and 1880s when the town's population was only a fraction of what it was in 1860s. Because many of the earlier burials had wooden headstones that have rotted away, or fancy marble headstones that have been stolen, the location of possibly hundreds of additional gravesites, including Aurora's Paiutes and Chinese, remain unknown.

Directory

William E. Carder was killed by Moses Brockman in front of the Exchange Saloon on December 10, 1864. The *Esmeralda Daily Union* called Carder one of the "most desperate characters we ever knew" and a jury found Brockman's action "justifiable homicide." Although badly broken, this beautiful marble monument is the only surviving tombstone from Aurora's booming 1860s.

33

CHINESE

Unlike the Paiute Indians, Aurora's Chinese residents did not think of Aurora as their home. Their intent was to earn enough money so they could eventually return to China and live relatively well off with the money they earned in America. Because the Chinese typically did not speak English and generally kept to themselves, they had little social contact with Aurora's citizens. A good example of this is the complete lack of Chinese participation in Aurora's 1864 Independence Day celebration when virtually everyone in the town, including the Paiute Indians, had some role to play in the festivities (see page 65).

In October 1863, there were about 50 Chinese living in Aurora, which represented only about 2% of the town's population of 3,500. However, with more and more Chinese arriving every month, and a prevailing atmosphere of prejudice among the white majority, the City of Aurora passed an ordinance in April 1864 requiring that all Chinese live out of the commercial and residential center of town which by then was west of Roman Street along Spring Street. However, by June the legality of such an ordinance was coming under suspicion:

> *CITY ORDINANCE NO. 32.— This ordinance, passed by the Board of Alderman on the 7th of April, makes it a misdemeanor for any person of the Mongolian or Chinese races to reside within certain limits of the city without a special license. Many doubt the legality of the Ordinance, averring that it contravenes certain provisions of the Constitution of the United States as stipulations in the treaty between this Government and that of China. The first trail for a violation of this ordinance came up before his Honor, Judge Moore, to-day, the prosecution being conducted by the City Attorney, Mr. Seawell, and Messrs. Kendall, Hayden and Palmer appearing for the defense.* (Aurora *Esmeralda Daily Union*, June 16, 1864)

The outcome of this case is unknown. The section of Spring Street west of town soon became known as "China Garden" for obvious reasons:

> *An unusual number of citizens are preparing grounds for gardens in the suburbs of town, and the Chinamen are going into business quite extensively, with the intention of supplying the town with all the right vegetables required.* (Sacramento *Daily Union*, May 5, 1867)

Although we know relatively little about Aurora's Chinese population, they were unquestionably an important part of the community as they served as cooks in local restaurants, household servants, woodcutters in the nearby pinyon pine forests, laundry workers, and independent merchants.

CHURCHES

The first religious services in Aurora were held in the middle of Antelope Street just north of the Flag Staff at 11 am on June 14, 1863. Rev. J. B. Saxton, who arrived in town for the first time only five days earlier, presided over the gathering. After repeating the services at the same location a week later, the congregation moved to the courtroom of Judge Tyler on June 28 where services were held every Sunday for six weeks. On July 14, 1863, members of the congregation (J. B. Saxton, Charles Cate, Amos A. Mower, S. F. Platt, Hugh Glen, Amos Farnsworth, and F. Haley) agreed to organize and build a Baptist Church in Aurora. Although the building was not finished, services were held for the first time at the 1st Baptist Church of Aurora on August 9, 1863. In an effort to expedite the completion of the church, The Trustees of the Church and the Trustees of the Public School reached an agreement to share the costs and use of the new church for one year until October 12, 1864. On October 23, 1863, Rev. Saxton received a commission as minister from the Baptist Home Mission Society with a salary of $1,200, half of it to come from local donations.

Baptist (52) - Except for a few rusting square nails, nothing remains today of this wooden structure that once was so important to the citizen's of Aurora.

> *On the 4th, the foundation was commenced for the First Baptist Church, under the superintendence of Rev. J. B. Saxton, of Oaklin* [sic], *twenty-five feet fronting Winnemucca Street, and thirty-eight feet deep.* (San Francisco *Alta California,* August 12, 1863)

> *Peace and quietude prevailed throughout the city, for the sturdy miners, instead of idling about the streets, went to some one of the various churches in town, which were all well attended. The Baptist church, on Winnemucca Street, was so crowded in the evening as to render it difficult to obtain a comfortable seat.* (Aurora *Esmeralda Daily Union,* April 18 1864)

> *Baptist.— Divine services will be held at the Baptist Church, on Winnemucca street, to-morrow, at eleven o'clock a.m., and at a quarter to eight p.m. Sunday School and Bible class at the close of the morning service.* (Aurora *Esmeralda Daily Union,* July 2, 1864)

Catholic - Although construction of a Catholic Church was started in November 1864, the building was never completed. Aurora's third church was to be located on Father Cotter's lot just south of the Fashion Stables on the east side of Esmeralda St.

Methodist Episcopal (29) [R] – Rev. H. D. Slade presiding over Aurora's second church:

The Methodist Episcopal Church going up on Aurora street, between Silver and Court, is a handsome brick edifice, and, when completed will be a splendid ornament to the town. (Virginia City *Daily Union*, January 8, 1864)

Preaching at the M. E. [Methodist Episcopal] *Church, on Aurora street, to-morrow at eleven o'clock a.m. and at 8 p.m. Morning subject— "The Blessed Nation, etc." Sunday School at 2 p.m.* (Aurora *Esmeralda Daily Union,* July 2, 1864)

Most miners and prospectors believed that once schools and churches were under construction their chances for "striking it rich" were over and it was time to move on to a new prospect. Therefore, when Aurora's first church was under construction in August 1863, the town's population began its inexorable decline from its peak of about 5,000 only a month earlier.

View of Aurora and Lovers Leap from Last Chance Hill.

The Esmeralda County Courthouse stood in the foreground for almost a century until contractors tore the structure down and hauled off the bricks to Bridgeport, California, in the early 1950s. Aurorans were understandably proud of this building as it served their community for almost sixty years. The view is looking west and Pine Street is on the right.

COURTHOUSE

The 60 x 40 ft. courthouse, a three story (two stories with a basement) brick building **(1) [R])**, was the largest structure ever built in Aurora. Originally known as "Preble & Devoe's Hall" after the original owners, the building was completed in October 1863 and was home to at least three businesses including saloons in both the basement and the first floor. The second story was finished for courtrooms and various county offices and included a large open hall used for many social parties and community meetings. Esmeralda County leased the second floor as their first courthouse after Aurora was found to be in Nevada Territory during September 1863 (see

Directory

page 57). The former Mono County courthouse "shanty" was a small wooden building owned by A. M. Wingate directly across the street from Preble & Devoe's Hall (the future Esmeralda County Courthouse) on Silver:

> *Instead of holding Courts, as heretofore, in a shanty, open to every wind of heaven, with Judge, jury, bar, Clerk, Sheriff, witnesses and spectators sitting around on benches, dry goods boxes, broken chairs, and three legged stools, these dignified officials and attendants will be furnished comfortable and commodious quarters.* (San Francisco *Alta California,* October 4, 1863)

The former Esmeralda County Courthouse (right) was briefly known as the "Esmeralda Hotel" in the early 1900s. The view is looking east down Pine Street in the early 1930s. (Author's collection)

According to a March 1864 Grand Jury report, the building had a few problems:

39

> *The Court room and various county Offices are leased from Preble Devoe & Co., by the County Commissioners, for the sum of $250 per month, the owners thereof reserving to themselves the right to lease or let the center or Court room at any and all times, provided they do not interfere with any Court of record. The floor of the room occupied by the County recorder, as also that of the Probate Judge, is of such a character that we beg leave to call attention thereto. It contains great openings and not a few holes, through which come noises from a saloon below, to the disturbance and annoyance of those engaged in making Records, whereby mistakes are liable to occur.* (Aurora *Esmeralda Daily Union,* March 31, 1864)

In addition to serving as a courtroom, the open second story hall was used for many important meetings and lectures. J. Ross Browne, noted mining engineer and author, gave a series of lectures at the hall in the fall of 1864:

> *J. Ross Browne.— It will be seen by advertisement in another column, that this eminent traveler and writer will deliver a lecture on Thursday evening next, at Preble & Devoe's Hall, for the benefit of the Sanitary Fund. Subject, "Experience and Travel in Foreign Lands." We bespeak for Mr. Browne a crowded house.* (Aurora *Esmeralda Daily Union,* September 5, 1864)

Amazingly, the hall could accommodate 350 people:

> *Union Meeting.— A large and very enthusiastic Union meeting was held at Preble & Devoe's Hall on Saturday evening last. About 350 men were present. Eloquent and patriotic speeches were made.* (Aurora *Esmeralda Daily Union,* October 24, 1864)

During the Civil War, a series of fund raising promotions to help sick and wounded Union soldiers traveled to Aurora. A 50-pound specimen of gold and silver ore from the Wide West mine was auctioned during the fall of 1864 and Edwin A. Sherman, the owner of the *Esmeralda Star* newspaper, had the highest bid. He took the ore specimen to his home state of Massachusetts and exchanged it for a piece of the Plymouth Rock which arrived in Aurora during February 1864. The following is his recollection of the event 43 years later:

> *As the fair was closing business, and nobody wanted to buy that fine gold and silver specimen, I applied for it, as I was going east, and if possible exchange it for a piece of Plymouth rock to be placed in the corner of the now "Old Court House," then to be erected. It was given to me and I took it to Plymouth* [Massachusetts] *and presented it to M. Davis, the vice-president of the Pilgrim Society, whose guest I was while there, and he gave me in return a fine piece of the Plymouth rock, which I immediately sent to Aurora and it was placed in the corner of the old courthouse, cemented in with the brick wall, and is there to this day and will be until the building is torn down or falls into ruins. If taken down, that piece of Plymouth rock should be carefully perservered and placed in the state cabinet at Carson City, and sacredly kept for all time.* (Reno *Evening Gazette*, January 6, 1906)

On December 19, 1864, Preble and Devoe's Hall was sold to Esmeralda County for $12,000. The courthouse served the citizens of Esmeralda County until 1883 when the county seat was moved to Hawthorne. During December 1905, the Esmeralda County Board of Commissioners authorized the sale of the "old Aurora court house." A former resident of Aurora said the building was in very good shape:

> *'The old court house at Aurora is still a good building,'* remarked James McCleary, one of the men who went to Aurora in the early days. *'It was built in the early sixties at a cost of about $75,000, and furthermore, it was honestly built. It is a two story structure and today is better built than the one that was put up at Hawthorne after the county seat of the county was removed.'* (Reno *Evening Gazette,* January 1, 1906)

According to "Death Valley Days" radio show writer Ruth Woodman, J. S. Cain and his son Victor bought the courthouse because it was thought to have a piece of the Plymouth Rock within its cornerstone. This purchase may have occurred immediately after the above mentioned sale by Esmeralda County in 1906.

The courthouse's Plymouth Rock fragment was the subject of a search some seven decades after it was placed in the building's cornerstone. According to the August 19, 1936, edition of the *Mineral County Independent News,* a large group of citizens from two states gathered at Aurora to find the famous piece of the Plymouth Rock. The search was organized by David Victor Cain of Bodie after he had heard the story about Aurora's piece of the Plymouth Rock from Ruth Woodman. Woodman visited Aurora in October 1834 to gather information for a future program she was planning to write for the popular "Death Valley Days" radio show.

Although the fifty or so searchers organized by Cain failed to locate the Plymouth Rock cornerstone, the mystery may have been solved when fellow searcher 87-year-old Sam Kelso recalled that the courthouse cornerstone had been stolen in the late 1880s. However, the article went on to say that Kelso's recollection did not deter the searchers. To this day, the piece of Plymouth Rock once attached to Aurora's courthouse has apparently never been found.

On January 28, 1939, the "Death Valley Days" radio show aired Woodman's story about Aurora and its piece of Pilgrim history to a nationwide audience in the program entitled "Nevada's Plymouth Rock." This show was apparently very popular as Woodman rewrote the program seventeen years later for the "Death Valley Days" television series that aired on February 13, 1956.

In 1955, Ella Cain told Mrs. Woodman that the Cain family had the courthouse torn down and the bricks moved to Bridgeport. The ultimate fate of these bricks is unknown. Since Cain's search party and his brick contractors never found the piece of Plymouth Rock attached to the courthouse, watch your step during your visit to Aurora as you may be walking on a piece of Pilgrim history.

The 50-pound chunk of gold and silver ore given to the Pilgrim Society in exchange for the piece of Plymouth Rock is also missing. Although an item described as "#12 Silver Ore from Aurora, Nevada presented by the New Englanders in Aurora" was listed in the *Cataloge of the Historical Collection and Pictures in Pilgrim Hall* published in 1906, a recent inquiry to the Pilgrim Hall Museum revealed the piece was likely "de-accessioned/discarded during the 1940s-1960s, along with many similar pieces."

As if having a piece of the Plymouth Rock within its cornerstone was not interesting enough, the courthouse was home to "ghostly apparitions" according to Aurora's only newspaper in 1881:

> *The sacred precincts of that sacred temple of justice have been and continue to be nightly invaded by spectre spirits who have long since passed over the dark and surging tide and through the gloomy valley to the farther side. Pandemonium seems to have let loose at times, and scenes that once were enacted in the flesh are now being re-enacted by these ghostly maskers. They roam through the corridors.....and then betake themselves to the basement, where stands the long disused and almost forgotten gallows upon which Johnny Daly, Masterson, Buckley and Three-fingered Jack expiated their crimes, and there the blood-curdling scenes are again gone over, amid the clanking of chains, the twisting and tightening of ropes, the groans and agonizing tortures of that long ago.*
> (Aurora *Esmeralda Herald*, March 12, 1881)

An 1864 Directory and Guide to Nevada's Aurora

The article appears to take the ghosts seriously as it claims "our county officials dare not venture within the portals of the courthouse after night shuts down upon it...and if their ghostships continue to hold high carnival as at present the officials will have to move to more congenial quarters." Two years later, the court did move when the county seat of Esmeralda County was changed to Hawthorne.

Regarding the fate of the records once held in the courthouse, most of Aurora's official records from the early 1860s through September 1863 now reside in the Mono County Courthouse in Bridgeport, California, whereas the records from late 1863 through the 1870s now reside in the Esmeralda County Courthouse in Goldfield, Nevada.

David Victor Cain's search party looked in vain for the famous piece of the Plymouth Rock at Aurora's old courthouse in 1936, which was about the same time this photo was taken. The person in the lower left may be Walter McKeough (Kenneth's father) who was a member of Cain's search party.

(Kenneth L. McKeough; see page 204 for information on the McKeough family)

DANCE HALLS

Cardinell's - Construction on this open brick hall, located on the east side of North Antelope **(16) [R]**, was started in August 1863. Work on the structure, however, was suspended for unknown reasons three months later. Sometime during 1864 construction resumed and by November 1, 1864 the 40 x 60 ft. "commodious" dance hall was scheduled to open.

> *Dancing Academy.- By reference to advertisement on the second page, it will be seen that Mr. Charles Cardinell will open his new Dancing Academy on the first of November next. His commodious hall is in every way suitable for the purpose, being forty feet wide by sixty long. Mr. Cardinell, as a teacher of "the light fantastic," has no superior on the Pacific Coast, and we are sure he will have a large school.* (Aurora *Esmeralda Daily Union,* October 24, 1864)

Because the hall had more floor space than Wingate Hall, the new brick building soon became a favorite for meetings, parties, and of course, dancing lessons. Governor Nye addressed a Union Rally there in November 1864. By December, Cardinell's dancing school was open for business:

> *CARDINELL'S DANCING SCHOOL— Mr. Cardinell's new hall has become a very fashionable place of resort, and is crowded every Monday and Friday evening with a large class of ladies and gentlemen who are taking lessons in the elegant accomplishment of dancing. Generally speaking, Aurora is a poor place for amusements, as we have no theater and are seldom visited by theatricals, but the want of such recreations is, in a great measure, compensated by Mr. Cardinell's pleasant semiweekly soirees.* (Aurora *Esmeralda Daily Union,* December 7, 1864)

DANCING ACADEMY.

Chas. Cardinell,

BEGS LEAVE TO INFORM THE LADIES AND GENTLEMEN OF AURORA AND vicinity that he will open his Academy for dancing at his

NEW BRICK HALL ON ANTELOPE STREET, AURORA,

ON TUESDAY EVENING, NOVEMBER 1st, 1864,

Where he will teach all the FASHIONABLE BALL-ROOM DANCES. Those desirous of taking lessons would do well to commence on the evening of beginning. ☞ No admission will be granted any person who does not become a scholar for the full term.

☞ Evenings of Tuition, Mondays and Fridays. ☜

CARDINELL'S BALL— The ball at Cardinell's Dancing Academy on Monday evening was one of the grandest affairs that ever came off in Aurora. The large hall was filled almost to overflowing, and satisfaction beamed on every countenance. Dancing was kept up 'till the breaking of the gray dawn' ere the festive dancers dispersed and sought the embrace of the drowsy god. An unusually large number of ladies graced the festive scene with their smiling countenances. (Aurora *Esmeralda Daily Union,* December 28, 1864)

Aurora's "social elite" were determined to have a good time even while their mines were closing:

The Masquerade Ball.— Not withstanding the dullness of the times the people of Aurora are determined to be merry. Last evening Mr. Cardinell gave a grand masquerade ball, to which none were invited but the most respectable portion of our citizens. There were about sixty gentlemen and ladies masked, all of whom assumed characters foreign and unique. Nearly all the nationalities on the globe were represented in a creditable manner. (Aurora *Esmeralda Daily Union,* February 15, 1865)

Hurdy Gurdy Dance House - owned by Chatterton and Parlin on the northwest corner of Juniper and Silver. It is interesting to note that J. W. Chatterton also once served as Aurora's City Marshal.

A Hurdy Gurdy Dance House was a musical saloon specializing in dancing where miners paid up to a dollar to dance with young women, known as Hurdy girls, who generally came from Germany. Selling drinks, however, was their main goal as the women made a commission on every drink a miner bought. Hurdy girls traveled to all the active mining camps in Nevada and California where they could average as many as 50 dances on a busy Saturday night. It is said their arrival in town always produced "great happiness among the miners."

DENTIST

Mastny, Dr. M. (2)

DENTISTRY.

Dr. Ma. MASTNY,
Silver Street—Pioneer Bakery, Aurora,
Is prepared to perform all operations pertaining to the Teeth, in a careful and skillful manner.
Prices moderate. All operations warranted.

DRUG STORES

Green's Drug Store (18) - wooden building owned by G. Shier fronting Pine Street by 25 feet.

Pioneer Drug Store (36) - owned by C.F. Collins and Dr. Reims in a 15 x 22 ft. wood building on a lot owned by E. D. Barker.

Woodcliff, T. - drugs, books, and stationary on the lot on Antelope owned by S. Davis.

ESMERALDA CAMP

Located about two miles south of Aurora, Esmeralda Camp was the first settlement for the miners who founded the Esmeralda Mining District in the fall of 1860. Its existence was short lived as by December of 1860, most miners had migrated down the canyon to Aurora:

> *They have two towns (or cities) here. The first* [Esmeralda Camp], *is upon the top of the mountain in the neighborhood of the Great Esmeralda Lode, the other, in the valley, about two and a-half miles below, and is named Aurora. The former can boast of seven or eight buildings, the latter has about sixty.*(San Francisco *Herald and Mirror*, December 15, 1860)

Although nearly abandoned by early 1861, Esmeralda Camp was the site for Perry's Esmeralda stamp mill and the Esmeralda Brewery by 1862. Both facilities relied on dependable water from nearby permanent springs (see photo on page 26) that are now used occasionally by wild horses on their way to the Brawley Peaks area.

ESMERALDA MINING DISTRICT

Gold was first discovered at Esmeralda Camp during August 1860. The three prospectors to make this lucky find were E. R. Hicks, J. M. Cory, and James M. Braly. In honor of their discovery, three prominent peaks in the vicinity of Aurora now bear their names (Brawley Peaks, Mt. Hicks, and Corey Peak). After a brief stop in nearby Monoville, Cory, Hicks, and Braly returned to Esmeralda Camp with 15 men who together organized the Esmeralda Mining District, adopted mining laws, and elected a recorder on August 30, 1860. The miners elected Dr. E. F. Mitchell as their first President, and James M. Braly as their first Secretary and Recorder.

The Esmeralda Mining District was created to enforce and oversee the district's mining laws established by the miners within the district, and was on equal legal footing with local government. The Recorder, arguably the most important job in Aurora, was the person a miner went to see in order to "record," or document, a new mining claim. The Recorder was also responsible for the volumes and volumes of records associated with Aurora's mining claims:

> *There are some six thousand claims taken up here, and each has a different name. Miners who locate claims now find themselves lost for the want of a name, as, after deliberating for hours, and spending a sleepless night, they go to the Recorder's to name their mine, thinking, no doubt, that their christening has never been thought of before, when they find, much to their discomfort, that the name has long since been recorded.* (San Francisco *Daily Evening Bulletin,* February 3, 1863)

During 1863, E. L. H. Gardiner was the District Recorder with his office in a cabin on the east end of Pine Street **(3)**. A deed written in 1863 for this small wooden cabin noted: "a one story frame building now occupied by the [Esmeralda Mining] District

Recorder's Office." This cabin was none other than the famous Mark Twain Cabin that was moved to Reno in 1924 (see page 101).

The Esmeralda Mining District's Recorders office on Pine Street was known as "Mark Twain's Cabin" during the early 1900s.
(Harper's Monthly Magazine, February 1912)

FIRE COMPANIES

By 1863, Aurora's fire department had two companies: the 65 man Esmeralda Engine Company No. 1 equipped with a pumper wagon; and the 80 man Deluge Bucket Company No. 1.

The Firemen too, who form quite a noble band of men, when clad in their handsome red flannel shirts, will enliven the scene on Christmas Eve, by a ball, which will be given in Armory Hall. There are two companies of firemen in Aurora, and an engine will soon be by this side of the mountains, so as to give the boys the hang of something when they turn out again. (San Francisco *Alta California,* January 1, 1863)

During the summer of 1862, Aurora's fire department was called the "Duane Engine Company" and was located in a firehouse on the east side of Court just south of Pine. However, by late 1863, the company became known as the "Esmeralda Engine Co, No. 1," and their firehouse had moved to the corner Antelope and Aurora Streets **(25)**:

The members of the Esmeralda Engine Co. No. 1 turned out on Saturday evening, in full numbers, for the purpose of receiving the set of hose purchased by the ladies of Aurora for their new fire engine. The company formed at the engine house on the corner of Antelope and Aurora streets, and with their hose carriage marched down Antelope and up Pine Street to the residence of A. Mack, where the committee of ladies were assembled, with the City Fathers, to present to the Fire Department the set of hose. Dr. Pugh— a member of the company —in a neat and impressive speech received the hose on the part of Esmeralda No. 1. Three cheers and a tiger were given by the company for the ladies of Aurora, and three cheers for the City Fathers, and the boys marched off in triumph with their new hose attached to their carriage, down to Sam Davis's saloon. (*Aurora Daily Times*, December 1, 1863)

Both the engine and bucket companies participated in Aurora's 1864 Independence Day celebration. The Esmeralda Engine Company No. 1 assembled at their firehouse at 9 o'clock for the parade according to the following advertisement:

FIREMEN'S' MEETING
The regular monthly meeting of Esmeralda Engine Company No. 1 will be held at their engine house, Antelope street, on Saturday evening, July 2nd, at 7 ½ o'clock. Every member is requested to be present. The members are also notified to appear at their engine house, in fill uniform, on Monday morning, July 4th, at 9 o'clock by order of Wm. Wilson, Foreman. (Aurora *Esmeralda Daily Union,* June 29, 1864)

FLAG STAFF

Widespread patriotic sentiment among Aurora's Union supporting citizens led to the erection of a towering flag staff at the town's busiest road intersection—Pine and Antelope Streets—on May 31, 1861. The $275 cost for both the "liberty pole" and the huge American flag was raised by the "cheerful contributions" of the 1,400 citizens gathered to honor the occasion:

A fine liberty pole, nearly 100 feet long, was erected, from which a large flag, made here, was thrown to the breeze, amidst the firing of cannon and other tokens of rejoicing. In the afternoon a staging was erected at the junction of the two principal streets [Pine and Antelope], *and the people having collected, R. M. Howland was chosen Chairman, and F.K. Bechtel Secretary. A patriotic song was then sung by a choir of young men, after which Rev. C. Yager offered a fervent prayer for the preservation of the union and the restoration of national harmony. The "Star Spangle Banner" was then sung, the audience joining in the chorus, when Dr. Mason, the orator of the day, pronounced a spirited oration which was received with frequent outbursts of applause.* (San Francisco *Alta California,* June 9, 1861)

We are to have a great 'Union" meeting here this week, on the occasion of the erection of the city flag-staff and the raising of the banner. The flag has been ordered from San Francisco, and is to 36 feet long. The pole and topmast are 95 feet clear, surmounted by a ball and star, making 3 feet additional. (San Francisco *Daily Evening Bulletin,* June 1, 1861)

After over a year's delay, Aurora's new American flag finally arrived:

The loyal men of this town have a magnificent American flag, 20 by 40 feet, with its stripes all bright and its stars undimmed, floating in beauty from their flag staff. It came by Express, Monday evening,... (Sacramento *Daily Bee,* September 6, 1862)

The flag must have grown a few feet in the next week or so because according to the *Alta California* of September 16, 1862: "business is very lively here since the raising of the fifty-foot flag on the Liberty Pole."

FRATERNAL ORGANIZATIONS

Masons- Although not officially chartered in Aurora at the time, Masons from other lodges in California and Nevada Territory now residing in Aurora held an oration and party in early 1862:

> *Day before yesterday—it being St. John's Day—the Masons of this place enjoyed an oration at the [Mono County] Court House, and afterwards a dinner at Mr. [John S.] Ross's house. The oration was delivered by the Rev. R. C. Yager, who dwelt on the uses and beauties of the Mystic tie. The Gov. Nye, who was present, made a short speech in the usual happy style. At dinner, James Stark favored the company with several recitations. In the evening they had a social party and dance, which did not break up until the "wee sma' hours" were passed away.* (San Francisco *Daily Evening Bulletin,* January 8, 1862)

According to the July 26, 1862, Nevada City *Transcript,* the Masons had 95 members by the summer of 1862. A little over a year later, the first Masonic lodge in Aurora was organized under the auspices of Grand Lodge of California. The "Esmeralda Lodge U. D." convened for the first time on October 10, 1863, with the following members:

> *Worshipful Master James Stark, Henry W. Leech, Jos. H. Richardson, Albert Mack, James Waiters, Isaac S. Rowman, E. E. L. Meek, A. C. Morse, Hiram Huster, Wm. P. Jones, Wm. Tyler, E. M. Bacon, Clinton H. Patchin, J. W. Deering, A. D. Allen, G. Kaufman, W. S. Stanley, John R. White, E. J. Mathews, Rudolph Shibler, D. H. Haskell, Isaac Harris, Thos. I. Wilbur, George Hacker, Geo. W. Bailey, Joseph P. McCoy, J. M. Barlow, Lewis Hanscomb, Peter Ingrehem, and John Carter.* (History of Masonry in Nevada, C. W. Torrence)

Directory

About a year later, a new charter was registered on the California registry under the name of "Esmeralda Lodge No. 170." Three months later, the charter was registered with the Nevada Grand Lodge and became the "Esmeralda Lodge No. Six."

During 1863, Aurora's Masons met on the evening of the third Thursday of each month in the hall above Kimball and Canfield's brick store **(23)** on Antelope Street. In 1864, Wingate Hall on Pine Street was rented and spruced up by lodge members for their meetings:

> *No expense was spared to make the new quarters* [at Wingate Hall] *comfortable; the latest in lodge furniture was installed, and a beautiful carpet, in which was interwoven Masonic emblems, covered the floor.*

Among the Esmeralda Lodge's more prominent members over the years were: A. M. Wingate, John S. Mayhugh, R. K. Colcord, Charles P. Shakespeare, D. H. Haskell, F. K. Bechtel, Judge E. W. McKinstry, Martin K. Harkness, Charles C. Dodd, M. Y. Stewart, Robert M. Howland, James Stark, Joseph H. Richardson, Michael A. Murphy, Wm. Van Voorhies, and John Neidy. With only five members left, "Esmeralda Lodge No. Six" surrendered its charter in 1888.

I.O.O.F (Independent Order of Odd Fellows) - meetings held every Wednesday evening in the same hall used by the Masons. By July of 1862, Aurora's *Esmeralda Star* stated that the Odd Fellows had about 60 members.

FUEL WOOD COMPANIES

Aurora was (and still is) particularly blessed with extensive nearby pinyon (or spelled piñon) pine forests ideal for the fuel wood needs of home and industry. The nutritious pinyon pine nuts was a basic staple for the native Paiute Indians for thousands of years before the miners cleared virtually all the large cone bearing trees near Aurora by the mid 1860s.

Pinyon pine wood sold for only $5 per cord at Aurora during 1862:

> *We have plenty of excellent fuel, furnished by the scrubby pine* [pinyon] *that covers about one quarter of the country hereabouts. The trunk of this tree, although small,—not growing more than twenty or thirty feet high, and seldom being over a foot through at the butt—throws out a great number of branches, making a large bulk when they come to be worked up into cord-wood. The timber is solid and full of pitch, burning for a long time, and throwing out a great deal of heat, being alike serviceable for domestic purposes and making steam. This wood can be delivered in town at $5 per cord— less than half what a similar article costs at Virginia* [City] *or Gold Hill. There is enough of this timber within a convenient distance of Aurora to answer requirements for years, unless the mills and smelting works shall be multiplied beyond expectation.* (San Francisco *Daily Evening Bulletin*, January 2, 1862)

Both the indigenous Native Americans (see page 86) and Chinese woodcutters began harvesting these abundant resources soon after Aurora boomed in the early 1860s:

> *WOOD AND THE RED SKINS.— By amazing energy and uncountable perseverance the Pi-Utes, supported by the Washoes, their collaborers, have kept "poor white trash" in fuel for several months past. They monopolize the market. The Caucasian race, of Anglo-Saxon and Celtic and Slavonic origin, could not compete. None except swarthy, tawny aborigines will haul wood to town at such ruinous low prices as $30 per cord. John Chinamen and Mexicans undertook it in the fall. It was a failure. While China and Mexico employ donkey power, the Indians relied on squaw power, and*

carried the day. (San Francisco *Daily Evening Bulletin,* April 16, 1862)

But less than two years later, fuel wood was disappearing fast:

From all appearance fuel will be very scarce in Aurora in a short time. If the small, stunted species of pine, called Pinyon, disappear from the hill-sides as rapidly for a year or two to come, as it already has since Aurora has grown into existence, there will not be a cord of fire-wood left within thirty miles of the place. (Stockton *Independent*, September 30, 1863)

GOVERNMENT OFFICIALS

From its founding in late 1860, Aurora was believed to be located in California even though the boundary between the two states not yet been established on the ground. That three-year misconception would finally be corrected on September 16, 1863, when California Surveyor General J. F. Houghton walked into Aurora's Mono County district courtroom and declared the town was officially in Nevada.

Because the issue of whether Aurora was located in California or Nevada had not been settled by September 2, 1863, when the terms of the Mono County officers elected in 1861 were due to expire, the powers-that-be decided that dual elections would be held on the same day. The election for the Mono County slate of candidates was held at the jail, while the election of Esmeralda County officials was held a short distance north up the hill at Armory Hall. On September 16, 1863, the boundary issue was finally settled. On that day, the Kidder and Ives survey team arrived in Aurora and declared the city was unquestionably located in Nevada. Three days later, Governor Nye appointed the following officials elected for Esmeralda County during the dual elections of September 2, 1863:

State Senator- Coddington, J. J.
State Assemblymen- Calder, J. W.
County Commissioners- Randall, P. W., Green, G. A., Whitney, G.
Probate Judge- Peck, A. S.
District Attorney- Mesick, R. S.
Sheriff- Francis, D. G.
Under Sheriff- Teel, H. J.
Deputy- Demming, L. L.
Clerk- Dickinson, E. B.
Recorder- Hawkins, Cyril
Treasurer- Rhodes, E.
Assessor- Smith, J. H.
Superintendent of Schools- Saxton, J. B.
Surveyor- McBride, Wm. (see page 137)
Justice of the Peace- Moore, J. T.
Constable- Stewart, M. Y.

One of the first orders of business for the new Esmeralda County Commissioners was to lease the second story of the large two story brick building on the corner of Pine and Silver from Preble and Devoe for their new courthouse.

Aurora's size and importance led Nevada's governor and legislative assembly to authorize the incorporation of Aurora from a "town" to a "city" on February 9, 1864. The act prescribed that the present Board of Trustees consisting of A. M. Wingate, Wm. Hughes, B. C. Fowler, E. Rhodes, and A. Mack now become the Board of Alderman responsible for governing the new city. Ramon Sanchez was the mayor. Although Aurora is now in Mineral County, Nevada, the town was once part of Carson County, Utah Territory; Calaveras County, California; Mono County, California; and Esmeralda County, Nevada.

Directory

GRAND CELEBRATION OF JULY 4, 1864

The following excerpts from the June 29th, July 2nd, July 5th and July 6th 1864 editions of *Esmeralda Daily Union* describe Aurora's July 4th "Grand Celebration." These particular issues of the *Union* were lost for over 130 years until they were found in 1999 inside a sealed tin can "time capsule" placed in the foundation of Aurora's first public schoolhouse in 1864 (see page 116). These lost editions are now preserved on microfilm at the Nevada Historical Society in Reno. For a description of the previous year's Independence Day celebration at Aurora, see the Sacramento *Daily Bee* of July 21, 1862.

The July 5th edition of the *Union* included a transcription of the keynote oration by the Honorable George Turner who was appointed Chief Justice of Nevada Territory by Abraham Lincoln when the Territory was created in 1861. According to Sam Davis' *History of Nevada,* Chief Justice Turner earned a reputation "as the shallowest, most egotistical and mercenary occupant of the Supreme Bench." Mark Twain, who knew Judge Turner during his time in Nevada, wrote a parody of a Turner speech in a newspaper article printed in the Virginia City *Enterprise* entitled "Lecture of Mr. Personal Pronoun." Corruption charges brought to light by the *Enterprise* during 1862 through 1864 eventually forced Judge Turner to resign his position as Chief Justice a little over a month after he gave this oration in Aurora.

Although pompous and long-winded, the following excerpts from Judge Turner's oration (starting on page 66) have been included because they reveal (at least to the author) a sophisticated understanding of Greek, Roman, American, and biblical history as well as a lost world of passionate patriotism, community organization, religious devotion, social comradery, and good will unexpected from a 19th century rough and tumble mining camp. Turner's speech appears to have been well received by the 500 Aurorans in attendance (about one third of the town's total population) as it "*was received by universal applause."* According to the editors of the *Esmeralda Daily Union*, his speech "was not only surpassingly beautiful, abounding in classic allusions, apt illustrations, legal lore, splendid imaginary, deep pathos, and lofty patriotism, but it was just in the right time and place."

***Esmeralda Daily Union*, June 29, 1864 -**

[Advertisement]

1776   Grand   1864
Celebration
of the
Eighty-Eighth Anniversary
of
American Independence
in the
City of Aurora
July Fourth, 1864
Form of Procession
Right Resting on Pine Street in front of Rangers'
Armory, facing west.
At Ten O'clock, A. M.

First Division:

Marshal, N. Steiner,
G. W. Bailey, Aid
Esmeralda Brass band, Esmeralda Rangers,
Aurora City Guard.

Second Division:

F. K. Bechtel, Aid:
President and Vice Presidents, Orator and

Chaplains, (in Carriages), County Officials, Mayor
And Alderman, Masons and Odd Fellows.

Third Division:

G. A. Whitney, Aid:
Fire Department--Engine Company No. 1
Deluge Bucket Company N. Sunday School
children, Miners, bearing emblems of the implements
used in their avocation, Citizens on foot, Horsemen.

Officers and Committees
Chairman of the General Committee, John S. Mayhugh.
Secretary, Jacob Levison.
Treasurer, E. B. Dickensen.
President, E. F. Mitchell.
Grand Marshall, N. Steiner.
Aid of the First Division, G. W. Bailey.
Aid of the Second Division, F. K. Bechtel.
Aid of the Third Division, G. A. Whitney.
Orator, Hon. Geo. Turner.
Chaplains, J. B. Saxton and I. P. Hale.
Reading the Declaration, Capt. Palmer.

Route of Procession

Down Pine to Mono, up Mono to Aurora, along
Aurora to Wide West, down Wide West to Court,
along Court to Pine, down Pine to Silver, up Silver to
Aurora, along Aurora to Antelope, thence
along Antelope Street to Travis Street, up Travis
Street to Silver, and thence to Armory Hall,
where the following exercises will take place:

Order of Exercises:

First—Music by the Brass band.
Second—Prayer by Rev. J. B. Saxton.
Third—Music by the Brass Band.
Fourth—Reading of the Declaration of Independence, by Capt. J. A. Palmer.
Fifth—Music by the Brass band.
Sixth—**Oration by Hon. George Turner.**
Seventh—Music by the Brass Band
Eighth—Regular Toasts.
Ninth—Benediction by Rev. I. P. Hale.
After which the procession will reform and march to the place of starting, and then and there disperse.

Esmeralda Daily Union, July 2, 1864 –

Local Matters

Decorations.—The business houses on Pine street have nearly all been decorated with evergreens which give the street a cool, refreshing and beautiful appearance. Grand preparations are being made in every part of the city for the Fourth and it is expected that we will have a good, old-fashioned celebration. Armory Hall, where the exercises will take place, is being fitted up with great care and taste.

The Public Schools will form in the procession on Monday. A banner appropriately inscribed is being prepared. Thirteen girls have been selected to represent the original thirteen States and one as the

Goddess of Liberty. We understand that the exercises are to be enlivened by the merry voices of the children in a patriotic song.

I. O. O. F.—Esmeralda Lodge No. 6 will meet at the Hall on Antelope street on Monday morning, July 4th, at nine o'clock for the purpose of joining in the celebration of the day. All members in good standing are invited to be present.

Baptist.—Divine services will be held at the Baptist Church, on Winnemucca street, to-morrow, at eleven o'clock a.m., and at a quarter to eight p.m. Sunday School and Bible class at the close of the morning service.

Preaching at the M. E. [Methodist Episcopal] Church, on Aurora street, to-morrow at eleven o'clock a.m. and at 8 p.m. Morning subject—"The Blessed Nation, etc." Sunday School at 2 p.m. L. P. Hale, P. C.

Fireman's Meeting.—Esmeralda Engine Company No. 1 will meet at 7 ½ o'clock this evening and will meet, in full uniform, on Monday morning, at 9, to join the procession.

Close Up.—The Committee of Arrangements desires us to renew the request that all business houses and saloons be closed on the Fourth from 8 a.m. till 3 p.m.

City Guard.—This Company will meet at their Armory to-morrow at twelve o'clock m.[sic] for drill and on Monday morning at 8 for parade.

No Paper.—We will not issue any paper on Monday as we believe that all business should be suspended that day.

Presbyterian services at Preble & Devoe's Hall to-morrow at eleven o'clock a.m. Preaching by Rev. C. Yager.

The Oration.—A rich treat may be expected in the oration to be delivered by Judge Turner at the coming Fourth.

Esmeralda Daily Union, July 5, 1864 –

The Fourth

Yesterday was a proud day for Aurora. The celebration exceeded in interest, the expectations of the most sanguine, eliciting an enthusiasm for the glorious old flag that ought to strike terror to the hearts of traitors, and fill with gratitude and hope those who love their country and its free institutions. The committee to whom the arrangements for the day were entrusted deserve great credit for the efficiency and thoroughness with which their duties were preformed. No pains were spared in perfecting every provision requisite to success, and nobly have the Committee been rewarded by the beauty and grandeur that characterized all exercises of the day. A salute of thirteen guns by Capt. Rabbitts ushered in the day, after which quiet reigned, resembling that of the holy Sabbath in a New England village, till about 9 o'clock. Then with one consent the masses began to move. The streets of the business part of the city had been ornamented by evergreens presenting a beautiful appearance, and men, women, and children thronged them vieing [sic] with each other in doing honor to the day we celebrate. At ten o'clock the procession formed under Marshal Steiner and his efficient aids. The Aurora Brass Band led the procession, and during the day acquitted themselves with their accustomed skill, eliciting the praise of all who heard them. Next came the Esmeralda Rangers, a splendid cavalry company under Capt. Teel. Then followed the Aurora City Guard under Capt. Palmer, exhibiting and efficiency in drill truly credible for the time they have devoted to the exercise. Following them were Vice Presidents (the President Dr. Mitchell being absent on account of sickness), Orator and Chaplains (in carriage), Odd-Fellows, the Fire Department, Public Schools, miners, citizens and horsemen, nor would we omit the tribute paid to civilization by the company of Pi-Utes, who, with flowing banner, followed the grand procession of American Freemen, as they marched through our principal streets. Long live "Heap Good Union Pi-Ute," and having sipped at the fountain of intelligence and felt the fires of Patriotism, may the time come when they may share our hopes of immortality also. About twelve o'clock the procession reached the Hall, and as the throng were filling it and the spacious veranda, prepared in front, Capt. Rabbitts fired the mid-day salute which wakened response to the thrilling notes of joy and freedom in the distant hills. The Pi-Utes through an opening in the crowd, with flowing banner, on which was the following inscription: "Heap Good Union Pi-Ute," and halting in front of the speaker's stand, by order of the Captain, Jacob Levison, they faced about, gave three rousing cheers for the Union, wheeled into line, marched out to the rear of the audience, indulged for a few minutes in a Pi-Ute dance, accompanied by the soft sweet cadences characteristic of the tribe, after which they quietly retired, leaving the rest of the exercises to be conducted by their white brethren. By this time the vast concourse had become quietly seated, and the exercises began. The Brass Band performed their part exquisitely, eliciting enthusiastic applause. The opening prayer was offered by Rev. J. B. Saxton. The Declaration of Independence was read by Capt. Palmer, after which Judge Turner, Orator of the day, was introduced by J. G. Canfield, acting President. The enthusiastic cheers that greeted the speaker gave evidence of the welcome he had found in the hearts of the people. His address needs no eulogy from us. It was received by universal applause. In our judgment it was not only surpassingly beautiful, abounding in classic allusions, apt illustrations, legal lore, splendid imaginary, deep pathos, and lofty patriotism, but it was just in the right time and place. By the politeness of his Honor we are permitted to present our readers a full outline of the production which we are sure will be read with interest and profit by all:

Judge Turner's Address.

In the commencement of his address the speaker spoke of the pleasure it afforded him to mingle with the festivities of our people, and then he alluded in the following language to the procession:

"It was a beautiful sight, fellow citizens, to look upon your brilliant procession, in its line of march. First came your admirable band discoursing of thrilling harmony: then came the cavalry, the Esmeralda Rangers, sitting upon their steeds like Castor and Pollux, their shoulders glittering with jewels and their heads bounding with patriotism; then followed the City Guards, with their blue uniforms and their hearts of oak; then the carriages with your officers and guests; followed these came the Odd-Fellows society, one of God's own orders; next to these the firemen, with their shirts as red as the fires they quench—these civic soldiers, who fight a superhuman foe—nature's fiercest element and God's chosen means of destroying the world. These heroes win laurels in civil conflict and illustrate the sentiment that "peace hath her victories no less renowned than war." God bless the noble firemen. After these came the children from the public schools, clad in hues of glory, "red, white and blue," singing their cherub hymns of patriotism; and at the end of all came a scene which could be witnessed in no other country under heaven, a band of Pi-Ute Indians, clad in parti-colored uniforms, their hats adorned with feathery ornaments of barbaric hue and gaudiness. The sentiment of this exhibition was truly remarkable. They were there a voluntary obeisance paid by savagery to civilization; they came next after the common schools—ignorance following education; they were last in your procession; barbarism bowing reverently to civilization and Christianity."

After other remarks befitting the occasion, the speaker spoke of the propriety of celebrating the Fourth of July, and said:

"It is meet [sic] that we should celebrate this day. Shall the Greek celebrate the birth-day of Athenia? Shall the Romans celebrate their Carnival and the triumphs of the heroes? Shall the Mohammedan celebrate the Hegira of his Prophet? Shall the Hindoo [sic] celebrate the birthday of Vishnu, and the Egyptian that of Isis and Osiris, and we sons of Columbia, fail to celebrate the birthday of out National Independence? Nay, rather let us add a new luster to the day; let us give a new zest to our rejoicings; let the shrill fife tell it to the breeze, and the sonorous drum echo it to the distant hills; let that deep-mouthed cannon, whose black throat immortal Jove's dread clamors counterfeit, sent it to the remotest recesses of the Sierras."

"Hang out your banners on the outmost walls; The cry is still we're free."

After speaking of the landing of the landing of the Pilgrims upon Plymouth Rock, and Captain John Smith and his party upon the banks of the James river, he spoke with some mirth of the Blue Laws, and the queer habits of those singular but wonderful people. The orator then spoke of the efforts of our ancestors in the Revolution to achieve their independence. Upon this subject he said:
"It was a peculiar period in the world's history when our evolution commenced. Struggles for freedom had always proved fruitless, and the tyrants of the world had ever rested from the toils of battle with the triumphant worlds, "Veni, ridi, vici." Glance at the history of the world for a moment. Israel had enjoyed a kind of freedom, but the Babylomish empire and neighboring monarchies soon absorbed it. The Greek States were partially republican in form, but an internal and external foe destroyed them. Phillip of Macedon fulminate over Greece from the Bosphorous [sic] to Artaxerxes' throne, and Xeres, with his Persian hordes, marched down upon them, commanding Mount Athos to bow his head before his conquering hosts, and casting iron fetters into the sea to signify his triumphs. Rome at times was free, but the kingdom, the consulate, and the empire absorb almost twelve centuries of her history. France struggled for it in vain while blood flowed shoe-mouth deep in the streets of the imperial city. England, too, had bright glimpses of freedom. She was glorious when the Barons upon Runnymede snatched Magna Charta from old King John. Cromwell and the Commonwealth gave the people much that was beautiful in freedom; but none of these were thoroughly

republican. After this brief review let us look at the present state of Europe, and there we will find little to encourage us. Italy lies in chains, with the foot of France upon her neck and a bayonet at her breast. Poland is torn and rent and bleeding.; while blue-eyed Hungary has sat her down to weep, with dust on her forehead and chains on her feet. I am not, however, fellow-citizens, among those who think that tyranny ever shall thus triumph. I believe that freedom shall yet walk abroad through the gardens of Europe; that her blue eye shall yet rest upon the snow-drifts of the north; that her fair hand shall yet pluck the green grapes of the South, and that the shouts of regenerated men shall hereafter follow the sun and keep company with the hours, while the song of jubilee shall go round the world like a hosannah! But I was endeavoring to prove that struggles for freedom had always before been fruitless, and that our forefathers still had faith. They believed that

"Freedom's battle once begun,
Bequeathed by bleeding sire to son,
Tho' baffled oft is ever won."

And accordingly, through eight long years of blood and poverty and toil, they struggled into light. At Princeton, at Trenton, at Valley Forge and at Bunker Hill, they achieved victories that needs but the antiquity that hovers over Mars and Mercury and Jupiter to elevate them to Olympus.

I propose to speak of America, her origin, her history, her destiny. I have said that we were God's chosen people; that we were as certainly raised up by Providence to prove to the world, the possibility of liberty when coupled with virtue, just as certainly as blood-stained France, with its Guillotine and Auto-de-fe, was designed by Providence to prove it impossible when coupled with vice; and I assure you, my friends, that in this land [we] are dwelling now, that people who have been anointed as the ancient sons of Levi were of old, to be the chosen guardian's of the Ark of God's liberty amongst men; the Ark of the Covenant, the Urim and Thummin of

Civilization and Christianity, are in your sacred keeping; guard well the holy trust.

Let me point to the Bible; let me ask you to run rapidly through the various prophecies of that sacred book, and see if America is not the child of prophecy; God's own peculiar country. What says Isaiah, Daniel, and Ezekiel? they speak of "that Nation which is to be born in a day." That people "who dwell in the land between the seas and east of the Great Sea." America is the only country east of the Pacific—they describe it as "a land where the son of the stranger is made citizen." A people whose ruler is chosen from among themselves; it is said to be a country where the "inhabitants thereof dwell in unwalled cities." This prophet never saw an unwalled city save in his apocalyptic vision of America. Again it is said to be "a land where all nations of the earth shall go up thereto." Lieutenant Maury has demonstrated that by the oceanic currents every Nation goes up when they come to America. The prophet further says that it is to be a country "where the chariots run like torches and smoke like fire and jostle each other in the streets." This pictures the railroad and locomotive beautifully. It is said that "in the land and in the midst thereof is the valley of the passengers between the Great Seas." This refers evidently to the Mississippi Valley. It is further true that by the best approved system of prophetic computation now extant, that starting from the time in Daniel when "the sacrifices ceased in Jerusalem" until the number of prophetic weeks had escaped, as described therein and making careful computation of the time, allowing for sabaticol [sic] weeks as is done, the time when "that Nation" shall be born is brought down precisely to the 4th of July, 1776. But this too recondite for me, and my scriptural learning is too limited to demonstrate it. Of this, however, I am certain, that the sacred book expressly says that "the lion and the leopard and the bear shall go up to contend with the eagle." The lion of England, the leopard of Austria and the bears of Russia, and I thank God and take courage, when I further read "that the eagle shall triumph."

The speaker then rapidly sketched our history down. He alluded to the war of 1812, the Mexican war, and then this great rebellion. He spoke with feeling of Fort Donelson, Wilson's Creek and Shiloh—of Vicksburg, Gettysburg, and Fredericksburg—of the battles of Chancellorsville, Fair Oaks, and the contests upon the Peninsula. He then alluded to the heroes who had fallen, and used the following language:

"Look at that youthful hero, as he bounds up the steps of that hotel in Alexandria and tears a rebel flag from its insolent standard. He descends the steps with his trophy in his hands, but ere he reaches the earth a cruel rebel shot him through the heart, while an avenging hand in a moment slew his executioner. I allude to the first offering of the war, the gallant, beloved Ellsworth. Look yonder at Southern Missouri. See that little band of men, struggling day after day without receiving succor from St. Louis, against four times their number. They now start for another charge upon the foe, four-fold stronger than themselves. Their gallant leader rides in front with his cap upon his sword, crying, "Follow me," but alas! as their shout of victory rends the air, a duplicate bullet pieces the heart of their leader. He sinks upon his horse. A friendly arm supports him while he asks, "General, are you hurt?" "Not much," was the reply, as he sank into death. Oh, no! it was "not much." The casket was shattered, but the jewel was unharmed. The earthly house of his tabernacle was dissolved, but he had a building of God, a house not made with hands, eternal in the heavens.

Sleep Lyon, sleep in honored rest,
Your fame and valor wearing,
The bravest are the tenderest,
The loving are the daring.

Again let me point you to northern Mississippi. See that gallant Colonel in an ambulance. He rides three miles in front of his regiment, with only three friends beside him. Suddenly a band of guerrillas surround his carriage; one cruel hand draws a pistol from his holster, and shoots him to the heart, and as another draws his weapon he exclaims, "Don't shoot, my friend, I am already killed." Then, sinking into the arms of his companion, he murmured in death,

"Charley, I am very young to die—but this country is worth ten thousand times ten thousand such poor lives as mine." I speak now of an old fellow lawyer of Cincinnati, the last man with whom I transacted legal business in Ohio, a friend of my early youth—Colonel Bob McCook, of the Ohio Ninth. "Peace to his ashes." Yet, once again, and finally, I would point you to that man, who was not a Senator from Oregon alone, but a representative from the whole Pacific coast. He dropped the toga of the Senator for the sword of the Hero, and early in the fight went down to the dust of death. I point you now to that figure bathed in the blood at Ball's Bluff, the gallant Colonel Baker."

The speaker went quite fully into the achievements of our men. He paid a handsome tribute to the valor of the privates and non-commissioned officers, who he styled "the unnamed heroes." Our orator then alluded to some objections to the Government, in brief but pointed terms. "It has been said, remarked the speaker, "that this war has cost mountains of gold and oceans of blood, but the government is worth it all. As to money the country never was so rich," and as to the death of soldiers he exclaimed:

"But whether on the scaffold high
Or in the army's van,
The fittest place for man to die
Is where he dies for man."

He spoke of coercing States as being like all the exercises of law, which only guilty men object to. As to the idea that the Union is already dissolved, he answered it by a beautiful tribute to its indestructibility. To the objections of those who pray for peace, he quoted these beautiful lines:

"Better that all our ships and all their crews
Should sink to rot, in ocean's dreamless ooze
Each torn flag waving challenge as it went,
And each dumb gun a brave man's monument,

> *Than seek such peace as only coward crave,*
> *Give us the peace of dead men or of brave."*

The speaker also spoke of the objection that Mr. Lincoln had violated the Constitution and added the weight of his personal and official authority to the assertion that Mr. Lincoln had never violated one single letter of the Constitution regarded in the light of the laws of war, and this, too, in view of habeas corpus suspended. Copperheads imprisoned, Fugitive Slave law suspended, and the proclamation of freedom issued. Slight departures may be tolerated when the Government is in danger. It was said of Pericles that he found Athens of brick and left it of marble, "and were I Mr. Lincoln," said the speaker, "I would ask no prouder epitaph upon my tombstone than this: 'Here lies the man who bent the Constitution to save the Commonwealth."

He closed by alluding to the life, history and character of U. S. Grant, and the victories of the past, which give such high promise of the future. He paid an earnest compliment to the citizens of Aurora for their $6000 subscription to the Sanitary Commission, and concluded by a comparison of this conflict to the Crimean campaign, which thrilled all hearts:

> *"The brothers close up nearer,*
> *Press hard the hostile powers,*
> *For another Ralaklava*
> *And the Malakoff is ours."*

At the close of the oration three cheers proposed by Major Sherman for the orator, and responded to by the audience with a hearty good will. Music by the Band, a patriotic song by the Public School children, conducted by Miss Anna Canfield and Benediction by Rev. I. P. Hale closed the exercises.

The evening was enlivened by bonfires, ascent of rockets, and the sailing of three large balloons from the corner of Pine and Silver streets. Two of them darted up with great velocity till the current of air caught them and wafted them Northward till they dwindled to the size of appearance of stars, and finally were lost in the distance. The third arose fitfully, careened like a ship in a storm, caught fire, fell to pieces, and descended at no great distance in fragments to the earth. Many interesting incidents of the day might be gathered up but for want of time, we are compelled to omit them. One thing however, is worthy of notice. The most perfect order crowned the day. Scarcely a drunken man could be seen during the day or evening. No quarreling, disorder or strife existed except the strife who could do most honor to the anniversary of our glorious Republic. Despite of all the sand and sage brush, the summer snow storms and frosty dog days we felt proud yesterday of our adopted home. It is mind and heart after all that make a country like ours what it is, a pride and joy among the civilized powers of earth.

Esmeralda Daily Union, **July 6, 1864 -**

News of the Day

We had the honor on the Fourth to dine with invited guests of the Aurora City Guard at the [Merchants'] Exchange [Hotel]. The guests met at the Armory at half past four P. M. and were escorted to the Exchange dining room by the Brass Band, and the Guards commanded by Capt. Palmer. A sumptuous repast was provided and the occasion proved to be a very happy one. After the cruel war on the formidable line of edibles was over, the feast of reason and flow of soul ensued, during which we are happy to say, the flow of wine was light. How far this fact was attributable to the example of his honor Judge Turner we do not pretend to say, but it was noticeable that he abstained entirely from the stimulating beverage. We are unable to present anything like a just idea of the pleasantry of the occasion, in language. Major Sherman read a very beautiful poem composed by one who has given his life to his country's cause upon the battle field. The name of the author we did not hear but we were impressed by the reading of the production with the conviction that the writer must have possessed a strength of mind and depth of patriotism fitting him alike for the active duties of our stern age and for her heroic martyrdom to his country's weal [sic]. Many toasts were given and responded to with patriotic ardor. Only a few of the sentiments offered can we give as we write from memory. Judge McKinstry offered as a toast the "Women of the Revolution," prefacing it with a characteristic speech, witty, oily, and polite, showing that his claim to be considered a lady's man is well founded. The usual toasts to the day we celebrate and The Father of his Country were offered. "The Public schools of America," "The Public Press," "The Hay Press," "The City Guards," "The Aurora Brass Band," "The Sanitary Commission," "The Esmeralda Mines," together with many other topics received attention, eliciting the greatest enthusiasm from gentlemen present. The exercises were interspersed by the music of the Band, the mirth and wit, courteousness and candor, dignity and affability of our District Judge adding greatly to the pleasure of the occasion. The following sentiment from Judge Turner closed the agreeable entertainment, in honor of the procession: "May the Guards guard the city and the Rangers range the hills, and the Odd Fellows and Masons protect the lives and the Firemen the property of our citizens, may the children learn wisdom and Pi-Utes nobly follow their example."

HOTELS AND BOARDINGHOUSES

American Hotel (47)

Aurora House- located on Silver between Pine and Aurora Streets. W. A. B. Cobb, was proprietor of this "first class hotel where all the comforts of a home may be found."

>   **American Hotel,**
> North side Pine Street, Aurora California.
> WM. MILLER................ Proprietor.
>
> Board and Lodging, per Week,........$10 00
>   "   "   "   Single Room 12 00
>   " Without Lodging, per week,..... 9 00
> Single Meals,........................... 75 cts.
> Lodging, per night................... 50 cts.
> Aurora, April 4th, 1863.   n1

Barnum Hotel (37) - operated by J. Bellinger on the second floor over the Washington Baths in a wood building owned by Grey and Martin.

Herbert House (45) - B. Bird proprietor.

Merchants' Exchange Hotel (49) [R] - a 28 x 50 ft. three story brick building on a 50 x 50 ft lot owned by Tranovich and Morris; H. K. White and P. Mitchell were the hotel's proprietors.

> *Some heavy grading is being done for the foundations of a large three-story brick building, sixty by eighty feet, on the corner of Pine and Winnemucca streets, to be used as a hotel. I have been informed by the proprietor that it is his determination to arrange the order of his rooms so as to give the most extensive accommodations to the traveling public. The rooms will be large and well ventilate. A hotel of the above kind is much needed in this burg.* (San Francisco *Alta California,* May 2, 1863)

The Merchants' Exchange Hotel opened its doors to the public in November 1863. The hotel had a bar where one could find the "choicest wines, liquors, and cigars" as well as a "No. 1 Billiard

Table," and one of the "most commodious and elegantly furnished restaurants in the Territory."

The Merchants' Exchange Hotel, Aurora's largest and finest hotel, also served as the town's stage stop. Its opening in the fall of 1863 ushered in a new level of elegance and sophistication to rough and tumble Aurora. (*History of Nevada with Illustrations and Biographical Sketches of its Prominent Men and Pioneers*, 1881)

    The Merchants' Exchange Hotel served the town for almost twenty years until it was destroyed by fire in 1882. The building, however, remained standing but vacant for another seventy years after the fire. Brick contractors descended on the structure in the early 1950s and today only piles of broken bricks remain to remind us where this magnificent structure once stood. Aurora's first authorized archaeological excavation was conducted at the Merchants' Exchange Hotel in 1999 and 2000 by Jessica Kinchloe Smith, a graduate student from the University of Nevada, Reno.

Directory

Monroe House - large brick hotel or boardinghouse on the north side of Wide West Street owned by Col. U. P. Monroe

St Charles Hotel (30) [R] - brick hotel, Mrs. B. Schram proprietor.

San Francisco House (26) - brick hotel owned by F. Pardoe.

Tremont House (25) - on the lot owned by P. Radovitch. A. C. Judy was listed as the proprietor on the 1864 Esmeralda County tax roll but M. E. Blaney & Co. were the proprietors according to an add in the November 18, 1863 *Esmeralda Star*.

JAIL

Located on the hill just north of Pine Street, Mono County's first jail was completed around the first of April, 1862 **(14) [R]**.

REPORT OF THE GRAND JURY— On examining the county jail, they find nothing to condemn in the manner in which it is kept either in cleanliness or in the treatment of the prisoners. They do not think the building safe. The walls are badly sprung and cracked, owing probably to the insecure foundation in front. The ties which are supposed to hold the front to its place, they do not consider any security or benefit, and it would not surprise them any day to hear of its falling and especially when the snow begins to melt in the spring; neither do they consider it a secure place to keep a prisoner without a guard. If the building is to be used for the purpose of confining prisoners they would recommend and press upon the proper authorities that they do cause to be built two or three substantial cells therein so that persons confined on criminal charges should be kept separate from other prisoners. This is not only a duty due the prisoners, but it would materially conduce on their safe-keeping and save the county the expense of a night watch. (Aurora *Esmeralda Star*, September 20, 1862)

LAUNDRIES

City Laundry - owned by Tomas Newman on Winnemucca.

McCarty, L. - laundry south of St. Charles Hotel.

LUMBER YARDS

Magilton & Yaney- lumber yard on the northwest corner of Aurora and Court.

Pioneer Lumber Yard- owned by C. D. Wingate on the south side of Spring Street across the street from the Union Mill.

The earliest mill to serve Aurora was likely the Green Mill at Sweetwater Canyon owned by Amos Green. However, Aurora's lumber yards got most of their timber from sawmills operating in the old-growth Jeffrey pine forests along the eastern slopes of the Sierra Nevada Mountains on the west side of Bridgeport Valley. According to Frank Wedertz in *Mono Diggings*, one of the earliest mills in this area was the Tuolumne Mill Company owned by Zach B. Tinkum, which was located at the east end of Lower Twin Lake at Robinson Creek. Another mill further down Robinson Creek was called the Moses Robinson (for whom Robinson Creek is named) and Hubbard mill. Nearby Buckeye Canyon was the site of the Buckeye Mill Company's sawmill, which was originally owned by Berry, then Towle, and finally by 1862, Napoleon Bonaparte Hunewill, the first Hunewill to settle in Bridgeport Valley. It is interesting to note that

Directory

the 1864 Esmeralda County Tax Assessor's Roll map shows two structures owned by "Hunniwell" along Spring Street about a mile west of town, which could possibly be a lumberyard owned by N. B. Hunewill.

Another important mill was owned by I. P. Yaney (for whom Yaney Canyon is named) and his partner Magilton. It was located where Patterson Creek intersects U.S. 395. The following newspaper accounts describes some of these early logging operations:

> *Mr. Elliott* [of Aurora] *informs me that the lumber business is far greater than I anticipated. There are four saw mills, which produce in the aggregate 20,000 feet of lumber daily, which at $40 per thousand, is the neat sum of $800. About one hundred men are daily employed in connection with the mills. There are over thirty teams constantly engaged in hauling lumber to Aurora.* (Stockton *Independent*, September 30, 1863)

> *About three miles beyond the Springs* [Fales Hot Springs], *we found a party of Columbians erecting a shingle mill which they intend to drive by steam power. They have also a water-power, on which they propose to erect a saw mill for lumber, by and by, I was told that short shingles are now selling in Aurora for $14 per M, and common lumber for $90 per M. There is a fine lot of timber here, the principal part of it secured by this company. Four miles farther down the same valley is Magilton & Yaney's saw mill. This was started by Magilton & Heslep, and, I think, was the pioneer mill. There are three others now, on adjacent streams, making four in all, as yet in operation, with an aggregate capacity of about a hundred thousand per week. The Pioneer Mill cut out 30,000 feet the week before we passed along. These mills, and two others, situated in another direction, supply all the timber for Aurora and the neighboring country. The timber sells for $60* [per M or thousand board feet] *at the mills, and $30 is*

79

allowed for hauling to Aurora. Two or three miles further on, the stream on which these mills are located, find their way into the East Walker; or its branches, at a prairie called The Big Meadows [Bridgeport Valley]. (Sonora *American Flag,* November 5 1863)

Aurora's hay also came from Bridgeport, California:

BRIDGEPORT— This town, at present the county seat of Mono County, Cal., is one of the handsomest places east of the Sierra Nevadas, excepting, o' course, the old established towns of the Atlantic States. The people of the town derive their support chiefly from the hay and lumber trade. There are six saw-mills and shingle factories within the limits of the township, which until recently have been doing an extensive business. The sawmill of Tinkum & Co., at Twin Lakes, is one of the finest we have ever seen. It is complete in every respect, and reflects great credit upon the enterprising and worthy owners. (Aurora *Esmeralda Daily Union,* August 15, 1864)

MEAT MARKETS

Aurorans ate a lot of meat which primarily came from cattle raised in Owens Valley located about 90 miles south of Aurora. These cattle were processed in local slaughterhouses along Spring Street (see page 120). Pieces of sawed-off cattle and sheep bones scattered everywhere among Aurora's ruins today attest to miners living "high on the hog" during the town's boom.

Centre Meat Market (15) - owned by Richard Barlow.

City Meat Market (4) [R] - also known as "Bradford's Store" or "Bradford's Brick Store," the two-story building had a brick-faced stone first floor, and a wooden second story. The remains of the building's stone sidewalls are some of Aurora's only building features left standing today.

Davis, Moses - butcher shop on E side of Winnemucca.

Livermore Bros. - meat market on south side of Wide West Street.

Nowlan, J. - butcher shop on Antelope.

Sigmund, Wm. - (or spelled Siegmand) butcher in Sommers brick building immediately north of the Merchants' Exchange Hotel.

Silver Street Market - meat market on east side of Silver, owned by Bradford and Bros.

Union Meat Market - owned by T. Burt & L. Dorn on a lot owned by B. G. Parker and the west side of Antelope.

MINES AND MINING COMPANIES

The hills around Aurora are covered with hundreds of exposed gold-bearing quartz veins and during the early 1860s, mining companies headquartered in San Francisco owned and actively mined most of them. These companies issued stock that was bought and sold in Aurora and San Francisco. The rapidly increasing demand for Esmeralda's mining stocks led in part to the organization of the San Francisco Stock and Exchange Board by the fall of 1862. Nearly everyone in California was involved with the "speculation mania" created by Nevada's mining stocks during 1863:

> *Not only the capitalist and the banker, but the wholesale and retail merchant, the lawyer and the physician, the preacher and the editor, the carpenter and the blacksmith, the jeweler and the hotel keeper, the tailor and the shoemaker, the*

> *drayman and the stevedore, the clerk and the laborer, the milliner, the teacher, the manservant, and the maidservant-all own share in some silver mine. It is a rare thing to meet a man who has not a certificate of stock in his pocket.* (San Francisco *Alta California,* October 29, 1863)

Aurora's three most important mines during the boom years of 1863 and 1864 were the Antelope, Wide West, and Real del Monte. Sadly for investors, they mined only enough gold to create a brief sensation and never returned one cent to their hapless stockholders.

During 1863, Aurora was infested by all sorts of "seedy-looking Nabobs" from San Francisco's Montgomery Street who were looking to either locate or buy and sell claims:

> *EDITORS ALTA: Every body, for the last week, seems to have gone 'daft.' Every day the hills around are covered with hunters for new ledges. Everything that looks like an 'indication,' is eagerly pounced upon, and located for a gold or silver Company, out of which all connected are to be millionaires in the spring. The mild season has brought us any number of comers— 'rolled up,' 'muffed up,' 'long' and 'short' coated gentry— who have a mysterious look about them. They seem to know everybody, and the way they 'liquor' the 'natives' of Aurora is a caution. Among them I see a good many Montgomery Street chaps, who, when there, were pretty seedy-looking individuals; but presto! change; here they are scattering around any amount of loose change, dressed like Nabobs, driving fast teams, riding splendid horses, and faring on the best that be had for money.. Get rich, fat and saucy, is the motto of the new comers.* (San Francisco *Alta California,* February 3, 1863)

Esmeralda's highflying mining stocks were much in demand even though few knew anything about the true underlying value or potential of the mine. But the "carnival time" of rampant speculation would soon end leaving many "fearfully demoralized:

> *At the start everyone bought almost anything that was offered them in the shape of mining stock, some of which were gotten up on paper in a style absolutely stunning. A wood-cut of an honest miner, with long boots, and a pick in hand, striking with fearful effect at some of the most astonishingly large chunks of gold, would readily command from ten to twenty dollars per share. A lithograph certificate, representing a huge monster vomiting forth bran new twenty-dollar pieces with an expertness and rapidity that would put to blush your Branch Mint, would bring almost any price…This was carnival time with those splendid modern 'soldiers of fortune' entitled 'jay hawkers,' and many is the poor fellow who fell early in the action, hit in the most sensitive and vital portion of the body, the pocket, by these expert sharpshooters; while others, who did not come out dead-broke, were fearfully demoralized.* (San Francisco *Alta California,* July 12, 1863)

But unlike Esmeralda's unscrupulous mining companies and stock brokers, her miners were typically hardworking and honest men many of whom were recent immigrants from mining regions in Europe. Aurora's miners typically lived in homemade cabins near the mines, and worked ten-hour days, six days a week. Their job was hard and dangerous but the pay was relatively high for the times:

> *About two hundred miners are regularly employed in taking out ore. The wages are $4 per day for work in the shafts or drifts; $3 per day for work at the windlass; or $1 per day less, if the employer provides board and lodging.* (San Francisco *Alta California,* October 29, 1862)

An 1864 Directory and Guide to Nevada's Aurora

J. Ross Browne was envious of the care free and independent life of miners when he visited Aurora's nearby neighbor Bodie in the fall of 1864:

> *These jolly miners were the happiest set of bachelors imaginable: had neither chick nor child, that I knew of, to trouble them; cooked their own food; did their own washing, mended their own clothes, made their own beds, and on Sunday cut their own hair, greased their own boots,...*

Miners pose with lunch pails in front of an impressive Aurora brick building during the early 1900s.

(Kenneth L. McKeough)

Directory

NEWSPAPERS

The *Esmeralda Star* was only five months old when this edition was published in "Aurora, Mono County Cal" by Edwin A Sherman and Co. Individual copies sold for 25¢ while a year's subscription cost $6.00.

Aurora Daily Times **(6)** - Published every evening (except Sunday) by Robert Draper in a 12 x 30 ft. wood building owned by C.D. Wingate, the *Aurora Daily Times* was the town's first daily newspaper. The newspaper originated as the *Aurora Weekly Times* when Robert Draper and Robert Glen first published the paper during April 1863. Due to its popularity, the paper began daily publication a month later. Because of the downturn in the town's fortunes, the newspaper ceased publication entirely during July 1865. Unfortunately, only a few issues have survived. Most of the ads displayed in this book are from the December 3, 1863, edition of

Aurora Daily Times archived at the Mono County Museum at Bridgeport, California.

***Esmeralda Daily Union* (33)** – The *Esmeralda Star*, Aurora's first newspaper, began publication on May 17, 1862. Edwin A. Sherman owned the paper while Aurora was thought to be in California. Sherman later sold his interest to John Hatch who, during March 1864, suspended the *Star* and began publishing the *Esmeralda Daily Union*. By the spring of 1864, Aurora supported two daily newspapers. The *Daily Union* ceased publication entirely during 1868.

PAIUTE INDIANS

Because the area in and around Aurora was once abundant with large game animals like bighorn sheep and pronghorn antelope, and once covered with plant resources like the bountiful pinyon pine tree, the native Paiute Indians hunted and gathered this rich bounty for thousands of years. The numerous flakes of locally quarried obsidian (a byproduct of making projectile points) one sees today scattered among the town's ruins attest to the occupation of Aurora by Native Americans long before the arrival of "civilization."

One of the earliest descriptions of how the Paiute Indians lived before their native way of life was transformed forever by white settlers comes from a correspondent writing from "Vining's Creek" at Mono Lake about his encounters with the Paiutes living at nearby Owens Valley:

> *The only animals owned by these people are a few small ponies, which they ride without saddle or bridle, and generally two at a time. They* [the horses] *are diminutive, but tough and docile creatures, are particularly used for moving camp and packing game, their owners being no great riders. Of game there is here a good deal—chiefly hare, with some*

sage hens, and a few deer and sheep in the mountains. The hars [sic] *are mostly caught in nets, and by other devises common among Indians. They have but few guns, the usual implement of the chase being the bow and arrow, in the use of which they are much more expert than that of firearms....They are also honest and industrious, never attempting to steal or purloin the least trifle, while they engage in any kind of work required of them with the least alacrity.* (San Francisco *Daily Evening Bulletin,* July 19, 1861)

The cutting of nearly all of the pinyon pine trees for fuel, as well as the slaughter of the big game herds for food by the miners, meant the Paiutes (spelled Piutes in the 1860s) who chose to stay had to adapt to a new way of life. Aurora's Paiutes were particularly resourceful as they soon learned how to make a meager living doing the hardest jobs, like gathering firewood in the winter, for Aurora's residents.

Col. Samuel Youngs, one of Aurora's most prominent and respected citizens (see page 102), noted an early performance by Paiute Indians in his journal entry of April 7, 1861:

Saw an Indian feast dance in town to amuse the citizens, who gave them a few shillings. 20 to 30 Indians form a circle, commence singing a humming nasal tune, stamp first one foot then the other, shaking their arms. Painted on faces, backs and bodies naked except cloth around their loins.

Mary Ellen Ackley, an Aurora who lived on Wide West Street in 1864 noted that the Paiutes were "peaceable and friendly" and generally very helpful around the house:

The squaws often came with baskets of faggots [bundle of sticks] *on their backs, which they would sell for 25 cents. I often had the Indian men shovel snow, cut wood and draw water from the well. One old Indian came every morning and filled my water barrel at the kitchen door.*

The hostilities with the Indians in Owens Valley occasionally spilled over to the outskirts of Aurora as reported by L'ARGENT:

Last night [April 19th] the whole town was aroused by a report that the Indians were threatening an attack upon Winter's Mill, about a mile distant, in Spring Valley, and the Esmeralda Rifles and a number of citizens hastily seized their arms and went out. They found no hostile act had been commenced, although the Indians had been there threatening and saucy. It would be surprising if we yet should have difficulty with them. These Pi Utes are strong, warlike, and courageous. (San Francisco *Daily Evening Bulletin,* May 4, 1863)

Aurora's Paiutes stayed on long after the town went bust:

The old Indians and squaws bring almost half a mule load of wood on their backs more than two miles into town. They have a rope around the wood and across their breast or forehead to hold it on their backs, and sell it for twenty-five cents per load. In case they don't sell it readily, they will stand holding it on their backs for an hour or more, not sitting down to rest. Yesterday I saw a half-grown girl with a heavy load of wood on her back, walking in the snow and ice with her feet wrapped in old rags. (Sacramento *Daily Union,* February 24, 1868 SD)

The Piutes are a useful class of people. They are willing to work for the farmers and families in the town doing washing, etc., for one dollar per day, or hog-a-dy (food) for small jobs. Their habits are very migratory. One month is about as long as they will work in any one place. They then go off for a while and return again to work. (Sacramento *Daily Union*, July 3, 1873)

They lived in the hills surrounding the town even in the coldest winter:

THE PIUTES.—These Indians are queer people. They "roost" on the highest hills, where their camp fires are visible through the stilly night, reminding one of the signal fires which blaze up in times of blood and terror. We seldom hear of a Piute dying from cold, although his shanks are often bare, even when 'tis cold enough to freeze the handle off a white man's face.' (Aurora *Esmeralda Daily Union*, January 21, 1865)

Their camps are about the hills far away from water, which they carry in jugs made with willow boughs covered with pitch from the pine trees. Their object in camping on the hills is probably on account of its being not so cold as the valley, or, as Kit Carson told me, the Indians always camped on the hills so that they could see all around them, while white men would camp in the valley and Indians could surround them before being seen. Their camps are small, about ten or fifteen feet in diameter, with cedar or pine bushes put up to keep off the wind, but nothing overhead to keep off the rain or snow. (Sacramento *Daily Union*, July 3, 1873)

Unlike the Chinese, the Paiutes were accepted into the community as evidence by their participation in Aurora's 1864 Independence Day "Grand Celebration" (see page 65).

Exactly how many Paiute Indians lived in the hills surrounding Aurora in the mid 1860s is not known. Newspaper reports and government estimates of the town's population at that time did not include Indians. The first accurate count of Aurora's

Paiutes occurred in the 1880 federal census. It noted 364 total Indians at Aurora of which 104 were men, 112 women, and 148 children.

PARKS AND RECREATION

Aurorans set aside a portion of their town as "Temple Chace Park" (see map on page 5) during 1861. Located in the saddle adjacent to the cemetery along the main road to Carson City, the park was used during Aurora's 1862 Independence Day celebration:

> *At ten o'clock the procession, having been formed in the following order, marched in Temple Chace Park, where coats were provided for the ladies, and where the oration was delivered, Declaration read, etc. etc. The procession numbered about 1,000 persons, including 100 ladies.* (Sacramento *Daily Bee*, July 21, 1862)

Aurora was not the kind of place one could find "rational amusements." As one reporter from "Aurora, Esmeralda, Calaveras County" noted in a letter dated February 20, 1861, amusements were limited:

> *As for rational amusements, there are none here: theatres, concerts, balls, etc., being out of the question. If we enumerate the music afforded at the saloons of the night, the miserable pastime of teasing a squaw, and an occasional dog fight, we shall have about exhausted the catalog of amusements common to this place. The boys, also, have a reprehensible practice of shooting at targets across the main street, a diversion not eminently calculated to soothe the nerves of one having the occasion just to journey athwart the line of their fire. The terror thus inspired, however, is supposed to considerably enhance the fascinations of the sport.* (San Francisco *Alta California*, March 8, 1861)

Directory

Although finding things to do after a hard day mining was limited to say the least, miners did find some of the town's "sporting events" to be worthy of their free time. One such event was the Sunday badger fight, which pitted a badger in a "fight to the death" with about a half a dozen dogs. The badgers were typically captured and sold to the miners for a few dollars by the local Paiute Indians. Such events drew large crowds and prompted heavy betting. At least one witness to this cruel event was J. Ross Browne who "turned away with a strong emotion of pity" and felt the whole business was "very much like murder."

In the winter, however, residents turned their attention away from such brutal events to more challenging and invigorating outdoor activities:

The weather for the past month has been truly wintry with frequent snowstorms accompanied by high winds which have drifted the snow badly, leaving it in many places six to eight feet deep...The citizens take advantage of the dull times enjoying themselves by sleigh riding. The almost constant and merry jingling of the bells gives a cheerful interest to the day, awakening associations to many of the days "when life was young and hope was bright." (Sacramento *Daily Union*, February 11, 1865)

W*INTER SPORT.— On last Saturday morning Mr. And Mrs. Fogus, Mr. and Mrs. T. N. Brown, Messrs. M. Y. Moore, C. I. Robinson, J. Finlayson, W. B. Lake, B. W. Peck, J. Blackman and others, whose names we did not learn, had a fine skating party in a small lake on the top of the mountain north of Fogus' mill. The treacherous ice flew up and hit several of the gentlemen on the head and we were informed that M. Moore had his chin badly cut.* (Aurora *Esmeralda Daily Union*, December 12, 1864)

"Snow shoeing," or skiing as we call it today, was also popular with miners who used their "shoes" to walk up, then slide down, Aurora's surrounding hillsides "at railroad speed." Aurora resident Col. Samuel Youngs noted such winter sports in his journal entry of January 7, 1862:

The citizens amuse themselves in going up the mountains on snow shoes about 8 to 10 feet long, four inches wide, turned up in front like a sled runner. Going up they use a pole, like pushing a boat, and then come down rapidly, more than a mile a minute.

PHOTOGRAPHER

Reed, W. LaRogue - photographer on the 2nd floor of Bradford's Store on Pine **(4) [R]**.

Mr. Reed is taking excellent photographs at his gallery over Bradford's brick store on Pine Street.

He transferred our 'sublime and elegant fetters,' (as Artemis would say) to a card the other day, and the picture looks exactly like us and so life like that a few, to whom we have granted the high honor of beholding our visage on the card, persist in saying that they can see the picture wink. It was a beautiful picture which is an entirely superfluous assertion if you recollect that we have already said it looks exactly like us. (Aurora *Esmeralda Daily Union,* April, 23, 1864)

Directory

PHOTOGRAPHIC GALLERY.

IF YOU WANT

A Good Picture

GO TO

W. REED'S GALLERY,

OVER BRADFORD'S BRICK STORE,

AURORA.

Where you can get anything in the Deguarrean line

ON SHORT NOTICE,

And in the best style of the art.

MR. REED contemplates leaving Aurora in a very short time, and now is your

LAST CHANCE

To get POTOGRAPHS taken to send to your friends

Call and examne specimens and judge for yourselves. All kinds of pictures taken at

LOW PRICES,

To suit the times.   W. REED.

An 1864 Directory and Guide to Nevada's Aurora

PHYSICIANS

Bacon, E. M. -

Chamblin, M. R. -

Collins, C. F. - owner of Pioneer Drug Store **(36)**.

Farnsworth - office on Winnemucca.

Eichelroth, Dr. William - office on W side of Antelope

Mason, B.S. -

Mayer, T. H. & Mitchell, A. H. - in wood building on lot owned by B. G. Parker on the west side of Antelope.

Pugh, John W. -

Reims, J. W. (36)- office in Collins Drug Store on Antelope.

Sill, H. C. - office on west side of Antelope.

Smith, Fisher C. - office on Pine, 2 doors down from Greens Drug Store.

Wilson, W. - office on Pine, next door to Wells Fargo &Co.

POST OFFICE

Aurora's post office was established on September 9, 1861, and letters going by the U.S. mail carried a 3-cent stamp marked "Esmeralda Cal." Prior to that date (and after that date as well), Wells Fargo, and Company's express carried their own mail, as well as the U.S. mail, but for a lot more:

There is some dissatisfaction in Wells, Fargo and Co. charging 25 cents for transmitting letters when the send to other parts of California for 10 cents. (San Francisco *Daily Evening Bulletin,* October 28, 1861)

In January 1864, Aurora's the post office mark was changed to "Esmeralda Nev." In 1866, letters were stamped "Aurora Nev" until the post office was closed in 1897. Due to the resurgence in mining in the early 1900s, the post office was reopened in 1906 only to close down forever in 1919 when the mines shut down and virtually everyone left town.

Between the place name change from Esmeralda to Aurora, and the California to Nevada switch in 1863, there was some misunderstanding about the proper way to address letters:

ESMERALDA POST OFFICE.—Much confusion exists with regard to the proper direction of letters for Esmeralda. They should be addressed thus: Mr.——, Esmeralda, Mono Co., Cal. There is only one Post Office in the County, and that is located in the town of Aurora. When the petition for an Office was sent to Washington, "Aurora" was named as the designation of the Office; but as that name is so common, the Department thought proper to adapt the name "Esmeralda." It would be well, we think, for the citizens of that enterprising mining camp to change the name of the town to correspond with the Post Office. (San Francisco *Mining and Scientific Press*, February 16, 1863)

An 1864 Directory and Guide to Nevada's Aurora

The Post Office Building (38) – Although the location of the post office moved frequently over the years this important institution was located in a single story wooden building owned by Grey and Morton on Antelope in late 1863. David A. Baum served as the postmaster.

Mail addressed to Aurora could either be sent by the U.S. Mail and picked up at the post office or by Wells, Fargo & Company and picked up at the Express Office.

Aurora's post office was located for a short time in the brick building pictured above once owned by John Neidy on Pine Street.
(Kenneth L. McKeough)

Getting mail at either location was the biggest event of the day for hundreds of lonely miners far away from home:

> *There is an exciting scene here every other evening on the arrival of the stage. Between the hours of 10 and 11, some quick ear catches the sound of the stage rumbling over the hills, and 'stage!' 'stage!' is heard reverberating along the*

declivitous streets of this usually quiet burg, and by the time the vehicle has fairly stopped, it is surrounded by a crowd of eager miners, all anxious to learn 'who's come,' and 'what's the news,' and in five minutes the Express and Post Office— now side by side— are thronged with the inquiring multitude, often numbering over a hundred. At the Express Office a letter list is speedily read over, and all who have letters or packages can receive them immediately, and have plenty of time to answer the same evening and at the Post Office, all who own boxes receive their letters at once, but the 'general delivery' crowd must study patience, and wait till 8 o'clock next morning, before they can get their missives of business or love. (Sacramento *Daily Bee*, August 20, 1862)

The purpose of these nightly gatherings at the post office, however, was more than just getting the mail. According to one particular member of this "inquiring multitude" who visited the post office while Mark Twain was a resident of Aurora in 1862, the building served as a venue for informal story telling and yarn swapping. In an article entitled "Salt Lakers Who Knew Mark Twain," which appeared in the April 23, 1910 edition of the *Salt Lake Herald* (two days after Mark Twain died), "octogenarian" Martin Harkness said that Aurora's post office was a "rallying place for narrators of yarns:"

During these periods [the long and particularly severe winter of 1861-62] *it was pretty hard matter for us to pass the evenings and, having no other place to go, we used to gather at the postoffice to tell stories and swap yarns. The postoffice was located in the only board shanty in town, and was about the most comfortable place in Aurora. Fred Bechtel, long since dead, was the postmaster, and among the names of the men who used to gather there were Mark Twain; Judge Boring,....*

> *In fact they were from all parts of the country and all good story tellers. Each man was given an evening, when he was suppose to tell stories and amuse the crowd, and the best of feeling prevailed at all times. Mark Twain fell in with the rest and when his evening came to entertain the crowd the postoffice used to be packed. Some stories were real and some were imaginary, and the gathering not only relieved the monotony of the long winter evenings, but they were the most enjoyable of any I have ever attended.*
>
> *Mark Twain, who had been a pilot on a Mississippi River steamboat, used to relate stories of river life that we all enjoyed and he in turn seemed to relish the stories the other members of the company told.*

If one is to believe Mr. Harkness, then in addition to beginning his literary career in a canvas-covered cabin at Aurora (see "Mark Twain's Aurora Cabins: Site of His First Success," *Nevada Historical Society Quarterly*, Summer, 2003), Mark Twain may have launched his extraordinary public speaking career as America's greatest humorist at Aurora's humble post office "shanty" as well.

RACE TRACK

Sometime during 1862, Aurorans cleared a race track for horses in the middle of a large meadow area about a mile and a half southeast of town just below Aurora Peak along the Aurora-Owens River Road. The track was likely straight and about a quarter of a mile long:

> *A horse race came off on election day, for a thousand dollars a side. All I know is that the gray horse won. They are to run again, in a few days, for a sum of two thousand dollars.* (San Francisco *Alta California,* September 16, 1862)

A race came off to-day in the suburbs of Aurora between two noted nags of this burg, whom we will call Old Whitey and Yellow. The race was for $500 a side— single dash of a fourth of a mile. Yellow came in nine feet ahead, winning for his backers perhaps $2,000. (Sacramento *Daily Bee*, October 10, 1862)

RESIDENCES

The majority of Aurora's population were miners who lived in a variety of self-built cabins located just outside the city limits. Most cabins were about 12 X 12 ft. in size, and were constructed with walls of stacked rocks covered with wood and canvas roofs. According to Mark Twain, these "cramped and wretched quarters" had dirt floors and were usually furnished with a small wood stove, bunk bed, and table. The hundreds of stone-lined depressions dug into the hills surrounding today's Aurora attest to the large number of miners who once worked in the area's underground mines.

One of the best descriptions of how these cabins were built was written by J. Ross Browne who visited Aurora and nearby Bodie, California during 1864:

Usually it is constructed of the materials nearest at hand. Stone and mud answer for the walls where wood is scarce; but if wood be abundant, a kind of stockade is formed of logs placed close together and upright in the ground. The roof is made of clap-boards, or rough shingles, brush-wood covered with sod, canvas, or any thing else that may be available. The chimney is the most imposing part of the house. Where the location permits, the cabin is backed up against a bluff, so as to afford a chance for a substantial flue by merely cutting a hole through the bank; but where such natural facilities do not exist, the variety of material used in the construction of chimneys is wonderful.

Chimneys were the "most impressive part" of a typical miner's cabin.

While miners lived pretty much everywhere in and around Aurora in these crude rock and wood cabins, most of the town's more prosperous citizens lived in stately brick buildings located in the town's "residential district" south of Pine, and west of Winnemucca.

Levy House (50) [R] - a single-story brick house occupied by the owners of Levy and Co.'s Store. By the early 1900s, the house was known as the "Cain House" after Jim Cain purchased it.

Directory

Mark Twain's Cabins (3 and 54) - Samuel Clemens, or Mark Twain as the world would come to know him soon after he left Aurora, was unquestionably the town's most famous resident. The 26 year-old Missourian moved to Aurora in April 1862 and worked as a miner. Although Clemens never owned any real estate in Aurora, he did share as many as three different cabins with his mining partners during the six months he lived in Aurora. His first residence was a cabin located on the north side of Spring Street west of town **(54)** just below the prominent rock outcrop known as Lover's Leap. This part of town was often referred to as "China Garden" because of the many Chinese who later lived there. His friend and fellow mining speculator Horatio G. Phillips owned this particular cabin. About the time Clemens was no longer "worth a million dollars" because his claim to part of the Wide West mine was "jumped" he moved in with his other mining partners Calvin Higbie and Dan Twing just west of the Phillips cabin. The City Brewery later occupied this site about a year after Clemens left Aurora. Toward the end of his stay in Aurora, Clemens and his friend Bob Howland may have shared a cabin at the east end of Pine **(3)**. By the late 1800s, this cabin was known as the "Mark Twain Cabin" (see photo on page 50) even though the evidence to support this claim was rather questionable. In an effort to preserve the now famous cabin, the structure was moved to a park in Reno in 1924. Vandals and souvenir hunters soon began to damage the building and by the early 1950s "Mark Twain's Cabin" was gone.

Sanchez, Ramon B. (51) [R] - large two-story brick house owned by Aurora's mayor and banker. For a detailed description of the Sanchez household, see pages 95 through 112 in Robert Stewart's *Aurora Nevada's Ghost City of the Dawn*.

Superintendents House (55) [R] - Located at the east end of Pine Street, this two-story Victorian-style brick house was the most prominent residence ever built in Aurora. Built by Michael A. Murphy in 1863, the house was later occupied by Roswell K.

101

Colcord, a former governor of Nevada, in the late 1800s. The J. S. Cain family of Bodie fame were the final owners in the early 1900s.

Walker, Fried (53) [R] - Although not a resident during Aurora's boom, Fried (short for Sigfried) Walker was one of a handful of colorful characters who inhabited Aurora after it became a ghost town in the early 1920s. He was born in Switzerland and immigrated to Aurora in 1903. Walker lived in town for over fifty years and was referred to by many as "the Mayor of Aurora." He was also considered the last resident of Aurora when he died at nearby Hawthorne, Nevada on February 20, 1955 at the age 91. His obituary in the *Territorial Enterprise* stated: "Many of its [Aurora's] buildings still stand, but with the death of Mr. Walker they are residence only for the jackrabbit and the tumbleweed."

Fried Walker at Aurora in the 1930s.

(Kenneth L. McKeough; also see photo opposite Preface)

Youngs, Samuel Col.- Youngs lived in a small 12 x 16 ft. brick cabin he built less than a quarter of a miles south of town during November 1863. He moved to Aurora during December 1860 making him one of Aurora's longest residing citizens by 1864. Youngs had a variety of occupations including prospector, businessman, and public official, and was arguably the town's most prominent resident. He is also well known because he kept a wonderful journal that fortunately has survived (see Stewart on page 206), served as Aurora's correspondent to the Sacramento *Daily Union* for many years, and lived in Aurora for almost 20 years long after the boom went bust.

Directory

RESTAURANTS

Antelope - owned by Stewartson and Warner in a wood building on the west side of Antelope.

Barnum (39) - wooden building on Antelope.

> **Barnum Restaurant,**
> (Formerly Restaurant de France,)
> ANTELOPE STREET, AURORA, CALIFORNIA,
> **VALENTINE BICK, & Co. Proprietors**
> HAVING Leased, enlarged and otherwise greatly improved the House formerly known as the "Restaurant de France," are now prepared to serve the old customers of the House, and all who favor them with a call, in a manner
> **Not to be Surpassed**
> On the Eeastern slope of the Sierras. Entire satisfaction guaranteed.

Exchange Dining Room (49) [R] - Located in the basement of the Merchants' Exchange Hotel (see page 75) on the southwest corner of Pine and Winnemucca, this "first class dinning saloon" was typically open till midnight:

> EXCHANGE DINING ROOM— We were greeted with a most cordial, smiling welcome from our hosts and seated at a table bearing a load of the staples and luxuries of life that could hardly be surpassed in San Francisco. We were especially surprised at seeing such a display of choice vegetables and fruits as were placed before us. That important condiment, the sparkling wine, was by no means lacking, and as everything else necessary for our enjoyment was there in abundance, we had a very pleasant time. We would advise all our patrons who are fond of good cheer to go by all means to C. P. Doubleday & Co's dining room, Merchants' Exchange Building, where the most fastidious epicure can be more than satisfied. (Aurora *Esmeralda Daily Union,* April 18, 1864)

In deference to the restaurant's importance to the city, Aurora's 1864 Independence Day "Grand Celebration" held its final banquet at the Exchange Dining Room. These festivities at the restaurant were described in detail in the July 6, 1864, edition *Esmeralda Daily Union* reprinted on page 73.

An 1864 Directory and Guide to Nevada's Aurora

The Exchange Restaurant was located in the basement of the three-story Exchange Hotel shown here vacant in the early 1900s.
(Kenneth L. McKeough)

Orleans- operated by Finnegan and Henderson in a wood building owned by J. Amsler on east side of Antelope.

Winters in Aurora were always cold, long, and dismal.
(Kenneth L. McKeough)

ROADS

When Aurora was first settled in late 1860, the only road in the Eastern Sierras went from Carson Valley to the placer gold mining camp of Monoville near Mono Lake. This crude wagon road went south from Carson Valley, to Smith Valley, Sweetwater, the East Walker River, Bridgeport Valley (or Big Meadows as it was called back then), over Conway Summit to Monoville. Aurora's incredible boom, however, led to the construction of five major roads leading to and from Aurora. Eventually, all roads east of the Sierras and south of Carson City led to Aurora. Short sections of many these early wagon roads may still be seen today in some of the more remote country surrounding Aurora.

Aurora-Big Meadows [R] - A toll road franchise was first granted by California to John Hawkins on December 19, 1862 for a toll road from Aurora to Big Meadows (Bridgeport). On April 4, 1864, California granted John N. Dudleston and D. H. Haskell the right to construct and maintain a toll road commencing from Bridgeport to the state line in Bodie Gulch over the same route granted to John Hawkins two years earlier. The road to Bridgeport split off to Bodie very near the state line. The road originally went west from Aurora directly down the steep canyon known as Esmeralda Gulch to Del Monte Canyon. This section of road washed out in the early 1940s and was later relocated out of the canyon.

View above is Esmeralda Gulch from the old Haskell tollhouse.

An 1864 Directory and Guide to Nevada's Aurora

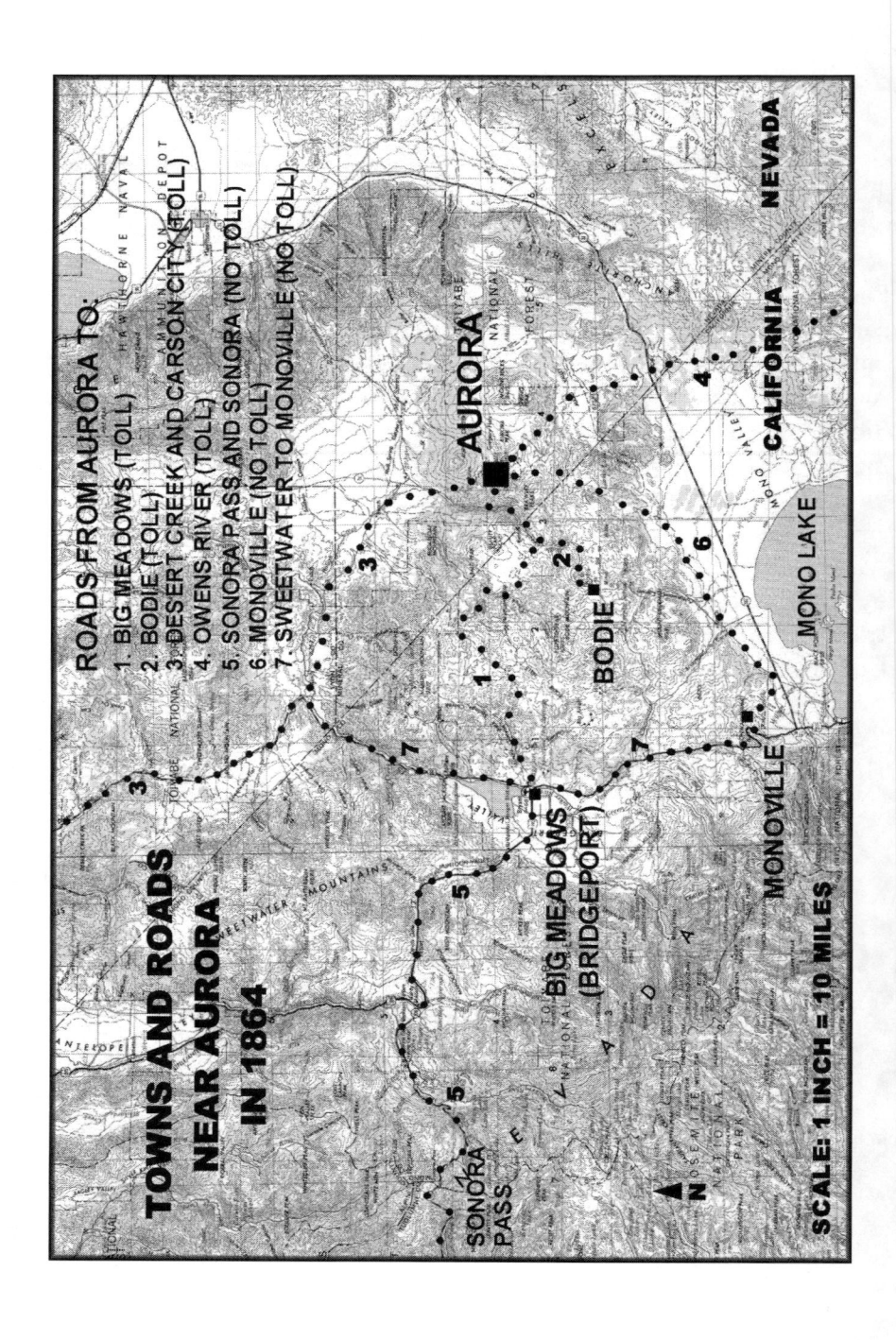

Directory

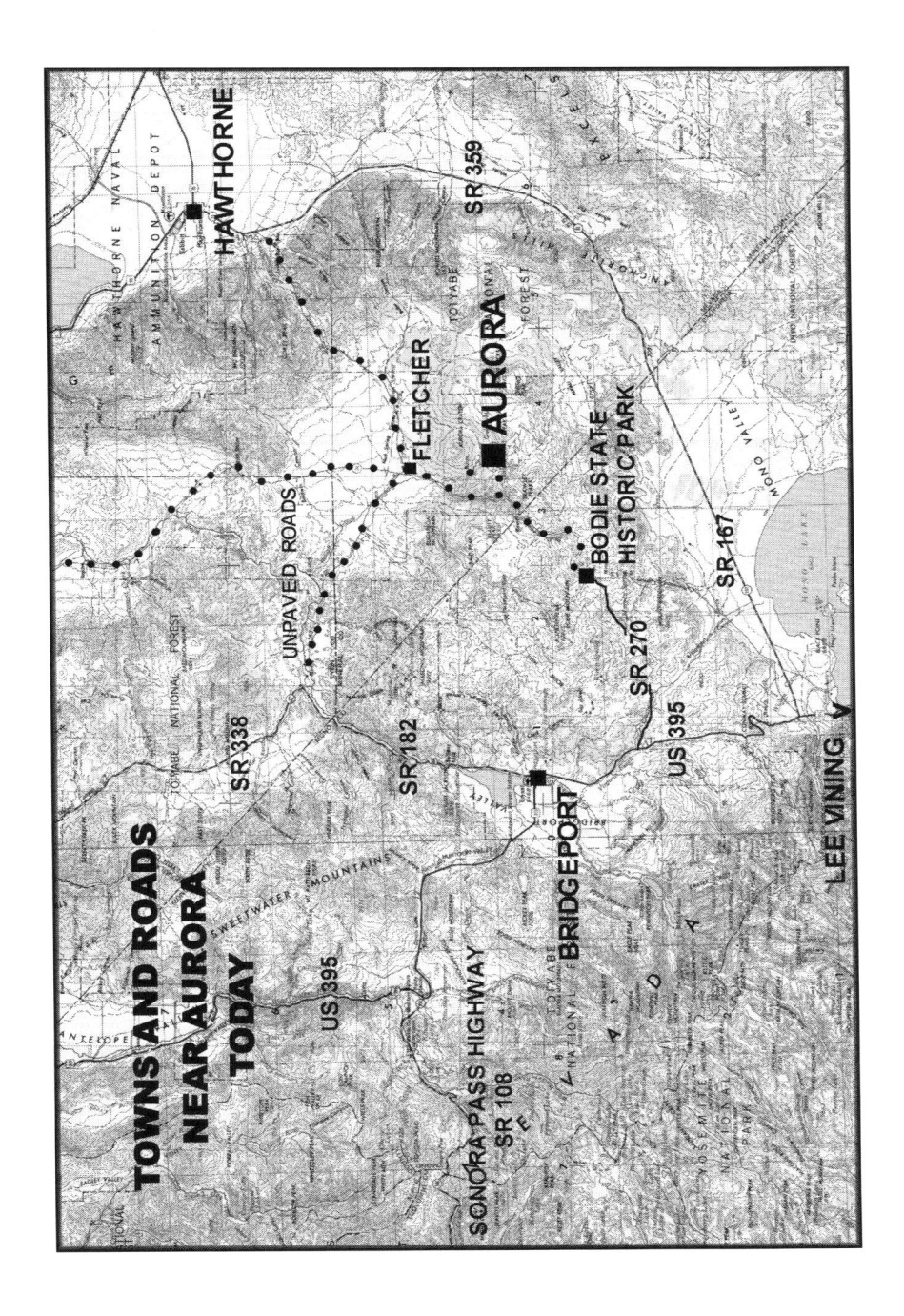

107

J. Ross Browne found refinement and intelligence when he visited the Haskell's tollhouse in 1864:

> *At Haskell's toll gate, about a mile from town, we halted a while to enjoy the hospitality of the worthy toll-keeper and his wife, who cordially invited us to stop and dine with them. I found here what I had not frequently before met with in the course of my travels through this wild region—refinement and intelligence. The cabin was a mere frame shanty of the rudest kind; yet it was clean and neat; nicely carpeted, and prettily ornamented with water-color sketches, very cleverly executed by Mrs. Haskell.*

Aurora-Desert Creek – On November 28, 1861, the Governor and Legislature of Nevada Territory passed an act giving William H. Dickson (also spelled Dickenson or Dickerson) the "right and privilege of maintaining a toll road" (referred to as the Dickenson Toll Road or the Esmeralda Toll Road) from Desert Creek in Smith Valley to Aurora via Sweetwater Creek, the Elbow, and Nine Mile Ranch over a route "established by Clayton [J. E.], Dickson and Company, and occupied and used by them as a toll road." Tollhouses were erected at the Elbow for traffic to Aurora, and about one mile north of town for traffic from Aurora. The act also provided for the following toll rates:

> *Wagon and one span of horses, two dollars*
> *Each additional animal, twenty-five cents.*
> *Man on horseback, twenty five cents.*
> *Each pack animal, twenty cents.*

The act required the toll road company pay Nevada Territory two percent of their gross toll receipts. Not to be outdone, the California Legislature passed a similar act on March 29, 1862. It authorized William H. Dickson, J. E. Clayton, and J. W. Pugh to

Directory

construct and maintain a toll road in Mono County "commencing at a point of rock, near where the Sweetwater [Creek] crosses the Aurora road" to Aurora "and connecting with the toll road established by Dickson" approved by Nevada Territory on November 28, 1861 "from Desert Creek to the Town of Aurora, in Mono County." Portions of the road still exist today as a dirt road maintained by both Lyon and Mineral County between Sweetwater and Aurora.

Aurora-Owens River [R]
Also known as the Aurora to Benton Road, this historic wagon road was completed in 1864 and today generally follows sections of DWP's (Los Angeles Department of Water and Power) Pacific Intertie high voltage electric power line from a few miles southeast of Aurora to Adobe Valley. The photograph on the right shows an old alignment of rocks that were removed from the roadbed and piled two to three feet high along the side of this once heavily traveled road.

AURORA AND OWENS RIVER ROAD- This enterprise will soon be completed, and a toll-gate erected thereon. It was commenced in 1862, and its proprietors have expended a considerable sum upon it but the travel to and from

109

Montgomery promises to make it a paying institution. (Aurora *Esmeralda Daily Union,* October 21, 1864)

Sonora and Mono Road- Early California immigrants heading to Sonora from the Midwest, as well as miners and prospectors heading to Aurora from Sonora, utilized an old Indian route crossing the Sierras a few miles south of Sonora Pass beginning in the early 1850s. The route, however, was unsuitable for the heavy freight-laden wagons needed to supply the growing new city of Aurora. Therefore, on March 31, 1863, the California Legislature approved an act "to provide for the construction of a Wagon Road from Sonora, Tuolumne County, to Aurora, Mono County." The act called for the selection of "Sonora and Mono Road Commissioners" by the Board of Supervisors from Mono, Tuolumne, Stanislaus, and San Joaquin Counties. Their job was to "locate, improve, and construct a wagon road, from the City of Sonora,... across the Sierra Nevada Mountains, to Aurora, in the County of Mono." The new road was to be funded by bonds issued by each of the four counties to be reimbursed later by the tolls collected for use of the new road.

The original Sonora and Mono Road, which generally followed today's Sonora Pass Road (California Highway 108), was one of the most ambitious engineering projects ever untaken in California up until that time. The road was open to wagons by late 1864:

COMPLETION OF THE SONORA AND MONO ROAD— We are happy to announce that this enterprise, so important to Esmeralda and the surrounding country, is complete. An excellent single track, with suitable turnouts, now connects Sonora with Bridgeport, and the road from Bridgeport to Aurora is one of the best that can be found on this side of the mountains. (Aurora *Esmeralda Daily Union,* October 22, 1864)

Directory

SALOONS AND LIQUOR STORES

"Saloons—saloons—saloons—liquor—everywhere" was what William Brewer saw when he visited Aurora in the summer of 1863. After a long day of prospecting or underground mining, miners had the choice of either retiring to a crowded boardinghouse, or worse, a cold and damp dirt-floor canvas hut, or visiting one of Aurora's brightly lit saloons. It's no surprise miners consistently chose the later where gambling was the order of the day:

> *The town, morally, is progressing finely— backward. We have two churches, one school-house, about 40 saloons, and several other public houses; any quantity of sports and plenty of sporting. Gambling holds its ravel day and night, and finds plenty of votaries. Pretty women deal the cards, and homely men rake the money in.* (San Francisco *Daily Evening Bulletin,* April 17 1863)

William Brewer also noted the proliferation of gambling at Aurora's many saloons during his visit in July, 1863:

> *Here are tables, with gold and silver piled upon them by hundreds (or even thousands), with men (or women) behind, who deal faro, or monte, or vingt-et-un, or rouge-et-noir, or who turn roulette— in short, any way in which they may win and you may lose.*

According to one former resident, nearby Bodie California was "mild and peaceable" when compared to Aurora during the early 1860s. Although somewhat tongue-and-cheek, this account belies Aurora's violent atmosphere particularly in its saloons during 1863:

> *Passing by a saloon early a few mornings since, which was being swept out, I counted among the rubbish no less than two noses and three ears. I looked around for an eye, and*

111

expressing astonishment to the proprietor of the broom at not finding one, was gravely informed by the philosopher that all the "bully boys" wore "glass eyes," which if knocked out were always properly replaced at the end of the fight, by their bottle-holders and friends. He was furthermore kind enough to inform me that "wax noses" were coming much in vogue among the "boys," it having been ascertained they were more nutritious to chew on than ordinary flesh and blood. (San Francisco *Alta California,* September 30,1863)

Bee Hive (13) - operated by Levison, J. and Co. just east of the Gem Saloon.

Clara's - liquors and bar fixtures owned by Madame Clara Cadame east of Bradford's Store.

Conner, H. - liquor store just west of Sommers brick saloon on Pine.

Danniz (12) - saloon in the basement of Neidy's brick building.

Del Monte Exchange (1) - saloon and liquor store owned by McMabeian in the basement of the courthouse.

Esmeralda Exchange (34) - Sam Davis proprietor.

Exchange (also known as the Bank Exchange or the Exchange Billiard Saloon) (20) - This 23 x 50 ft. brick saloon was owned by Chapin and Mathews in 1863 and was one of Aurora's earliest and most prominent drinking establishments.

Fagan, N . - liquors on Antelope.

Gem (13) - in 20 x 55 ft. wood building owned by O. Hoey and D. Davis on Bechtel's lot on Pine.

Directory

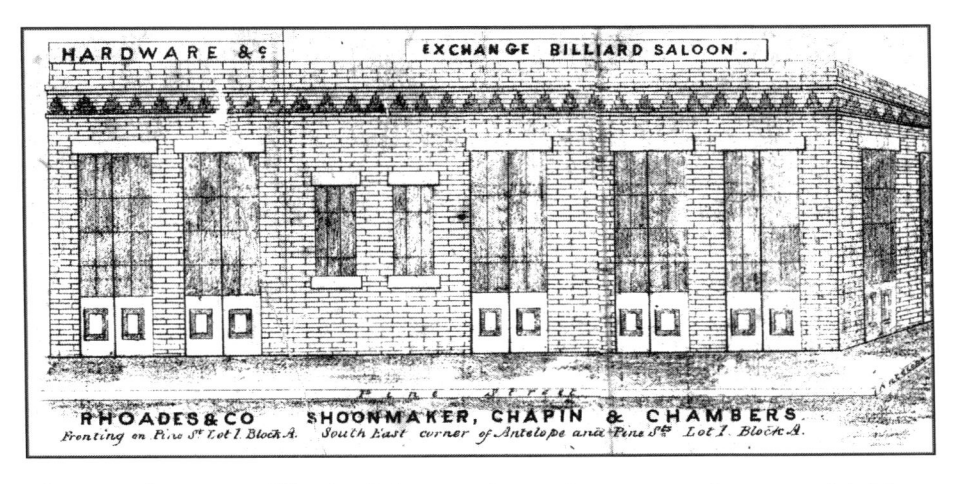

The Exchange Billiard Saloon, Aurora's most famous drinking establishment, was located on the corner of Pine and Antelope Streets. Erected in early 1862, the saloon was one of Aurora's first brick buildings.

(Detail from Brady's 1862 Map of Aurora and Esmeralda. Original at Nevada Historical Society; online image from Nevada in Maps collection, Mary B. Ansari Map Library, University of Nevada, Reno.)

Gibbins, J. - liquors and bar fixtures at Aurora and Wide West.

Glen Bros. (11) - saloon in the basement of Wingate's building on Pine.

Greely, T. - saloon on southwest corner of Pine and Silver.

Hefs & Demming (26) - liquors and bar fixtures in the San Francisco House.

Jacks & Decker -

Kennedy & Porter (24) - liquor store in a 25 by 40 ft. wooden building owned by Fleischman and Kaufman.

An 1864 Directory and Guide to Nevada's Aurora

Larkin - in Sommers brick building on the east side of Antelope.

Last Chance - owned by W. Price on Antelope.

> **RUNYON & HARKNESS,**
> Wholesale and Retail Dealers
> .... IN ....
> **Fine Wines, Liquors,**
> Tobacco and Cigars,
> East side Silver Street,
> Nearly opposite the Recorder's Office.
>
> WE HAVE JUST OPENED, and are constantly receiving, the finest assortment of
> **Wines, Liquors, Tobacco and Cigars**
> Ever offered in Aurora, consisting in part of
> **Brandies,**
> Champagne Vinyard, Otard, Hennessy, Old Sazerac, Pinet Castillion, Martelle, Pellvoisin, Seignette, French Mixed.
> **Whiskeys,**
> Old Government, J. H. Cutter, Ess. Old Virginia, Old Hanger, Hermitage, Old Ky. Bourbon, Corwin's case, Suit's case, Bininger's case.
> **Wines,**
> Champagnes of all brands, London Dock Port, Duff Gordon Sherry, Clarets, Sauternes, Hock.
> **Bitters,**
> Orange, Hostetlers, Sachem and Angostura Bitters
> Tennent's Ale,—Cigars and Tobacco of all brands

Levy & Bros. - liquors on Pine.

Martin, S. - liquors in saloon on the west side of Antelope.

Marks & Co. - stock of liquors in LaRue building on Pine.

McName, P. J. - 14 x 60 ft. wood building immediately south of Pioneer Drug Store on a lot owned by E. D. Barker.

Merchants' Exchange (49) [R] - located in the Merchants' Exchange Hotel:

White & Mitchell keep the best wines, liquors and cigars, that can be procured on the Pacific Coast. If you are in need of 'spiritual consolation' you can get it at the Merchants' Exchange for a 'bit' [25 cents] *a glass.* (Aurora *Esmeralda Daily Union,* April 18, 1864)

Plauf, F. - saloon in Sommers brick building just west of Bradford's Store.

Directory

Runyon & Harkness (2) - liquor store.

San Francisco (36) - owned by J. McNamee.

Teel & Wand (22) – saloon and billiards in a wooden structure fronting 16 feet on Antelope. The saloon became know as "Band Boys' Saloon" by September 1864 where "free' music by the Brass and String Band was offered every night.

Valer- liquors in a brick building attached to the north side of the Merchants' Exchange Hotel.

Sazerac (11) – located in Wingate Hall and owned by Steiner and Gaige.

SAZERAC SALOON.
PINE STREET, AURORA.

N STEINER,   M M GAIGE

Having recently taken possession of our new SALOON, and fitted it up in a style unsurpassed in this Territory, we invite the attention of the public to our stock of WINES and LIQUORS which we will sell at Wholesale and Retail. We have connected with our establishment a BILLIARD ROOM with three of the best BILLIARD TABLES ever manufactured in San Francisco.

STEINER & GAIGE.

SCHOOLS

Public (28) [R] – "School District No. 1" was formed by the J. B. Saxton, Superintendent of Public Instruction for Esmeralda County, during October 1863. A. S. Peck, G. W. Case, and J. B. Bradford were selected to serve on the Board of Trustees for the School District. Arrangements were made with the Baptist Church to share their new building on Winnemucca Street for one year. Dr. A. Farnsworth was selected as the first teacher. On May 30, 1864, the District's purchased a lot on the north side of Del Monte Street east of Silver and immediately began construction of Aurora's first public school house. In early June, a decision was made to establish a Primary School made up of "sixteen of the small children" who were taught by Miss Annie Canfield in separate school room on Winnemucca Street.

The historic two-room schoolhouse stood for almost 90 years until brick contactors tore down the building in the early 1950s. The schoolhouse was likely the last of Aurora's beautiful brick building to be destroyed. In 1999, a sealed metal "time capsule" containing various issues of the *Esmeralda Daily Union* and newspapers from Massachusetts (the former home of many Aurorans), and a five page hand-written note by the Benj. W. Peck, the Clerk of the Board of Trustees for the School District, was found in the schoolhouse foundation ruins. The miraculously preserved note summarized the activities of the Trustees since their creation in October 1863. The note ended with "Voted to accept this report and that the same be placed in the Tin Box within the foundation wall." The metal canister was likely placed in the foundation by the Trustees during a schoolhouse dedication ceremony in July 1864, where it remained hidden and sealed for the next 135 years. Fortunately, the tin can time capsule and its contents are now safely preserved at the Nevada State Archives in Carson City.

Directory

Aurora's schoolhouse in the mid 1950s just prior to its destruction.
(Mineral County Museum)

Schoolhouse ruins today.

117

> *The foundation is laid and the walls commenced for a brick schoolhouse, 20 by 40 feet. We now have about eighty school children attending schools in Aurora.* (Sacramento *Daily Union*, July 28, 1864)

The note in the time capsule noted who built the schoolhouse:

> *W. A. Dowd and Patrick Reddy took the contract to grade and lay the foundation* [of Stone] *for the School House and they also were the lowest Bidders for the Brick work and A. B. Williams for the Carpenter and Joiner work.*

Mr. Dudleston's private school - Aurora also had a private school on Aurora Street:

> *Mr. Dudleston's School— We had the pleasure yesterday afternoon, of being present at the weekly review in Mr. Dudleston's private school on Aurora Street. The pupils, though mostly small, exhibited a remarkable degree of proficiency for the short time they have been in school. The most exemplary order and quietude prevailed during the whole afternoon, and the close attention bestowed by the pupils upon their studies and the marked respect shown their instructor were truly commendable. Aurora may well be proud other educational facilities; for besides supporting two public schools, both of which are well attended, the private school of Mr. Dudleston is well supported.* (Aurora *Esmeralda Daily Union,* August 27, 1864)

Aurora also had a **Singing School-**

> *H. K. Gage has removed his singing school from the Methodist to the Baptist Church, on Winnemucca street, where regular lessons in music and singing, on Tuesday and Friday of each week until the end of the term, will be given.* (Aurora *Esmeralda Daily Union,* October 24, 1864)

Directory

SEWER SYSTEM

Because Aurora was built along two intermittent streams, flooding was always a potential problem. Recognizing this threat, the Mono County Board of Supervisors ordered the construction of flumes, or storm sewers as we call them today, under Antelope Street in 1862, and Pine Street 1863. The Antelope Street sewer was made of rock and wood, while the Pine Street sewer was made of brick.

The workman on the Pine Street sewer have struck the mouth of the old flume, at Antelope street, and made a connection therewith. This work is of no little benefit to the city. When finished it will drain and carry off the water from the streets, and by this means keep them in good condition, and making traveling easier and better. (Aurora Daily Times, December 3, 1863)

Aurora's sewers were not used to discharge sewage. Simple pit toilets, or "outhouses," were used for this purpose throughout Aurora's sixty year history. According to one report, the Aurora's storm sewers were built tall enough to "allow a man to stand up." Remnants of both structures which are now filled in with silt may still be seen today in the eroding ditch at the intersection of Pine and Antelope Streets.

SHOE SHOPS

Borger, J. - shoemaker on Spring St.

Fieffer, G. and Thomas, M. - southwest corner of Pine and Silver.

Rearden, D. - in 10 x 25 ft. wood building on lot owned by Williams and Stewartson on the west side of Antelope.

SLAUGHTERHOUSES

Parker, B. G. - in the ravine in back of Miller's brickyard on the south side of Spring Street west of town.

Nowlan, J. - north side of Spring Street at the end of Roman Street.

SOCIETIES

A substantial number of Aurora's "better citizens" were originally from New England. As such, they formed a society of New Englanders that celebrated the "Festival of the Pilgrims:"

> *Monday evening next is set apart by the sons and daughters of New England, to celebrate the anniversary of the landing of out Pilgrim Fathers on Plymouth Rock. Judging from the spirit which animates our citizens, whenever so worthy an object enlists their sympathy and attention, I can well promise myself a good time, as speeches are announced on the occasion, and music has volunteered her voluptuous swell.* (San Francisco *Alta California,* January 1, 1863)

There was also the Lady Washington Society:

> *A new society, consisting of ladies, and bearing the above name has been formed here quite recently, having for its object the alleviation of the sufferings of the poor wounded Union soldiers. While their purpose is a good one, and seems to be well patronized, I must say that these ladies have made quite a laughing-stock of themselves, as on last evening, after their adjournment, they marched singing—John Brown—but*

something very much like it, which no one could understand. (San Francisco *Daily Evening Bulletin,* February 11, 1863)

The Lady Washington Society gave a grand ball on the 1ˢᵗ inst., (May Day), for the purpose of procuring funds to aid and relieve the sick and wounded Union soldiers who are fighting to enforce the laws and to uphold the Constitution in all of its parts; the net proceeds will not fall short of $360. I understand the ladies of the society design to raise $1000, and then send it in the shape of a gold and silver brick. (San Francisco *Alta California,* May 13, 1863)

Aurora's lyceum was organized by the town's more educated and prosperous citizens in order to provide a venue for educational and inspirational lectures. William T. Gough, Aurora's most prominent attorney, presided over this most august organization:

Aurora, or rather its citizens, are making Herculean strides in the literary direction. Already it boasts of its Lyceum and Library Association, which does great credit to the literati of the place; and with the talented Gough as librarian, it is sure to be a success. A course of lectures is now being delivered for the benefit of the Association, the first of which came off a few nights ago, by W. T. Gough, Esq. Subject: "Geology, and its relation to the Bible." He handled his subject in the most masterly manner, and so enchained his audience that a pin could be heard dropped on the floor, until at the conclusion, one spontaneous acclamation went forth in honor of the orator. After the lecture came a tripping of the "light fantastic toe," to relieve the mind, by exercising the body, of the grand but eloquent subject they had listened to. (San Francisco *Mining and Scientific Press*, March 10, 1866)

SODA FACTORY

Parsons, C. & Co. **[R]** - brick "soda factory" on the south side of Wide West Street. "Soda! Soda!! Soda!!!" was available at Green's "New" Drug store on Pine according a newspaper add from 1864.

STABLES

Bodea - owned by R. Elstner and located just west of the City Brewery on Spring Street.

Exchange Liberty (43) – owned by Cobb and Brady located on Pine Street just west of Fleishman and Kaufman's Store. In the 1930s this stable (photo on the left) was owned by A. Taylor

(Kenneth L. McKeough)

Fashion (32) -owned by Converse and Horton.

Union (46) - owned by Robinson & Pearson.

Directory

STAGE LINES AND STOPS

During Aurora's boom, stages arrived from Carson City every day with mail and hoards of new immigrants. They soon left fully loaded with gold bullion and disheartened miners.

Wells, Fargo & Company (17) - The "Express Office" occupied the wooden building owned by G Shier fronting 25 feet on Pine.

> *I have observed, with listless curiosity, from day to day and from month to month, the same stereotyped bipeds rush frantically, upon the arrival of the stage, and block up the Express office with a mob of eager and gaping humanity. Now not one man in ten of these restless and excited sons of Adam ever have received a letter since they struck this mining Mecca; not one in seven have any reasonable right to expect that anyone has written to them. And at a moderate estimate, not more than every other man could spell out a letter if anyone should ever be guilty of punishing him with such a serious task as a correspondence to decipher: And yet these same men will crowd and elbow in every day, and stand there like a mass of gaping pigs until Mr. Garesche, the Express agent, and the clerk, Col. Jamison, have read aloud the addresses of the letters over and over again, until they are hoarse enough to sing basso in the highest-toned musical circles.* (San Francisco *Alta California,* June 15, 1863)

Most of Aurora's gold bullion left town on Wells Fargo stages:

> *From the books of Wells, Fargo & Co., as furnished me by the gentlemanly agent of that house here, I find that the shipment of bullion from that firm alone, to San Francisco, from here, for the months of May, June, and July, last past, amounted to $130,000. The fact that five of the mills here have been working steadily since the first of the present month' and are*

123

likely to continue so up to the end of the month, it is quite certain to result in a yield of bullion exceeding $100,000 for August. (San Francisco *Alta California,* August 26, 1863)

> **CARSON AND AURORA STAGE,**
>
> **THROUGH IN ONE DAY**
>
> From Virginia City.
>
> ---
>
> CARRYING U. S. MAIL AND WELLS, FARGO & CO'S EXPRESS.
>
> ---
>
> Leaves Carson City Daily,
> On arrival of Stages from Virginia City, connecting at GENOA with the
>
> **Pioneer Stages from California.**
> Arriving in Aurora on the evening of the same day.
>
> ---
>
> Through from San Francisco
> **IN TWO DAYS!**
>
> ---
>
> RETURNING,
> Leaves Aurora, daily, at 7 o'clock A. M.
>
> ---
>
> **Through to San Francisco in 58 hours.**
> G. E. WELLINGTON,
> Agent.

Esmeralda Stage Line (AKA Carson and Aurora) - According to this November 1863 newspaper add, George E. Wellington was the Agent who had an office at the Merchants' Exchange Hotel. The add also indicated their company carried the U.S. Mail and Wells, Fargo & Co.'s Express, and connected with the Pioneer Stage Line leaving Genoa for California.

Nine Mile Ranch Stage Stop- The most important stage stop near Aurora was located along the main road to Carson City at Rough Creek, which was only nine miles northwest from town. The ranch was owned by "Mr. Gardiner" in 1862 according to Mark Twain in *Roughing It.* According to the 1864 Esmeralda County Tax Roll, Moses Wiley owned the Nine Mile Ranch a year or two after Gardiner. The impressive stone house you see today at the Nine Mile Ranch was completed in 1880 according to the *Esmeralda Herald* of March 6, 1880.

Known as the Nine Mile Ranch for obvious reasons, the site was visited by J. Ross Brown in 1864. Brown later described his adventures in the "Walker River Country" chapter in his 1869 book *Adventures in Apache Country*. Although he incorrectly calls the following "oasis in the desert" the "Elbow" (which was actually located another seven miles past Nine Mile Ranch) in his book, the mileage he noted from Aurora for this stop—four miles past the Five Mile Station—indicated the station he visited was nine miles from Aurora, the precise location of Nine Mile Ranch.

> *...four miles beyond this station* [Five Mile Station near Fletcher] *, we reached another oasis in the desert, where we concluded to camp for the night. A good and substantial frame house, with stables, corrals, and various out-buildings, has been erected here for the accommodation of travelers; and the scene, upon our arrival, was lively and characteristic. Freight trains were drawn up in front of the tavern, the teams tied to the wagon-poles, with piles of hay before them which they were devouring with great relish; groups of dust-covered-teamsters sitting around the glowing camp-fires; an emigrant family a little to one side, weary and way worn, but cheered by the prospect of soon reaching the end of their journey; a stage just arrived from Wellington's, with a noisy delegation of politicians from Carson; some half a dozen stray miners on broken-down horses, from unknown parts, and bound to unknown districts; while here and there dust-covered pedestrians, whose stock in trade consisted of a pick, shovel, pan, and blanket, were scattered about on the ground, taking their ease after their dreary walk across the deserts.*

STAMP MILLS

Aurora's mining companies built a total of seventeen stamp mills to remove gold and silver from mined quartz ore at great cost to their shareholders. Their existence, however, was short-lived as most of the following stamp mills were dismantled and moved to nearby mining regions after the gold ran out in the mid 1860s. Because most of these mills were made of locally manufactured brick and stone, the ruins of many of these once impressive structures may still be seen today particularly in Esmeralda Gulch and Del Monte Canyon.

1- Antelope "New" [R] - 20 stamps, cost $150K, located in Del Monte Canyon across Bodie Creek from Real del Monte Mill. The current county road maintained by Mineral County goes directly through the western half of the mill's ruins.
2- Antelope "Old" [R] - 8 stamps, cost $30K, brick mill about a mile west of town down Esmeralda Gulch.
3- Coffee- 4 stamps, cost $20K, located next to the Union Foundry.

The Durand stamp mill's ruins along Bodie Creek about a half a mile south of the Real del Monte mill look like walls made by the ancient Inca Indians.

Directory

4- Durand [R] – located in Del Monte Canyon above the Antelope and Real del Monte mills. The mill burned under "suspicious circumstances" in late 1864.

5- Fogus [R] - 12 stamps, cost $50K, about a half a mile west of town.

The Fogus stamp mill site as it appears today; and in 1864 (bottom).
(*Harper's New Monthly Magazine*)

6- Gibbons[R] - 4 stamps, cost $15K, located about a half a mile west of town.

7- Gregory & Belton also known as the Spring Valley, Claytons, Peck & Co, Lambs) – 12 stamps, cost $30K, located about a mile east of town.

8- Moses (also known as the Youngs) **[R]** - cost 20K, located in town.

9- Napa [R] - 8 stamps, $20K, located about a quarter mile west of town.

10- Perry's Esmeralda [R] - located two miles south of town at Esmeralda Camp.

11- Pine Creek (also known as either the Dows; Bodies; or Brodie's Story's and Lufkins) - 10 stamps, cost $40K, located in Del Monte Canyon.

12- Pioneer (also known as Green's) **[R]** - 8 stamps, cost $25K, was Aurora's first mill, located quarter mile southeast of town on Wide West Street across from the Wide West mill.

13- Real del Monte [R] - 30 stamps, cost $250K, Aurora's biggest and costliest mill located where Esmeralda Gulch intersects Del Monte Canyon across Bodie Creek from the Antelope Mill. J. Ross Browne visited Del Monte Canyon in September 1864 and noted the new Real del Monte and Antelope mills:

> *We stopped awhile at the foot of the grade* [at Del Monte Canyon] *to visit the magnificent quartz-mills of the Real del Monte and the Antelope Mining Companies, of which I had heard much since my arrival in Aurora. Both of these mills are built of brick on the same plan, and in the Gothic style of architecture. Nothing finer in point of symmetrical proportion, beauty and finish of the machinery, and capacity for reducing ores by crushing and amalgamation, exists on the eastern slopes of the Sierras.*

14- Tucker & Stark (also known as the Aurora) - 10 stamps, $50K, located in Del Monte Canyon.

Directory

This engraved block of granite was once the cornerstone for the Wide West Mining Company's stamp mill. Although this important piece of Aurora's history is likely the oldest inscribed stone monument remaining in the Eastern Sierra region, it now serves as a stepping-stone for Bodie State Historic Park's museum. (Top photograph by Leeann Murphy)

15- Union (also known as the Johnson) - 8 stamps, cost $20K, located in town. This mill was reportedly "torn to pieces simply for the purpose of securing large quantities of amalgam wasted around the battery and pans" in 1868.

129

An 1864 Directory and Guide to Nevada's Aurora

16- Wide West [R] - 20 stamps, cost $150K, located quarter mile southeast of town on Wide West Street directly below the Wide West mine. The tunnel referred to in the following description of the Wide West stamp mill led directly from under the Wide West mine on Last Chance Hill to the stamp mill:

The Wide West Mill— bldg 60' by 124', built of granite and brick, tin roof, cost about $150,000, 20 stamps, commenced running about April 1863. They have a tunnel 7' high, 71/2' wide for a double track now in 200'. Capacity of the mill is 30 tons per day.

The new mill rarely reached its capacity of 30 tons of ore per day because shortly after it started operating nearby wells ran dry:

They have a splendid twenty-stamp mill, which, with a foresight worthy of the immortal Bunsby, was placed at a glorious point to run short of water,... (San Francisco *Alta California,* July 12, 1863)

17- Winters (Independence) - 16 stamps, $90K, located mile northeast of town. The site is now occupied by a modern mill.

STORES

The following list of 43 stores is derived from the 1864 Esmeralda County tax roll and does not include the previously listed bakery shops, drug stores, meat markets, and liquor stores:

Ackley & Cooper - groceries in Taylor's brick building on the south side of Wide West.

Barnum (11) - Cigars and tobacco in the Sazerac Saloon in Wingate's building on Pine.

Berliner, A. - clothing store on the lot owned by A.M. Wingate northeast corner of Silver and Pine.

Bloomingdale, N. & Co. (11) - store on the first floor of the courthouse.

Caro, Galland & Co. (44) [R] - one story brick store with basement. The large concrete wall seen today at the corner of Antelope and Pine was added to the building's interior in the early 1900s when the building was converted to a power substation.

Carter & Crocker (35) - grocery, liquor, and clothing store in a wooden building.

CARTER & CROCKER,

.... DEALERS IN ....

Groceries and Provisions,

West side Antelope street, Aurora.

KEEP CONSTANTLY ON HAND a large assortment of

Groceries and Provisions,

Of the best quality, such as—

Flour and Corn Meal,
Potatoes and other vegetables,
Bacon, sides and Hams,
Fresh Butter and Lard,
The best Golden Syrups,
Sugar, of all kinds,
Coffee, Tea and Spices,
Barley and other Grains,
Mining Tools and implements,
Bar Steel,
Hammers, Picks and Shovels,

Together with every article of convenience or service to the Miner or Housekeeper. Their Stock is being constantly supplied from below, and they are determined to make their establishment second to none, both in price and quality.

Aurora, April 4th, 1863.

Castro, N.- fruit store in wood building on north side of Pine just west of the Dublin City Store.

Cohn & Co. - cigars, fruit, and stationery.

Cordez & Brickwell - liquor and grocery store on the north side of Wide West east of Conner lot.

Crofts & Dumay - groceries and liquors on the east side of Silver.

Dreyfus & Lauer (9) [R] - one story brick store with basement. During the early 1900s, this building served as the post office.

FLEISHMAM & KAUFMAN,
DRY GOODS,
Clothing, Boots and Shoes,
Groceries and Provisions,
Hardware, Crockery and Queen's Ware,
SADDLERY, Etc.

MONEY SAVED, IS MONEY MADE!

We take this method of informing the people of Aurora and Mono County, that our Winter Stock is now all in Store, consisting of a complete assortment of

GROCERIES, AND PROVISIONS, HARDWARE, SADDLERY, CLOTHING,

☞ DRY GOODS and FANCY GOODS,

In fact *every thing* a Miner, Rancher or Family needs.

Those who wish to lay in a supply for the coming Winter would do well to give us a call as our Goods are laid here fully fifteen per cent cheaper than any other stock in Aurora, and we will sell accordingly.

Dublin City Store (47)- owned by R. M. Kearney. Store was also known as Kearney, R. M. & Co's Store.

Elliot & Co. - brick store on east side of Court just south of the Keppler & Mack store.

Ennor, W. - grocery, fruit and vegetable store in wooden building owned by Hutchinson and Rhodebank fronting 28 feet on Pine between Wells Fargo **(17)** and Green's Drug Store **(18)**.

Excelsior Book Store (44) - books owned by E. Berg in Caro's store.

Directory

Fleishman & Kaufman (42) – wholesale and retail dealers in groceries, provisions, hardware, dry goods, clothing, and crockery in a store known as the "Pioneer Brick Store."

Freidman's - fruit and confectionary in Manard's wooden building on Antelope.

Gallick, J . - groceries, dry goods, and clothing immediately west of the Exchange Stables. By July 1864, Gallick moved his store to the site "formerly occupied by of Shier" on Antelope just south of Pine.

Garland - fruit and vegetables on south side of Pine.

Geneley (1) [R] - brick grocery store.

Gillig, Mott & Co. - hardware in brick building on Pine.

Hass & Finlayson - dry goods and clothing in stone building owned by J. Booth on Pine. The partners also owned merchandise in Neidy's brick building **(12)**.

Hafky, J. - of goods in Martin's building on west side of Antelope.

Harrison, E. (24) - jeweler in Kennedy and Porter's Saloon on Antelope.

Huber, C. - gun shop on the north side of Pine.

Keppler & Mack – groceries, liquors, and hardware on the southeast corner of Pine and Court.

Kimball & Canfield (23) [R]- clothing in a prominent two story brick building. According to an add in the Esmeralda Daily Union, the store was located under the Masonic and Odd Fellows Hall, and carried a wide variety of items including "Fine Dress Coats, Pants and Vests, Business Suits (Summer and Winter), All Variety of Shirts, Hosiery of Every Kind, Handkerchiefs, Boots, Shoes, Hats, Pipes, Smoking Tobacco, Cigars, and Stationary."

Latez & Roeffe - merchandise on the west side of Antelope, north of Pine.

Levy & Co's "Aurora Emporium" (40) [R] - dry goods, clothing and groceries in a one story brick building with basement.

> **MOLINEUX & CO.,**
> DEALERS IN
> **HARDWARE,**
> Stoves, Tinware, Iron,
> Steel, Gas Pipe, Lead Pipe, window Glass, Putty, Oils, &c.
> CROCKERY AND GLASS WARE,
> BELLOWS, ANVILS,
> BLACKSMITH AND CARPENTERS' TOOLS,
> LAMPS AND LAMP FITTINGS, PACKING RUBBER AND HEMP,
> STEAM COCKS,
> STEAM FITTINGS, DOORS AND SASH.
>
> All kind of Job Work in Sheet Iron, Brass, Tin or Copper done with dispatch and in a workmanlike manner. Quartz Screens of all sizes on hand.
> Sign of the Big Tea-Kettle
> Pine street, Aurora.

Linton, C. B. & Bros. - groceries on east side of Court.

Molineux & Co. (10) [R] - hardware in a two-story brick building.

Morrison, Miller, and Haley - clothing, groceries, and hardware in Hull's building on the east side of Court.

Newman, M. - clothing store on southwest corner of Pine and Silver.

Pioneer Book Store (38)- owned by J. A. Armstrong in the Post Office Building during late 1863. By July 1864, the store was located on Pine and owned by Lake and Stewart. Some of the items for sale included: "Stationary line, penny-a-line, or fishing line [available] cheap for cash or greenbacks at market rates; blank books, poetical works of Lowell, Poe, Ossian, Shakespeare, Holmes, Bryant, Milton, Byron; periodicals, magazines, histories, blank forms, red and black ink, envelopes, seals, water stamps, gold and steel pens and pen holders." Lake and Stewart also offered a lottery:

Mr. Alexander, a tailor who keeps a clothing store opposite the Post office, held ticket No. 131 [first prize], which he received for mending a man's vest a few days ago. R. H. Leonard held ticket No. 22 [second prize], which drew the $50 greenback.
(Aurora *Esmeralda Daily Union*, December 7, 1864)

Rhodes & Co. (19) - hardware in a one-story brick building fronting Pine Street by 22 feet.

M. SCHWARTZ,
DEALER IN
Books and Stationery,
NEXT DOOR TO WELLS & FARGO'S EXPRESS OFFICE,
AURORA, ESMERALDA.

I have lately received the largest and best assortment of Goods, in the Stationary line ever brought this of the Mountains such as

STOCK & BLANK BOOKS, LAW BLANKS, MINING AND QUIT CLAIM DEEDS, ALBUMS, PHOTOGRAPHS, WRITING FLUIDS, INKSTANDS, &c. &c. &c.
DIMOND POINTED GOLD PENS,
OF THE BEST MAKERS.

BOOKS, BOOKS, BOOKS!

A most select assortment of

LITERARY WORKS,

By the best Authors.

ALSO A

CIRCULATING LIBRARY.

Filled with the choisest literature of the day, kept at this establishment. All the leading

ATLANTIC PAPERS AND MAGAZINES,

Received by the earliest conveyances.
Having the
AGENCY
for the Principal
CALIFORNIA & TERRITORIAL NEWSPAPERS,
I will deliver the same to the residences of subscribers without extra charge.

Saulsbury & McKinsley (1) - merchandise on the first floor of the Courthouse.

Searing, Dorn, and Co. - liquors, groceries, clothing, and mining tools on the north side of Wide West.

Shier (21) - dry goods, liquors, and clothing in a brick building fronting 16 feet on Antelope.

Schwartz Books (17) – see add on page 135.

Taylor - brick store on the south side of Wide West.

Watson, R. - cigar stand in Martin's saloon on the west side of Antelope.

Williams, J. (20) - cigars and tobacco in Exchange Saloon.

Wingate's Store (11) [R] - groceries and miner's goods on the first floor of Wingate Hall owned and operated by A. M. Wingate. The Wingates were one of the first to establish a "trading post" at Aurora:

> AN ESMERALDA PACK TRAIN.— *Wingate & Brothers' pack train, consisting of 55 mules and 6 muleteers, encamped on the Piaza, at Sacramento, on the 3d February, says the News, of that place, preparatory to a trip to Aurora, the city of Esmeralda mining district. The brothers Wingate are about to establish a trading post at Aurora... They will pack 42 mules, each bearing 350 pounds, or in the aggregate 14,700 pounds. Their cargo consists of groceries and liquors, and a few incidental article necessary on the route and to be used at the trading station.* (San Francisco *Daily Evening Bulletin*, February 2, 1861)

SURVEYORS

Aurora was fortunate because Joshua E. Clayton, a civil engineer from Mariposa, California, originally laid out the town's streets and lots according to an accurate survey. He located the town's sixty-foot wide streets in a north/south east/west grid in late 1860. Every resident in the Esmeralda Mining District was allowed to select and buy these newly surveyed town lots by paying the surveyor $5 and the Recorder $2.

> *Two towns, names respectively Esmeralda and Aurora, have been regularly laid out there by J. E. Clayton, formerly of Mariposa.* (Sacramento *Daily Union*, November 6, 1860)

> *Map of Esmeralda.—Mr. Clayton, a competent civil engineer, has prepared a map of Esmeralda mining region, in which all the silver leads are accurately defined. He states that, from a careful survey, he finds that all the diggings are in California...*(Visalia *Weekly Delta*, February 2, 1861)

About a year later, Clayton collaborated with William McBride to provide the information needed for Brady's Map of Aurora and Esmeralda (see page 4). Clayton, however, was not Mono County's first elected surveyor. That honor went to L. Tuttle who was elected to this post during Mono County's first election during June 1861. During that year, Aurora's surveyor surveyed the new cemetery, the lot for the first jail, and the storm sewers on Pine and Antelope Streets. By 1863, Mono County residents voted William McBride as their county surveyor.

The Mono County Board of Supervisors declared "all roads now used as such and all streets in any surveyed or laid out town in the county are hereby declared Public Highways" in June of 1861.

An 1864 Directory and Guide to Nevada's Aurora

TELEGRAPH OFFICE

On June 9, 1863, a 90-mile long telegraph line was completed between Genoa and Aurora. The telegraph office was located in the eastern portion of the brick Exchange Saloon building **(20)** just west of Rhoades & Company hardware store **(19)**.

> *About five o'clock this afternoon this place was alive to the great importance of having the telegraph line from Genoa to this place completed, which puts us in instant communication with San Francisco, and takes us within the magic circle of telegraphic communication. As soon as the wire reached the office the room was crowded to its fullest capacity. The citizens made the necessary preparations to celebrate the completion of the enterprise. At 7 o'clock, P. M. a large crowd assembled in the plaza. W. T. Gough was loudly called for, when he came forward and entertained them in a short speech touching the importance of the town of Aurora being connected by telegraph to the bay city, and also the relative position the enterprise of the Telegraph Company has placed Aurora with the eastern slope of the continent.* (San Francisco *Alta California,* June 10, 1863)

Touting Aurora's rich new mining strikes for only $2.50 per message soon became the telegraph's main purpose:

> *Our sage-brush has been struck by lightning last week, and the whole camp was alive with the pleasing evidence of our progress. We are now within speaking distance with all our relations on the whole continent, and the outside world may know in a trice whether our feet* [shares of mining stock] *are on the top, the bottom, or inside of the famous hills with which we are surrounded. On the evening of the telegraph everybody was anxious to be the first at the office to send a dispatch to the Bay to let his friends know that Aurora is no*

longer shut out from civilization and the world. It is mighty convenient thing to be able to inform your friend in the city that a heavy ledge has been struck rich, and by this little investment of $2 50 be enable to realize thousands. (San Francisco *Daily Evening Bulletin,* June 18, 1863)

UNDERTAKERS

Kelly and Vernon, Aurora's best-known architects and builders, also attended to the dead according to their July 1864 newspaper add:

Kelly & Vernon, Undertakers.
We are prepared to do all kinds of work in the above line, at short notice. We have a first class hearse which can be had at any time, on reasonable terms.

There is a possibility that Kelly & Vernon's hearse now resides at Bodie State Historic Park. The hearse pictured in a photograph taken by Shorty Harris at Aurora in the 1920s (see Death Valley Region Photo Collection, Utah State University's Digital Library) looks remarkably like one of the two hearses now displayed at Bodie's museum.

WATER AND GAS COMPANIES

In addition to relying on natural springs along Spring Street within the city limits, Aurorans constructed numerous wells in town to supply their stamp mills, and for their drinking water:

The Aurora Water Company's tunnel, which has been run day and night since it was commenced, is now in the hill west of

> *town about 150 feet. They have already found some water, and expect soon to strike the springs which are known to exist in the hill, within the next 50 feet, and seem very confident of finding in that distance a sufficient quantity to supply at least the present wants of the town with pure and wholesome water. I think it will prove a profitable investment for the owners.* (Sacramento *Daily Union*, April 20, 1863)

Because most of these wells and springs eventually dried up, at least three water companies were formed to transport water in horse-drawn water wagons from nearby springs below Brawley Peak to the town's many cisterns:

> *We have suffered from the want of water, but since the mill owners have gone to work in earnest to obtain it, there is no lack of it for their use. The artesian well of the Wide West Company has increased their supply, and they now have all they need; but they are still boring deeper, to make a sure thing of it. Our City Fathers are relying on the water companies— of which there are three or four— to bring water into the town for the use of the Fire Department. A small amount expended for sinking old wells deeper and digging new ones, would furnish all the water needed for that purpose. We are now supplied by water carts with as pure and clear water as the Sierras can produce. It is obtained from springs a little out of town. There are several large springs on Mount Brawley that a company secured for the purpose of bringing the water into the city, which can be done for comparatively little money. Another company design extending the Mono ditch to this place via Bodie.* (Sacramento *Daily Union*, August 6, 1863)

Aurora's Spring Street received its name for the numerous springs which sprang up along the roadway just west of town. One of the town's main water sources was located at one of these springs:

Passing up Bodie Gulch, to the edge of town we stop at a brickyard to try the water from a spring gushing from the ground by the roadside. The first drought contradicted all the stories about which I had heard about the bad water of the place. It was as good, cool water as any to be had in Sonora. A large tank has been prepared and persons are employed to haul this water all over town for sale. No one need drink bad water in Aurora now, unless he chooses to do so. (Sonora *American Flag,* November 5, 1863)

In 1862 and 1863, the Aurora Gas Company was authorized by both California and Nevada to provide Aurora with "illuminating gas." Although officially in California at the time, the Governor and Legislature of Nevada passed an act on December 19, 1862, creating the Aurora City Gas Company. F. K. Bechtel, D. C. Croker, and John S. Mayhugh were designated the principals of the new company which was given the "exclusive privilege of supplying the Town of Aurora, in the Territory of Nevada, and the inhabitants, residents, and people of said place, with illuminating gas."

Not to be outdone, the California Legislature approved an act on March 28, 1863, "granting F. K. Bechtel, and others [John S. Mayhugh, and D. C. Croker] the right to erect Gas Works and lay Gas Pipes, for the purpose of supplying the Town of Aurora with illuminating gas." The act also authorized Bechtel, Mayhugh and Croker to form a corporation called the "Aurora Gas Company." However, because Aurora's use of gas lighting was never reported in any newspaper account during the 1860s, it is unlikely the Aurora Gas Company ever completed their ambitious project.

An 1864 Directory and Guide to Nevada's Aurora

WIDE WEST MINE

Among the lucky prospectors to accompany Braly, Hicks, and Cory (the discoverers of the Esmeralda Mining District) back from Aurora to Monoville in the late summer of 1860 were George W. "Doc" Chase, a dentist from Mariposa, and "Professor" Joshua E. Clayton. According to the *Homer Mining Index* of January 5, 1884, Chase was the first to discover and make a claim on the Wide West vein on Last Chance Hill. Shortly after Chase claimed the Wide West, he reportedly sold out and became a very rich man. Clayton, who would later go on to becoming one of West's most respected mining engineers, stayed on and soon surveyed Aurora's lots and streets.

But according to Calvin Higbie, Samuel Clemens' mining partner from *Roughing It*, it was Alexander Gamble who first located the Wide West:

> *Alec Gamble had located the Wide West quartz mine, a large vein that cropped out very prominently, though not a color of mineral could be found on the surface. Hundreds of men had prospected the lode but didn't think enough of it to make a location.* ("Mark Twain's Partner." *Saturday Evening Post*)

However, there is no disputing the fact that the Wide West Mining Company was formed in San Francisco at the beginning of 1861:

> *The Wide West Mining Company was incorporated yesterday. Its purpose is to extract precious metals from the Wide West vein, at Esmeralda. The capital stock is $500,000, composed of 2,400 shares. Its first Board of Trustees is composed of John L. Murphy, Alexander Gamble, Wm. Norris, R. J. Vanderwater, and Lawrence A. Brown.* (San Francisco *Alta California,* January 17, 1861)

Directory

Most members of the Board of Trustees were residents of San Francisco. Alexander Gamble, one of their members and the master mind behind the Wide West, would play a pivotal role in the future development and promotion of Aurora, as well as the promotion of the Real Del Monte, the town's other major mine.

Gamble's Wide West mine became front-page news in the summer of 1862 when miners discovered incredibly rich gold and silver deposits while tunneling only 75 feet below the surface:

The next which demands our attention is the 'Wide West' and here we must pause, for it deserves our special care in observation, and the startling truths we are compelled to mention in connection with this ledge are astounding.... We have been in California since the spring of '49, visited many of the mines, but never saw anything to compare in richness with the ledge of the 'Wide West.' (Aurora *Esmeralda Star*, May 31, 1862)

According to eyewitness accounts, gold was visible along the walls of the Wide West's mining shafts and visitors fortunate enough to go inside the mine were astonished:

From the bottom of the shafts, drifts are being driven off upon the ledge, and holding a lighted candle in them, remind one of the fabulous tales of ancient golden caverns. (San Francisco *Daily Evening Bulletin*, June 5, 1862)

During June 1862, "Brady's Map of Aurora and Esmeralda" was published in San Francisco (see map on the next page). This was the first map to show the town's streets and lots in relation to all the major gold-bearing quartz veins in the Esmeralda Mining District.

An 1864 Directory and Guide to Nevada's Aurora

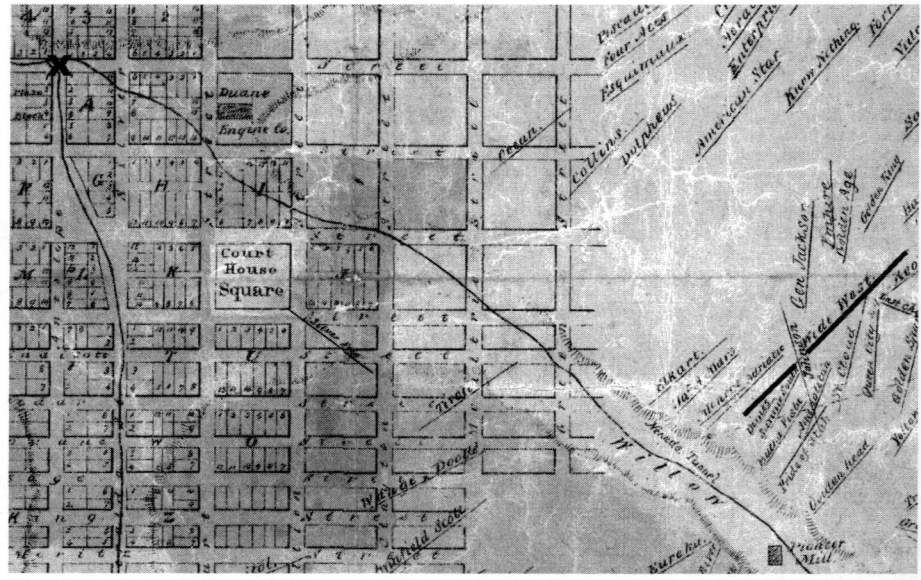

The location of the Wide West vein on Last Chance Hill (bold black line on the far right) in relation to downtown Aurora located at the intersection of Pine and Antelope (**X** symbol in upper left). Wide West Street, which would later connect the Pioneer Mill (shown on the lower right) in Willow Gulch to town, was not shown on this map. (Detail from Brady's Map of Aurora and Esmeralda found on page 4. Original map at Nevada Historical Society; online image from Nevada in Maps collection, Mary B. Ansari Map Library, University of Nevada, Reno.)

Mark Twain's mining partner Calvin Higbie stated that Gamble discovered "one of the richest chimneys of ore ever discovered in the state" within the Wide West mine. The amount of gold taken out of the Wide West was staggering:

> *Express wagons would haul great loads of these silver bricks downtown to the company's office, where they were stacked up like bricks in a brickyard. Extra foundations had to be put under the buildings to keep them from breaking down under the weight. All this time four and six mule teams with heavy express wagons laden with these bricks would be tearing*

Directory

across country to get them to San Francisco. ("Mark Twain's Partner." *Saturday Evening Post*)

These fabulously rich discoveries soon transformed Aurora from a mining camp of wood and canvas buildings to a booming city of brick and stone buildings overflowing with over 5,000 residents by 1863. Simply put, the Wide West put Aurora "on the map."

But it wasn't the Wide West's actual gold or silver bullion that caught the immediate attention of the average Californian—it was the pieces of paper on which shares of the Wide West's valuable stock were printed. The insatiable public demand for mining stocks from the Comstock Lode at Virginia City and Aurora's Wide West mine led to the organization of the San Francisco Stock and Exchange Board on September 11, 1862. According to a former member of the Board, the first stocks traded on the new exchange were from Aurora:

> *I am reminded of a few reminiscences when we first assembled for business.... The first two days we made no sales. The third day, Mr. P.B. Comwall and I arranged to do some business. I bought form him two purchases, five shares each, Wide West, and one purchase, Real Del Monte, of five feet, being the first records made.* (King's *History of the San Francisco Stock and Exchange Board*).

Money derived from the sale of Wide West stock gave the company the capital it needed to begin construction of a twenty stamp mill directly below the mine:

> *The Wide West Company is erecting a very extensive brick mill, 100 feet by 70 feet, in Willow Gulch, near their old mill* [Pioneer Mill]. *About two-thirds (of 75 tons) of their machinery has arrived. The engine and boiler are of the largest class capable of propelling 60 stamps of the largest size. The latest and most improved silver process will be*

used. (San Francisco *Daily Evening Bulletin,* November 10, 1962)

Mining stock was usually quoted as so many dollars per foot—a foot being a portion or share of particular mining claim. According to one report, Aurora's citizens had nothing but "feet" on their minds day and night:

Men talk feet, eat feet, drink feet, sleep feet, and—God help them— dream feet. They work feet, stake off feet, trade feet, jump feet, buy feet and sell feet. (San Francisco *Alta California,* March 14, 1863)

The Wide West Mining Company's stock reached its highest value during March of 1963:

The WW [Wide West] *was subject to considerable excitement on Monday. The stock suddenly rose to $500, but soon dropped to $395, and finally closed at $400, at which it may now be quoted.* (San Francisco *Mining and Scientific Press,* March 9, 1863)

Although stockholders usually expected dividends from successful mining companies like the Wide West, assessments (mandatory payments from stockholders required by mining companies to provide working capital) typically occurred far more often at Aurora. The Wide West's high valuation was not to last as the company unexpectedly levied an assessment only a month later:

Office Wide West Mining Company, 522 Montgomery Street, San Francisco, April 16, 1863.— An assessment of fifty (50) dollars per share has this day been levied on the capital stock of this company, payable in United States gold coin on of before THURSDAY, 23d inst. By order of the Board of Trustees. SOLON PATTEE, Sec'y. (San Francisco *Alta California,* April 30, 1863)

Directory

The value of Wide West stock soon plummeted and by July the stock was worth only a fraction of its April value:

> *I now come to explain why wiser and cooler heads, men of business capacity, have lost faith in Esmeralda mines. The mine which has been known more widely and dealt in more extensively by capitalists than any other in our district, is the 'Wide West.' It is a large company, and the stock has been put up at times as high as nearly $500 per share. Great things were expected of the 'Wide West.' 'Upon this rock I build my church,' exclaimed enthusiastic speculators in its stock,... I regret to state that the performance of the Wide West, up to this time, have been of anything but a satisfactory nature to its large and highly respectable audience. Indeed, I doubt not but that many would leave before the curtains rung down, if they could have their money returned to them at the door.* (San Francisco Alta California, July 12, 1863)

Stockholders were never sure if they had been swindled or the mine simply "fizzled out:"

> *But what about the Wide West? Honestly we cannot tell. It is apparently great swindle or a great fizzle; and yet, from all the facts accessible to an outsider, a Philadelphia lawyer could not decide which it is, or whether either.* (San Francisco *Mining and Scientific Press*, November 30, 1863)

In addition to the shady stock manipulations orchestrated by the likes of Gamble and some his San Francisco cronies, the Wide West Mining Company failed because the rich gold deposits first discovered near the surface were confined to only a few "pockets" which "played out" in less than a year. If that wasn't enough, the water wells constructed to supply the company's costly stamp mill ran dry shortly after they were completed.

An 1864 Directory and Guide to Nevada's Aurora

However, Alexander Gamble made a fortune on the Wide West just before the stock plunged in value in mid 1863. After selling his Wide West stock about the time the stock peaked in value, he invested heavily in the Real Del Monte mine. Here too he was involved with some questionable stock transactions. However, this time his creditors took a dim view of his activities and by the late 1860s, he was broke.

Just before Mr. Gamble died in 1899, a reporter from the San Francisco Chronicle interviewed him at San Francisco's almshouse and wrote an article entitled "Stripped of His Millions." This article was published in many newspapers across the country including the *Atlanta Constitution* of July 12, 1896. Although he was still alive at the time, the following except from this article reads like an obituary:

> *How fickle is the goddess of fortune was never better known than in the case of Alexander Gamble, a man seventy-three years of age, who is now an inmate of the city and county almshouse. Forty years ago he was reputed to be worth between $3,000,000 and $4,000,000, being reckoned as one of the wealthiest men in California, but today he in a superannuated dependent upon public charity.*
>
> *In 1849 Gamble came to California from Belfast. Me., bringing with him nothing but a pair of strong hands and a college education. He was sober and industrious, and within a few years by hard work, directed by superior intelligence, gained a controlling interest in several of the richest mines in Nevada. These were the Wide West, the Del Monte,...They were all at Aurora, Esmeralda County, Nevada.*
>
> *But just at the dawning of the '70s Gamble's fortunes was reversed. His mines depreciated in value, his creditors pressed him, he found himself unable to meet their demands, and the inevitable happened. His creditors sold him out, and he was left with what he had when he first entered the sate, twenty-five years ago—a pair of strong hands and a college education.*

Directory

However, it was Mark Twain who would make the Wide West one of the most famous mines in the American West. In his 1872 book *Roughing It,* Twain describes his association with the Wide West mine the most "curious" event in his life so far:

> *I now come to a curious episode—the most curious, I think, that had yet accented my slothful, valueless, heedless career. Out of a hillside toward the upper end of town, projected a wall of reddish looking quartz-croppings, the exposed comb of a silver-bearing ledge that extended deep down into the earth, of course. It was owned by a company entitled the 'Wide West.'*

Mark Twain's "reddish looking quartz-cropping" of the Wide West vein is visible as the dark line above Aurora in this 1890 close-up of Last Chance Hill. Also visible to the lower right of the exposed vein is a rare view of the Wide West Mining Company's stamp mill in Willow Gulch. The Real del Monte mine is located in the upper right and the courthouse is located in the lower left. (Nevada State Museum, Carson City)

149

Twain goes on to describe how he and his partner Calvin Higbie were "millionaires for a week" because they were temporary owners of a rich vein which ran right through the Wide West mine. After failing to do the required assessment work, their claim was "jumped" and later sold to the Wide West Mining Company for $500,000.

Although one can still see Twain's "wall of reddish looking quartz-cropping" on Last Chance Hill today, the only evidence of the Wide West mine itself is a few collapsed mining tunnels, piles of discarded quartz ore, and the crumbling foundations of its once famous, but now demolished, stamp mill. The mine that was responsible for Aurora's rise to prominence is now abandoned and forgotten.

Last Chance Hill today. The barren hillside now supports a thriving pinyon pine forest concealing much of the Wide West vein. This is the same view shown on the previous photograph.

WINGATE HALL

This two-story brick structure **(11) [R]** owned by A. M. Wingate was one of Aurora's largest and most important meeting halls. The Glen Brothers operated a saloon in the basement, the first floor was used as a grocery and miner supply store run by Wingate, and the Sazerac Saloon was located on the second floor. The second floor also served as a meeting hall for large gatherings including 350 "law and order citizens" of the Citizen's Safety Committee during the February 1864 vigilante uprising.

No expense was spared for this ornately decorated three-story structure:

> *A large number of new buildings have been contracted for, to be erected during the coming fall, and a large number are now being finished. There are also many buildings of cut stone and brick in the course of erection. The most prominent and beautiful one in Aurora is A. M. Wingate's large three-story brick building, fronting on Pine Street twenty-two feet. The Basement story is built of dressed stone-the wall two feet thick. The main store room is thirty-two by fifty feet, the ceiling thirteen feet six inches high from the main floor, and is supported by heavy iron columns. The third story forms a large and beautiful hall, of thirty-two by fifty feet, and is well adapted for a lecture room or billiard saloon-ceiling thirteen feet high. On the north end of the main building is added an L, twenty-four by twenty-four feet, three stories high, and is well arranged for a family residence. The interior of the main and front building is beautifully finished-all of the openings being enclosed with heavy iron doors, and the front is handsomely decorated with a splendid bracket cornice, making a happy combination of durability and beauty.* (San Francisco *Alta California,* September 4, 1863)

The spacious second story hall was the favorite meeting place for Aurorans for many years:

THE FESTIVAL AT WINGATE'S HALL. The festival of the Trinity Church Sunday School which took place last Saturday evening was one of the grandest affairs of the kind ever seen in Aurora. W. Van Voorhies, Esq., delivered a brief moral sermon, which was really better than nine-tenths of the sermons we ever heard preached by ministers of the Gospel in this city. At the close of the sermon the "reverend" gentleman was congratulated by his friends. The Christmas tree—the grand magazine of joy for the children—exceeded in beauty, richness, and variety, anything that could have been expected in this mountain town, so isolated from the more luxurious cities of the world. Alderman Mack officiated as Santa Claus, and it is no exaggeration to say that he "filled the bill" exactly. After the presents had all been distributed—making a load for each child of two or three times as much as he could carry—the little folks marched into a large room, where a most magnificent collation was awaiting them. (Aurora *Esmeralda Daily Union,* December 28, 1864)

After singing "America," the entire audience proceeded to Wingate Hall, where a most bountiful collation prepared by the ladies, awaited them....Almost the entire community gathered together at Wingate Hall, which was illuminated by the heaven-born hues of our starry banner, to say nothing of the bright eyes of fair women, there "tipping the light fantastic toe" to the time of most excellent music. (*Borax Miner,* July 15, 1876)

Wingate Hall was used for social gatherings and meetings through the 1870s until it was destroyed by fire in the 1880s. Unfortunately there are no known photographs of this important building.

DULL TIMES

Unlike her close rival Virginia City, Aurora's fabulously rich surface ore deposits unexpectedly ran out only one hundred feet below the surface early in 1864. This set off a panic to sell the once high-flying stocks of Aurora's biggest mines—the Wide West and the Real del Monte. "Reckless, bloody, extravagant" Aurora soon began to decline and by the summer of 1864, most of Aurora's expensive stamp mills ceased operation.

The Aurora debacle was well known to mining engineers and historians for many years after the collapse:

> *During the great stock fever of 1862, '63 and '64, the credulous and then comparatively inexperienced people of California were most wretchedly humbugged and swindled by having wild cats of all kinds, sizes and colors palmed off upon them as genuine mines by unscrupulous stock sharps and swindlers.* (San Francisco *Mining and Scientific Press*, January 23, 1875)

An 1864 Directory and Guide to Nevada's Aurora

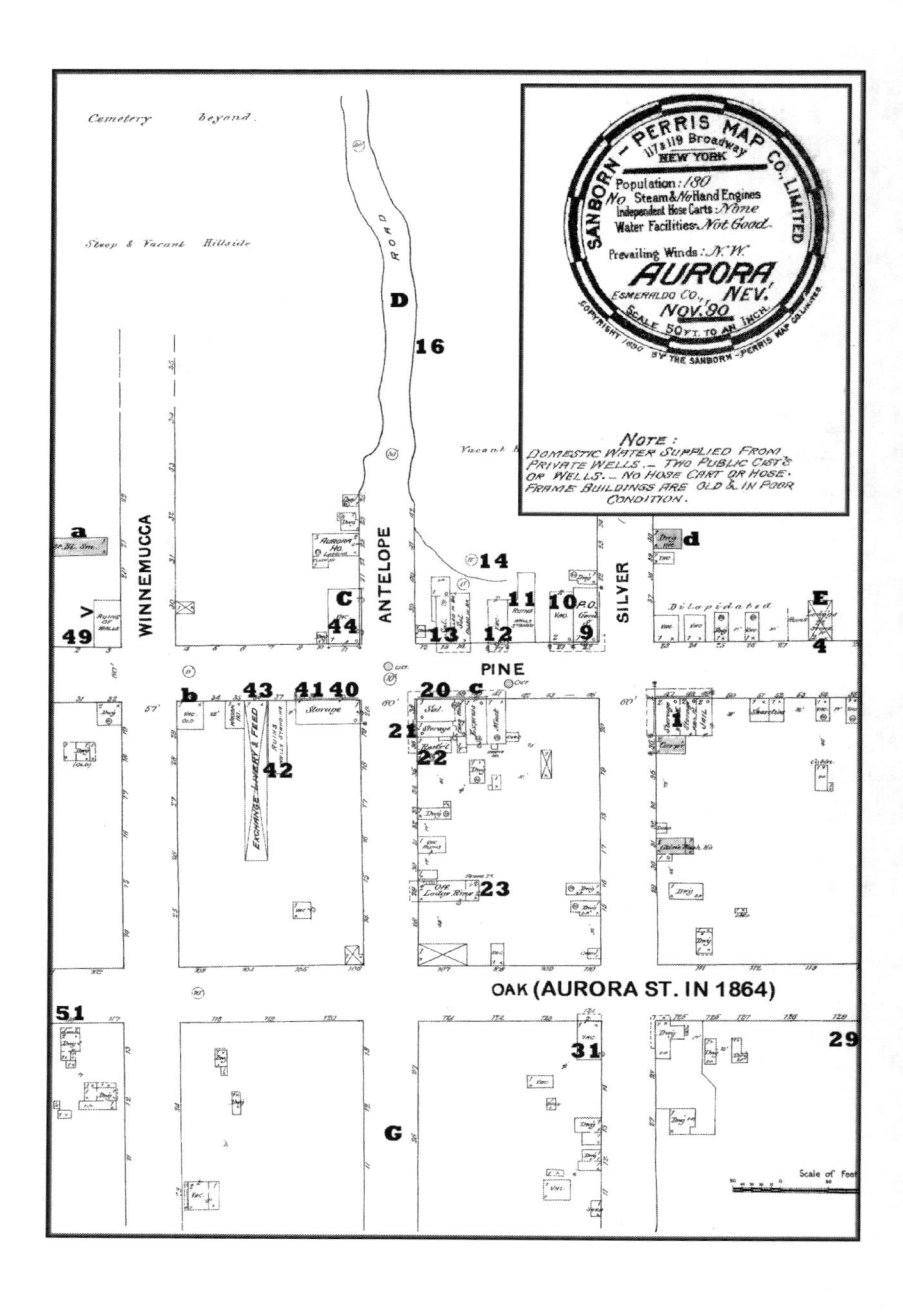

Dull Times

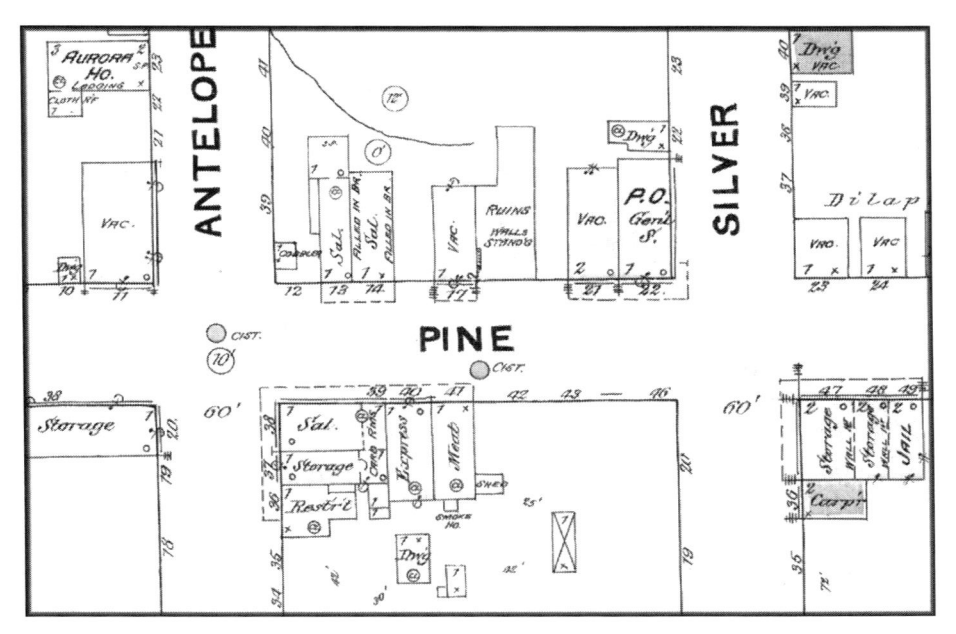

Above is a section of downtown Aurora from a fire insurance map prepared by the Sanborn-Perris Map Company in November 1890. The map on the left is a larger portion of the original map that includes numbered locations (placed by the author) that are keyed to the Location Index on page 11. Additional location symbols placed on this map include: a- Housley Blacksmith shop; b- Hass & Finlayson's Store; c- Rhodes & Co. Store that was the Express Office in 1890; and d- brick house owned by Edmund Green. The structures with location numbers generally date back to 1864 whereas many of the unnumbered structures labeled "vac," "shanties," and "dwg" in 1890 may have been constructed after 1864. This map was completed about the same time the photograph on page 9 was taken. The map does not show every building that existed in 1890. Notable omissions include all the structures along Spring and Wide West Streets, as well as the schoolhouse (location index #28); Levy & Co's residence (#50); and the Superintendent's House (#55). (Nevada in Maps online image collection from the Mary B. Ansari Map Library, DeLaMare Library, University of Nevada, Reno. The original map is from the Nevada Historical Society.)

155

Aurora produced the bulk of her gold and silver in 1863 and 1864 when most of the area's seventeen stamp mills and numerous mines were operating. Because the records regarding Aurora's bullion production during the 1860s have been lost, most historians base their bullion estimates of between $16 and $30 million on "recollections" from former Wells Fargo employees written long after they departed Aurora. If we rely on accounts written at the time of Aurora's boom, a bullion figure of $2-3 million is more likely (see page 204). When you compare this amount to the $300 million in bullion produced at Virginia City's Comstock Lode from 1859 to 1880, and Bodie's production of $15-18 million during her boom time from 1877 to 1888, Aurora's production is a poor showing for such a famous mining region.

Considering how many millions were spent developing Aurora and her mines and mills, such a meager showing establishes Aurora as one of the biggest mining scams in Nevada history. This fact was well known to mining historians like Charles Howard Shinn who singled out Aurora in 1910 as one of Nevada's greatest, if not the greatest, mining scams ever: "There is that Nevadan Golgotha of speculators, Esmeralda, where millions of dollars were wasted."

It is interesting to note what a rapid decline in a town's fate can do to a person's opinion of a place they once admired. Only a few years earlier, both visitors and residents alike had nothing but good things to say about Aurora. But with the boom over, the mood of residents like Mary Ellen Ackley began to sour in 1864:

> *As the mining excitement had died down, Wide West Mill had shut down. The town grew so dull that people were leaving everyday. I never liked Aurora. The climate was harsh; it snowed nearly every month in the year; not a tree nor flower in town; nothing but rocks, sagebrush and sand.*

Downtrodden Aurora also fell out of favor with California newspaper reporters who only a year earlier had praised the town's bright prospects on a daily basis. The following excerpt from an article by "Dogberry" was entitled "Sterility Everywhere:"

Aurora has neither trees, soil or vegetation, its appearance is not prepossessing. A very home-sick man would probably die here. The plan of the city can be imitated by scattering three or four hundred carpenter's blocks mixed with a few brickbats over a pile of building stones; then kick up the dust and gravel with your heels and hands, and keep the same in a state of perpetual suspension over said pile, and you have Aurora in miniature. Aurora was discovered by a man who was blown upon it by one of the vigorous zephyrs peculiar to these latitudes. On being deposited near the site of the town, he is said to have exclaimed, "Well, this is a roarer!" hence the name Aurora. (Stockton *Weekly Independent*, July 15, 1864)

Two years later, much of Aurora was destroyed by fire and by 1870 the town was down to a few hundred residents. The following description by Henry DeGroot sums up the sense of abandonment:

Journeying on by many a deserted claim and camp, we arrived in Esmeralda country—a very Golgotha of mining enterprise, and hope, and industry. In hardly any other district of Nevada has so much money been spent to so little purpose as here. The sums thrown away may be literally counted by the million. Aurora, once a large and lively town, wears now an altogether cadaverous aspect. Its streets are silent, its houses empty, and its businesses dried up.

Clarence King wrote the best epitaph for Aurora in 1872:

Alas for Aurora once so active and bustling with silver mines and it's almost daily murder. Twenty-six whiskey hells and two Vigilance Committees graced those days of prosperity and mirthful gallows, of stock-board and the gay delirium of speculation. Now her sad streets are lined with closed doors; a painful silence broods over quartz mills, and through the whole deserted town one perceives that melancholy security of human life which is hereabouts one of the pathetic symptoms of bankruptcy. The "boys" have gone off to merrily shoot one another somewhere else, leaving poor Aurora in the hands of a sort of coroner's jury who gather nightly at the one saloon and hold dreary inquests over departed enterprise.

Looking east down Pine to the "Superintendent's House" in the early 1900s. Electric power was extended to Aurora from Bodie and Hawthorne in 1909.
(Kenneth L. McKeough)

By 1890, Aurora's population was down to only 180. Although there was a brief resurgence of mining activity just before World War I, the mines soon closed again and Aurora became a permanent ghost town by 1920.

Dull Times

This view down Pine Street from the early 1930s shows the old courthouse on the left, and the burned out hulk of the Merchants' Exchange Hotel in the far distance on the right side of the road. (Library of Congress, Prints and Photographs Division, Historic American Buildings Survey, HABS, NEV, 11-AURO)

Nevertheless, Aurora lived on as one of Nevada's most visited ghost towns. Nell Murbarger, a visitor to Aurora in the late 1930's, noted: "The ghost town that lay before us was more extensive in scope and better preserved than any we had seen before, or I ever expected to see again!" Much to Nell's amazement, over one hundred buildings, thirty-five of which were large structures of brick and stone, still remained in the deserted town where "sagebrush grew more than man high in the streets."

An 1864 Directory and Guide to Nevada's Aurora

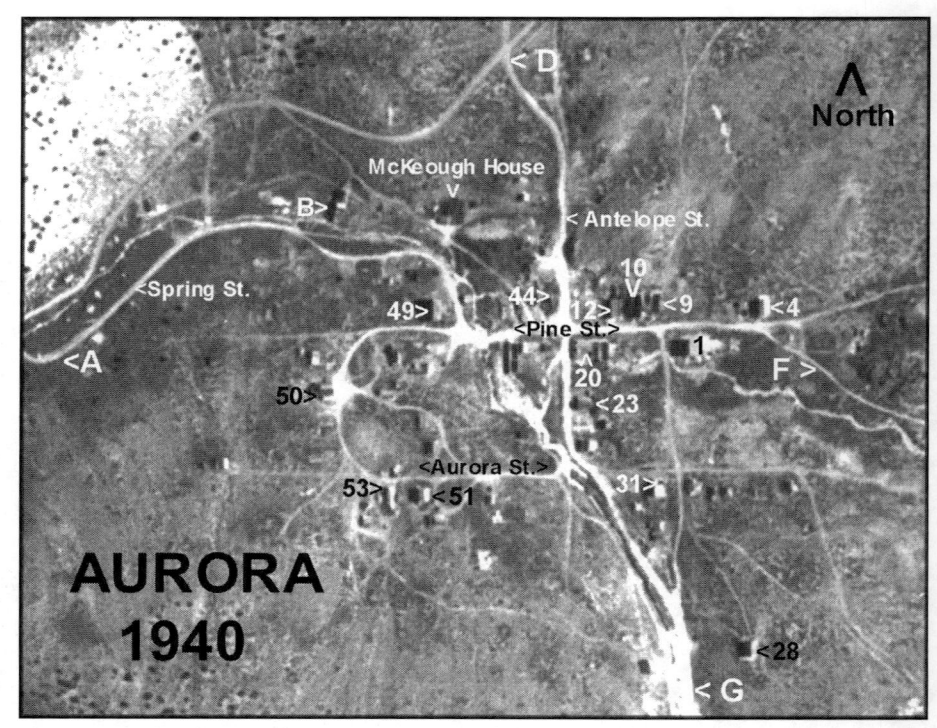

AURORA 1940

Aurora as it appeared almost 70 years ago on a 1940 aerial photograph. The numbers, which are keyed to the Location Index in page 11, indicate standing brick buildings and the letters indicate roads. By 1940, the town was abandoned except for the "McKeough House" and #53—Fried Walker's House. Nearly all of Aurora's buildings were gone in less than fifteen years.

The old abandoned houses, she noted, were still full of beautiful old-time furniture. Other homes had fifty year-old calendars still hanging on the walls, or faded newspapers with the latest news about some Civil War battle, plastered on the walls. Nell summed up her weeklong visit to Aurora by saying:

> *Everywhere we turned we were confronted by a wonderful wilderness of relics. In one day's time we could have loaded a*

railroad boxcar with material of museum caliber. Yet the grandest relic of all was the priceless old town, herself!

Aurora's glorious ghost town days were not to last. After commercial building contractors, or "brick thieves" as they were sometimes called, began tearing down the town for the used brick market after World War II, the town disappeared fast. By the time Aurora was added to the National Register of Historic Places in 1974, the only things left of this once prosperous city were piles of broken bricks, scattered heaps of old lumber, and a few surviving stone building foundations. Today's visitor to Aurora will feel much the same as Mark Twain did when he described a vanished early California mining town site in *Roughing It* over a century ago:

—you will find it hard to believe that there stood at one time a fiercely-flourishing little city, of two thousand or three thousand souls, with its newspaper, fire company, brass band, volunteer militia, bank, hotels, noisy Fourth of July processions and speeches, ...labor, laughter, music, dancing, swearing, fighting, shooting, stabbing.. everything that delights and adorns existence—all the appointments and appurtenances of a thriving and prosperous and promising young city,—and now nothing is left of it all but a lifeless, homeless solitude. The men are gone, the houses have vanished, even the name of the place is forgotten.

An 1864 Directory and Guide to Nevada's Aurora

View down Spring Street to China Garden and Lover's Leap.

RESIDENTS OF AURORA 1861-1864

Note- Each name is followed by a source abbreviation keyed to a list on page 207.

A
Ackley, George H. (P61); (E62); carpenter (R62).
Adams, G. (R63)
Adams, J. M. (M61)
Adams, Moses (R63)
Adams, Otis (R63); blacksmith shop in Willow Gulch (M62).
Addens, John house on Mono St. (M62).
Adkins, E. P. (M61)

Aitkin, R. A. (R63)
Ake, Sam ("Chinaman") house on Humphrey lot on Esmeralda St. (E64).
Albright, T. J. (R62)
Aldrich, A. D. (M61)
Alexander, W. (R63)
Allan, Chas. E. (M61)
Allen, A. D. (P61); (E62); miner (R62); (M61); mortgage from Sam Davis (E64), First Lieutenant of the Esmeralda Rangers

(G84), elected to the Territorial House of Representatives on 9/3/62 (N81).
Allen, George F. (M61); (R63).
Allen, H. F. (P61); (R62); (R63); (M62); (M61).
Allen, H. S. (M61); (P61); (R62); (M62); lot on E side of Silver (E64).
Allen, H. W. (P61); (M61).
Allen, R. N. (R63)
Allen, S. (R63)
Allison, W. D. (R63) jewler from New York.
Alliston, O (M61)
Alt, George (R62) [may be same as Ault, George]
Alvison, Albert (R63)
Amsler, Jacob (R62) miner; (M62); (M61); proprietor Orleans restaurant on E side of Antelope (E64); eating house (tax1864).
Ancin, John (M61)
Anderson, C. S. (M61)
Anderson, O. (M61)
Anderson, P. (R62)
Angeles, Chris lot and cabin on E side of Winnemucca (E64).
Angiers, Chris lots in Aurora (M62).
Anis, A. (R62)
Archer, J (M61)
Archibald, J. [spelled Archbald, James in (R63) and Archbold, J. in (M61)] (R62); lot on E side of Winnemucca (E64).
Archibald, James (P61)
Armstrong, A. S. (M61)
Armstrong, Chas. D. (M62)
Armstrong, J. A. broker in mining stocks, owner of Pioneer Bookstore in P. O. Bldg. (E64).
Arnold, Chas. (R63); C.H. (P61); (M61); (M62); (E62); (R62).
Arnold, W. A. (R63)
Arnold, W. B. (R63)
Arnold, W. F. (P61); (R62).
Arnott, S. G. (M61)
Ash, Fred (R63)
Asham, M.B. (R63); (M62).
Ashburn, D. (M61)
Aspen, Louis (M61)
Atkins, E. D. (R62)
Atkins, E. P. superintendent Antelope Mill (R63).

Atkinson, J. W. (R63)
Atwood, Thos. (R63)
Ault, A. J. stable on N. side of Spring between Blasauf lot and Bodie Stable (E64).
Ault, George [may be same as Alt, George] (M62); (M61); partner with Ault, A. J. (E64).
Austin, A. (M62)
Angine, C. (R62)
Angus, C. (R63); (M61).
Austin, G. L. (R63); works for the Wide West Mining Co. (E64)
Averil, A. (P61); or spelled Averill, A. (R62)
Aylward, Jas. (R63); (M62).

B
Bacigalupi, Gaitano "Italian Jim" (G84).
Bacon, E. M. M.D. (R63); lot on NW corner of Court and Aurora (E64).
Badgely (N81); (G84).
Bailey, G. W. (R63); appointed sheriff after Scott was killed by Indians (N81) (G84); on the Cotillion Part committee (T63).
Bailey, W. P. (M61)
Baker, A. (P61); (R62)
Baker, F. (M61); (M61); miner (R62).
Baker, F. A. (R63); four lots in town (E64).
Baker, Frank (P61); lot on W side of Antelope (E64).
Baker, J. (R62)
Baker, John (M61)
Baker, S. (R62)
Baker, Sam. (M61)
Baker, Samuel (P61)
Baker, W. (R63)
Baldwin, Judge Alexander Mono Co. Court Judge, held dual court with Turner (N81) (G84).
Baldwin, Wm. (R63)
Baling, M. L. (R62)
Ball, S. M. (R62); (M62).
Ball, Wm. H. (R63); adobe house on lot on E. side of Esmeralda (E64); house on Silver & Aurora Streets (M62).
Ballew, C. W. (R63)
Bane, Wm. (R63)
Banner, Anthony (R63)

Residents of Aurora 1861-1864

Bannister, [or spelled Banister in (M61)] John (P61); (E62); miner (R62); (R63); (M62); barbershop on SW corner of Pine and Silver (E64).
Barber, A. J. (R63); wood bldg on alley E. side of Silver (E64).
Barber, Jos. (R63)
Barbien, Joe brickyard and adobe house on E. side of Cottonwood gulch (E64).
Barclay, Capt. W. R. lot on SE corner of Pine and Silver (M62).
Barclay, Geo. R. (M61)
Barger, Samuel (E62); (R62)
Barker, Edw. D. (P61); (M61); (R62); (R63); (M62); four lots in town (E64); on the Cotillion Party Committee (T63).
Barker, F. A. lot on E side of Antelope W of Esmeralda (E64).
Barkwaltor, Daniel (P61)
Barlow, Richard "Centre Meat Market" on Antelope behind Armory Hall (E64); butcher (tax1864).
Barlow, Wm. (R63)
Barman, A. tobacco shop in Steiner's saloon (E64).
Barman, J. (R63)
Barman, J. P. (R63)
Barnell, Jno. (R63)
Barnes, Charles W. (R63); cabin E side of Roman, lot on W side of Mono (E64).
Barnett, S. D. (M61)
Barnett, W. H. (P61); (M61).
Barnill, Wm. (R63)
Barns, F lot on W side of Winnemucca (E64).
Barnum, P. cigars in Steiner saloon in Wingate brick bldg (E64).
Barstow, W. H. (M61)
Barten, I. P. (R63)
Barton, Jake (P61)
Basasid, F. (M61)
Batchelder, N. (R63)
Baughton, G. W. (P61)
Baum, David A. (R63); Postmaster (E64).
Bawden, J. A. (P61)
Bayer, T. A. (M61)
Bayer, Theo. [or Thos. per (M61)] (R63).
Bean, William (R63)
Beardsell, Luke (R63) [may be same as Birdsall, Luke]

Beardsley, B. miner (R62)
Beardsley, C. L. (M62)
Beardsley, R. (M61)
Beasley, T. (or F.?) M. (R62); (M61).
Bechtel, Frederick. K. (M61); (P61); (M62); 2nd Lieutenant (E62); Justice of the Peace (R62); Notary Public (R63); conveyancer (T63); Bee Hive Saloon on NE corner Pine and Antelope (E64); (G84); (tax1864).
Becker, H. L. (M61); (P61); (R62).
Beckitt, H. D. miner (R62)
Begnette, A. H. (R63)
Begole, C. D. (M61)
Beguette (spp?) H. D. (M61)
Beldon, H. (R62)
Beliner?, W. (or H.) clothing in Sam Davis bldg on W. side of Antelope (E64).
Bell, A. (R62)
Bell, A. Y. (M61)
Bell, Aaron (P61)
Bell, Alexander (P61); (M61); (R62).
Bell, R. (M61)
Bell, Robert (R63), house and lot on S. side of Antelope & house and lot on N side Del Monte, lot and house on S side of Aurora (E64).
Bell, S. H. (R63)
Bell, T. J. (M61)
Bell, William H. (R63); house & lot on E side of Esmeralda (E64).
Bellinger, J. owned Barnum Hotel located over the Washington Baths on Antelope (E64).
Bellow, H. (P61)
Bender, Jno. C. (R63)
Bennel, John lot E of M. Myers lot (E64).
Bennett, Captain (R63)
Bennett, T. (R62)
Bennett, Thomas (M61); (P61).
Benschoten, W.M. (P61); (M61); (R62).
Benson, G. (M61)
Bentley, H. R. (R62)
Benton, A. P. (P61); (R62); (M61)
Benton, S. S. (P61); carpenter (R62)
Benway, Charles (R63)
Berg, B. (R63)
Berg, E. (R63); Excelsior Book Store in Caro, Galland & Co. store on NW corner Pine and Antelope (E64); (tax1864).
Berger, S. (M61)

165

Berger, Samuel (M62)
Berk, P. (R62)
Berliner (or Bellinger), J. (R63), lodging house furniture over Washington Baths (E64).
Berliner, A (or H. ?) clothing store in Wingate's bldg on NE corner of Pine and Antelope (E64).
Berry, James (tax1864).
Berry, Margaret (R63)
Best, John B. (M61); (P61); (R62); (R63); (M62); house and lot on N side of Wide West (E64).
Bick, Valentine (R63); proprietor of Barnum Restaurant (T63); eating house (tax1864).
Bigelow, Dennis (M61); (P61); miner (R62); (M62); wood bldg on lot on S. side Pine, E. of Court (E64).
Bigelow, E. F. (R63)
Biggs, John (R63)
Bigsby, H. G. (P61); (M62).
Bilinas store on NE corner of Pine and Silver (E64).
Bill, Robert (M62)
Billings, W. (R62)
Billows, H. (M61)
Bimker, T. C. (M61)
Bird, B. B. liquors, lodging furniture in Herbert House, N. side of Pine, W. of Antelope (E64).
Birdsall, Luke (R63) [may be same as Beardsell, Luke]
Bishop, S. A. (M62)
Black, James V. (R63), lot on N side of Del Monte between Antelope and Winnemucca (E64); secretary Davenport G&SMCo.
Blackman, D. (P61)
Blackman, I. (M61); lot on the W side of N Antelope (E64).
Blackman, J. F. (M61); (R63).
Blackman, J. T. (P61); (R62).
Blackman, S. (R63)
Blackwell, E. H. (R63); cabin and lot on N. side of Wide West (E64).
Blake, C. C. (R63)
Blanchard, Charles (R63)
Blanchard, J. B. (R63), six lots in town (E64).

Blaney, B. D. (R63); wooden house on lot on NE corner of Court and Del Monte (E64).
Blaney (?), Mrs M. eating house (tax1864).
Blasauf (Blasif), Jno. (R63); brick house and brick "City Brewery" on N Side of Spring (E64); brewer (tax1864).
Blayin, P. miner (R62)
Blazier, Phillip (P61)
Blethin, A. G. (R63)
Blethin, H. A. (R63)
Bliven, Franklin in Bell's House on Del Monte St. (E64).
Blivin, C. (R63)
Blondin, Abraham (R63)
Bloomingdale, N merchandise in Preble & Devoe's bldg. on Pine & Silver (E64); (tax1864).
Boat, (Baab?), Elmer (P61)
Boatwright, W. (P61); (E62).
Bodell, J. (R62)
Bodine, A. (M61)
Bodine, A. H. (R63)
Bodine, J. A. (R62)
Bodle, John L. (R63); (M62); (M61); three houses on lot on N. side of Wide West (E64).
Boggs, G. H. (R63)
Boggs, J. M. (P61); (R62); (M61).
Boggs, T. W. (M61)
Boler, William (R63)
Bolinger, A. (M61)
Bolt, W. H. lot between Esmeralda and Silver (E64).
Bolton, ? (M61)
Bond, Cal. (R63)
Bond, H. E. (M61)
Bond, J. M. (R63)
Booker, Isaiah (R63)
Boonershin, J. (R62)
Booth, Geo. (R63)
Booth, James wooden bldg on lot on N. side of Pine (E64).
Booth, N. (P61)
Boothe, J. N. (M61); (M62).
Boring, Wm. M. [or H. in (R63)] (M61); attorney-at-law (R62); attorney with Hayden on Silver (T63) Justice of the Peace, elected Probate Judge on 9/7/64 (N81); on the Cotillion Party Committee (T63).

Residents of Aurora 1861-1864

Bornemann, W. C. & Co. Brokers (R63).
Boston, Geo. E. (M62)
Botsford, R. M. (M61)
Boughton, G. W. (M61), (R62).
Bowell, J. M. (R63)
Bowman, J. S. (R62); (M61); lot on N side of Aurora (E64).
Boyle, B. (R63)
Boyle, John (P61); (R62)
Boyle, Patrick (R63)
Boyle, T. works for the Wide West Mining Co. (E64).
Brackett, John B. (R63)
Bradford, G. S. (R63)
Bradford, J. B. & Bros. (R63); (T63); lot on W side of Silver, and Bradford's Store (aka City Meat Market) on N side of Pine, and house E side of Mono (E64); Notary Public (T63); butcher (tax1864).
Bradford, William H. (or B) (R63); butcher (tax1864).
Bradley, George (R63); house on E side of Silver (E64).
Bradley, James house on N. side of Pine (E64).
Brady, G. (P61);(R62).
Brady, George (R63); board house on lot on E. side of Silver (E64).
Brady, John B. (P61); (R62); house on N side of Pine (E64).
Brady, Thom. (M62)
Braly, James M. (M61), (G84), (N81) [Braley per (P61)]; ex-recorder (R62); one of the founders of the Esmeralda Mining District on August 25, 1860 (G84); lot on Silver (M62).
Bramley, Dr. (R63)
Brenham, O. S. (R63)
Brewster, John (R63)
Brickweder, J. (R63)
Brigby, J. C. (M61)
Brill, W. S. (R63)
Brimhall?, J. A. barn and hay on N side of Bodea [Bodie] Gulch W of Gibbons mill (E64).
Britell, C. K works for the Wide West Mining Company (E64).
Britton, E. (M61)
Brock, Daniel (R63)
Brockman, Moses killed Carder (G84).

Brodie, T. mill owner (R62)
Bronson, A. (M61); (R63).
Brooks, W. E. (R63)
Brookwalter, D. (M61)
Brown, Alexander (R62)
Brown, C. J. (P61); (E62); (R62); (M62).
Brown, Charles (R63)
Brown, David (M61)
Brown, E. C. (M61); (P61); (R62)
Brown, H. R. (M61); (R62).
Brown, J. B. [Broun per P61]; (R62).
Brown, J. H. (R63); brick cabin on E side of Silver (E64).
Brown, J. M. (M61)
Brown, Ja. (M61)
Brown, John (P61)
Brown, L. A. stock broker (M62); (M61).
Brown, T. N. (R63)
Brown, W. B. C. (M61)
Brown, Z. A. (R62)
Bryant, William works at Winter's Mill (E64).
Bryfoger, C. C. (M61)
Buckalaw, Mrs. cabin on lot on S. side of Aurora (E64).
Bucke, James (M62)
Buckely, Ed (R63)
Buckingham, John (R63).
Buckley, William member of Daly gang hung at Aurora on 2/9/64 (N81) (G84).
Bugbee, J. C. (R62)
Bullpit, Wm. [or spelled Bullpiet in (E64)] (M61); (M62).
Bulwer, A. J. (R62)
Bummerskin, J. H. (E62)
Bunker, D. C. (R62)
Bunker, T. C. (P61)
Bunt, James (R63)
Burgess, W. H.(or E.) ranch on E Walker River (E64); appointed County Commissioner on 4/5/64 but later rejected (N81).
Burke, [or spelled Burk (M61)] B. (P61).
Burke, Charles (R63)
Burkes, Samuel (P61)
Burnett, N. (R63); Burnett & Co. wood house and lot on W. side of Silver (E64).
Burnett, S. D. (P61); (R62)
Burnett, W. H. (R62)
Burnham, W. L.

167

An 1864 Directory and Guide to Nevada's Aurora

Burns, Jno. (R63)
Burns, Jno. W. (R63)
Burrill, John works at Winter's Mill (E64).
Burrill, William works at Winter's Mill (E64).
Burt, F. H. (M61); (P61); (E62).
Burt, P. H. (R63); or T. H. per (M62); of Burt & Dorn who owned Union Meat Market on W side of Antelope (E64); (tax1864).
Burt, T. F. (R62)
Burton, John (R62); (M62).
Burton, W. (M61)
Bussell, A. J. (R63)
Buster, H. C. (R63); lot NE corner Cedar and Winnemucca (E64).
Butler ? cabin on N side of Spring (E64).
Butler, C. W. (R63)
Butler, Charles (R63)
Butler, William (or Wilson) J. (R63); in Towles blacksmith shop at SW corner Pine & Winnemucca (E64).
Butterfield, O. (M61); (P61); miner (R62); (M62).
Byers, Joseph M. (M61); (P61); (R62); (R63); (M62).
Byrne, L. (R63)
Byron, A. L. (M61); (E62).

C
Cable, S. D. (M62)
Cadame, Madame Clara saloon E of Bradford's store (E64).
Cady, H. C. (M61)
Caffery, Peter (P61); (R62); (R63).
Caffrey, R. (M61)
Calaghan, D. R. (M61)
Calahan, W. (M61)
Calcott, W. (M61)
Calder, Joseph (or Jas.) W. (M61); (P61); (E62); (R62), of Rhodes & Co. hardware store on S. side of Pine (E64); elected to the Territorial House of Representatives on 9/3/62, elected Territorial Representative 9/2/63 (N81); formed Company F, Nevada Volunteers (G84).
Calderwood, A. (M61)
Caldwell, J. A. (R62)
Caldwell, W. J. (R63); East Walker River Ranch (E64).

Calisher, J. (R63)
Calkins, W. (R62)
Callahan, D. R. (R62)
Callen, C. (R63)
Calley, L. D. (R62)
Callman, T. (R62)
Calrick, W. H. (R62)
Calvin, C. works for the Wide West Mining Co. (E64).
Calvin, John board house N side of Spring west of Parker's lot (E64).
Cameron, I. B. (P61); (R62).
Cameron, J. B. (M61); (R63); (M62); cabin and lot on S side of Wide West and N side of Aurora (E64).
Campbell, G. E. (E62)
Campbell, J. C. (M62)
Campbell, John E. (M61); (P61); (M62); (G84); cabin S side of Aurora and two wood bldg (E64); was killed by H.T. Parlin on 6/6/64 (N81).
Campbell, Mrs. H. C. (?) now Mrs Craigore or Carnigue (E64).
Campbell, R. B. (P61); blacksmith (R62); (M61).
Campbell, W. B. (M61); (P61); (R62); (M62).
Canfield, J. G. 12/31/63 *Aurora Daily Times*; (tax1864)
Canley, W. works for Wide West Mining Co. (E64).
Cannon, J. works for Wide West Mining Co. (E64).
Caothers, J. S. (R63)
Carberry, Thomas "Irish Tom" (G84)
Card, W. S. (M61)
Carder, Annie wife of William Carder (G84).
Carder, William E. infamous gunfighter, candidate for Marshall of Aurora (T63); killed in Aurora on 12/10/64 and buried in Aurora cemetery (G84).
Cardinell, Chas. owned dancing academy that opened during November 1864 in brick bldg on E side of Antelope (E64).
Carl, W. S. (P61); miner (R62).
Carleigh, J. (P61)
Carlyle, S. S. (R63)

Residents of Aurora 1861-1864

Carnigue, Miss Hattie (formerly Mrs. H. C. Campbell) house on Mays property E side Winnemucca (E64).
Carpenter, Geo. W. (R63)
Carpenter, N. T. (P61); (M61).
Carpentier, N. F. miner (R62)
Carr, J. (R62)
Carran?, Hugh shoemaker's shop in tent on W. side of Silver near Pine (E64).
Carrick, J. (M61)
Carrick, W. (M61)
Carrol, Wilson (P61)
Carroll, Jas. (P61)
Carroll, Martin (R63); two wood bldgs on E side of Winnemucca (E64).
Carroll, W. (M61)
Carroll, William (M62)
Carson, Adelaide "Kit" Daly Gang favorite (G84).
Carter, E. W. (R62)
Carter, John L. (M62)
Carter, John miner (R63)
Carter, John S. (R63)
Carter, Sol. (R63); Carter & Crocker wood store on E side of Antelope, two other lots (E64); retail dealer (tax1864).
Caruthers, William M. (P61); (R62); (M62); (M61).
Case, G. W. (R63); (E64)
Cash, M. (R63)
Cassidy, M works at Winter's Mill (E64).
Cassidy. J. (R63)
Castor, J. W. (M61)
Castro, Nicholas (M62); house used as fruit store on N side of Pine (E64); retail dealer in liquors (tax1864).
Causland, D. M. (M61)
Center, M. (P61); constable (R62); (G84)
Centswig, D. (R62)
Chamberlain, A. (R63)
Chamberlin, H. M. lot with Parker on N side of Spring (E64).
Chamblin, M. R. (R63) M.D.
Champlin, J. F. (R63)
Chansen, C. at Hurdy Gurdy dance house (E64).
Chapin, E. W. (R63); owner of Exchange Saloon on SE corner Pine and Antelope (E64).

Chapin, G. S. (M61); saloon keeper (R62); 4th Sergeant (E62).
Chapin, Thomas R. superintendent of an Aurora Sunday school (G84).
Charles, A. B. (M61); (P61); (R62).
Chase, G. W. two wood houses SE corner of Cedar and Antelope (E64).
Chase, Isaac (R63)
Chase, R. A. (R63)
Chase, Stephen H. (R62); (R63); (G84); attorney; elected Prosecuting Attorney on 9/7/64 (N81). Born in Fryeberg, ME in 1813, Served as District Judge until 1869.
Chatterton, J. W. (R63); with Parlin owned "old Hurdy Gurdy dance house" on NW corner Juniper and Silver (E64); City Marshall of Aurora (T63); lawyer (tax1864).
Chaurne, Delos (P61)
Chick, G. W. (M62)
Childs, B. (M62)
Childs, J. A. (R62); cabin NE corner of Aurora & Winnemucca (E64).
Childs, R. H. (R63)
Chism, George C. (M61); (M62); carpenter on N side of Pine west of Court (E64).
Chole, Thomas adobe house on W. side of Silver (E64).
Chord, J. (P61); attorney, etc. (R62).
Chord, W. S. (R62)
Chorpenning, Dr. F. (M61); (R62); (M62); was acting Assistant Surgeon for Capt Rowe and was killed by Wm. Pooler on 7/28/62 (N81), (G84).
Chu Wing (Chinaman?) household of furniture and store on S. side of Pine east of Assay office (E64).
Church, D. W. (M61)
Church, G. L. (M61); (R62); (R63); elected Esmeralda County Recorder on 9/7/64 (N81).
Clanson, George (R62)
Clara, Madame Clara's Saloon on N side of Pine east of Bradford's store (E64).
Clark, A. (M61); (R62); toll road opposite Moses Mill (M62).
Clark, A. C. (R62)
Clark, Alex (P61)
Clark, Andrew (M61); (P61).
Clark, Dan'l (R63)
Clark, F. M. (M61)

169

Clark, G. W. wood house NE corner Sage and Antelope (E64).
Clark, James (P61)
Clark, Thomas (P61); (R62); (M62); (M61).
Clarke, Alex (R63)
Clarke, T. W. (R63)
Clayton, J. C. lot on NW corner of Silver & Aurora (M62).
Clayton, Joshua Elliot (M61); (E62); mining engineer, owned stamp mill at Aurora.
Cleaver [or spelled Cleever per (M61)], C. (R63).
Clemens, Samuel L. [or Mark Twain] miner who lived in various cabins on Spring Street from April to September, 1862 (G84).
Clemens, W. J. (R62)
Clement, B. (M61); (M62).
Clements, S. B. aged 52 years, stone store bldg occupied by Kaech & Co. on SE corner Aurora & Antelope, and one garden of 25 acres on Turkey Hill (E64).
Clemmens, Anthony miner (E64).
Clerk, T. S. (R63)
Clough, W. H. (P61)
Coates, N. (M61)
Cobb, L. D. brick house on SE corner Aurora and Winnemucca (E64).
Cobb, S. D. (M61)
Cobb, S. G. lumberman (R62); (R63).
Cobb, W. A. B. hotel owner (tax1864).
Cobb, Sylvanas (P61)
Coburn, N. F. (M61); (P61).
Cochrane, [spelled Cochran, Thomas (M62)] Thomas (P61); (R62).
Coddington, Joe J. (E62); elected Nevada Territory Councilman on 9/2/63 (N81); floor manager for the Cotillion Party Committee (T63).
Coe, Robert (R63)
Coff, S. D. (R63)
Coff, S. G. (R63)
Coffee, Geo W. (R63); (T63); Union Foundry N side of Spring, and residence N of mill (E64); manufacturers (tax1864).
Coffee, John (M61); (R62).
Cohn, J. (or D.?) (R63) of Cohn & Co. cigar & fruit store in Parker's bldg on E side of Antelope (E64); (tax1864).
Coland, Daniel (M62)
Colby, H. S. (M61)

Colby, L. D. (P61); (R63); lot on N side of Wide West east of Richardson (E64).
Colcord, Roswell K. former Governor of Nevada (G84). (see Marden, Horace)
Colden, J. W. (R63)
Cole, J. (M61)
Cole, J. J. (R62)
Cole, R. (P61)
Cole, Robert (R62)
Coleman (spp?) B. H. (M61)
Coleman, Thos. (R63); (G84).
Colen, T. (M61); (R63).
Colerich, W. H. (P61)
Coll, J. H. (R63)
Collard, Geo. (R63)
Collett, Wm. (M61)
Collier, Robert (R63)
Collins, C. (M61); (P61).
Collins, Charles F. Dr. (R63); physician and owner of Pioneer Drug Store on Antelope St. (T63); apothecary (tax1864).
Collins, D. (M61)
Colman, T. (P61)
Comstock, Peter B. (R63); elected Representative on 9/7/64 (N81).
Conklin, L. (M61); (P61); (R62); (R63); house and lot on E side of Winnemucca (E64).
Conley, A. (M61)
Conley, Wm. (R63); works for the Wide West Mining Co.
Connell, M. boardinghouse on lot 4, block W (E64).
Connelly, M. miner (R62)
Connelly, Martin (R63)
Connelly, Mitch (P61)
Connelly, W. (M61); miner (R62).
Conner, Edward (R63)
Conner, Franklin house on N side of Wide West (E64).
Conner, Henry half interest in saloon W of Bradford's store on N side of Pine (E64).
Conner, J. (R62); (E64).
Conner, J. J. (M61).
Conner, Jas. (P61)
Conner, John (R63)
Conner, John J. (P61); (R62); (R63); works for the Wide West Mining Co. (E64).
Conner, O. M. (R62)
Connolly, M. (R63)

Residents of Aurora 1861-1864

Connor, Franklin (R63); (E64)
Connor, Jerry (?) half interest in liquor store on N side of Pine (E64); liquors (tax1864).
Connough, J. (R62)
Converse, O. M. partner with Horton in Fashion Stable (T63).
Conway, Mich. (R63)
Cook, J. W. (P61); (R62).
Cook, J. W. (R62)
Cook, T. A. (M61); (P61); (R62); (G84).
Cook, T. A. (R62)
Cook, V (?). B. house on Blanchard's lot, E side of Court (E64).
Cook, V, B. house and oxen on Blanchard's lot on E side of Court (E64).
Cook, Y. V. miner (E64).
Coolidge, J. P. (E62); (R63)
Cooper, E. Bruce (R63) blacksmith?
Cooper, Jacob (M62); (R62); blacksmith.
Cooper, T. L. (R63)
Cooper, W. E. (M61).
Copeland, J. (R62)
Copeland, John (M61); (P61).
Copper, W. E. (P61); (R62).
Corbett, Wm. (M62)
Cordes, H. (R63)
Corey, L. (R63)
Cornell, C. O. (R62)
Cornell, Jas. (R63)
Corner, Thomas (P61); (R62)
Cortez, C. M. miner (R62)
Corwin S. (M61)
Corwin, Samuel (P61)
Corwin, Samuel (R62)
Cory, J. M. miner (R62); (M61); [or spelled Corey in (G84)] J. M., one of the founders of the Esmeralda Mining District on August 25, 1860 (N81).
Cory, Johnson [may be same as Cory, J. M.] lots in town (M62).
Cory, L. (M61); (P61); (R62).
Cosgrieff, J. E. (R63)
Cosgrove, John (R63)
Cotton, J. F. (P61); (R62); (J. A. per R63); cabin on lot on E. side of Esmeralda that was to have been the site of never completed Catholic Church (E64).
Countryman, L. (M61)
Cox, B. C. (P61); (E62); miner (R62).
Cox, B. E. (M61)

Coy, Jas. (R63)
Craig, J. (M61)
Craig, John S. (E62); (R62); (M62).
Craig, P. A. (P61); (R62)
Craigore, Mrs. Owns house, formerly Mrs Campbell (E64).
Craigue, J. S. (E62)
Craigue, S. W. (R63)
Cramer, [or spelled Creamer per (M61)] J. H. (P61); (R62).
Crane, L. W. (M61)
Craner, Henry (R63)
Creed, J. T. (M61)
Crenshaw, George H. (M61); (R62).
Crittenden, Howard (R63); younger brother of Laura Sanchez, bookkeeper at Wide West Mining Co. (Robert E. Stewart).
Crocker, A. W. (R63) Carter & Crocker
Crofts, ? ownes cabin on E side of Winnemucca (E64); liquors (tax1864).
Cromdall, R. (R63)
Cronan, D. (P61); (R62).
Crooker, D. C. (M61); (P61); (E62); Recorder's clerk (R62).
Crosby, Matthew (R63)
Crow (or Crowe), W. E. (M61); (R63); S side of Pine (E64).
Crowell, H. (M61); (P61); (R62).
Cullen, Phil. (R63)
Cummings, Wm. (R63)
Cunningham, M. (R62)
Cunningham, P. (M61); (R62).
Cunningham, S. (P61); (R62).
Cupid, Wm. (M62)
Curtin, Cornelius (R63)
Cushenbury, J. R. (M61)
Cutter, B. D. (R63)
Cutter, T. A. (R62); (M62); (P61); (R63); canvas house on lot on S. side Del Monte (E64).

D

Dacy, C. (R63)
Dacy, J. (R63)
Daily, John (M61) [may be same as Daly, John]
Dair, Dan'l (R63)
Dair, Thos. (R63)
Dally, A. (R63)

171

Dalrymple, W. H. (R63); lot and building on NE corner of Travis and Winnemucca (E64).
Daly, John [or spelled Dailey in (E64)] head of Aurora's infamous Daly Gang (i.e. paid gunmen for the Pond Mining Co.), Daly had two houses and two or three lots in town at time of his hanging on February 9, 1864 (G84); cabin on west side of Court S of Pine (E64).
Daly, T. (R63)
Damon, C. H. works for Wide West Mining Co. (E64).
Damond, C. A. *12/31/63 Aurora Daily Times.*
Danaigne (or Dancigne), Simon tailor in shanty on Murphy's lot S side of Pine (E64).
Daney, J. W. at Linton's store E side of Court (E64).
Danforth, N. (M61)
Danniz (or Danis or Dannis), A. J. saloon in basement of Neidy's bldg on N side of Pine, also saloon on Martin's lot on W side of Antelope (E64).
Danridge, Simon (R63)
Dargin, J. (R63)
Darling, Wilkie (or Wm.) (R63); lot on E side of Mono (E64).
Darnagh, J. A. (R63) Dr.
Darragh, J. C. elected Representative on 9/7/64 (N81).
Darwell, J. W. (R62)
Dasken, A. (P61)
Daub, J. W. (R63)
Dauchy, (or Duchey) H. O. (R63); butcher (tax1864).
Davis, D. C. (R62)
Davis, D. W. (M61); (P61); (R62); elected Esmeralda County Commissioner on 9/7/64 (N81); floor manager for the Cotillion Party Committee (T63).
Davis, E. P. (P61); (R62); (M61).
Davis, H. C. (M61); (R62).
Davis, Issac (M61)
Davis, J. A. (R63)
Davis, Jas. H. (M61); (P61); (R62).
Davis, Miss with Miss Snyder in Cases home on Antelope near Cedar (E64).
Davis, Moses butcher shop on E side of Winnemucca (E64); butcher (tax1864).
Davis, R. (M61)
Davis, S. E. miner (E64).
Davis, Samuel (R63); (M62); wood saloon known as Esmeralda Exchange saloon on NW corner Antelope and Aurora, also five lots and buildings in town (E64); on the Cotillion Party Committee (T63).
Davis, Wm. (R63); or W. C. Fashion Stable (M62).
Dawd, W. A. (P61)
De Kay H. G. (P61)
De Kay, A. A. (P61); (E62); (R62).
De Kay, Aug. D. (R63)
De Kay, M. (R63); (M62); W side of Antelope (E64).
De Kay, Wm. Dep. Co. Clerk (R62); (M62); (M61).
Dean, P. (M61).
Dean, Robert (P61)
Deanfeldt, B. (M61)
Dearborn, E. (M61); (P61); (E62); (R62).
Dearborn, L. H. (M61); (E62); (P61); (R63).
Decker, G. W. (R63)
Dedrick, M. (R63); (M61).
Deidrich, M. (R62)
Delancy, S. & Co. N side of Pine west of Merchants Exchange (E64).
Delany, S. (M61)
Demmers, L. L. brick house on SW corner of Aurora & Winnemucca (E64).
Demmey, John (M62)
Demming (or Demmers), L. L. (R62); (R63); lot SW corner of Aurora and Winnemucca (E64).
Demming, D. S. Deputy sheriff (G84).
Demont, Joseph partner in Searing, Dorn, and Co. store on Wide West (T63).
Demontt, John (R63),
Deneby, J. B. blacksmith on SW corner of Court and Pine (E64).
Denfell, P. (R62)
Denning, S. S. (M62)
Dennis, A. G. (R63)
Dennis, J. (M61); (R63).
Dennis, Jas. (R63)
Dennison, E. F. (R63); house known as Oriental Hotel on S. side of Wide West (E64).
Dennison, Eliza "Lizzie" (G84).
Denny, John W. (P61); (R63); (M62).

Residents of Aurora 1861-1864

Denslinger (or Denelenger), Jacob (M62); bake shop E side of Antelope N of Bechtel's property (E64).
Denters, R. D. (R63)
Denton, D. D. (R63)
Deo, John [or Joseph (M62)]; lot on S side of Aurora (E64).
Derby, G. B. (P61); or George (M62); Esmeralda Laundry (R62).
Derby, Wm. (P61); (R62); (R63).
Devere, E. W. (R63)
Devine, Patrick (R63)
Devoe, E. W. (of Preble & Devoe) lots on W side of Silver, NE corner Silver Antelope, SE corner Pine Silver, and owner of Preble & Co. brickyard up Cottonwood Gulch S of Barbien's brickyard (E64).
Devon, Henry (R62)
Dewey, J. W. (R62)
Dexter, B. (R63)
Dexter, E. (R63)
Dexter, J. G. (P61)
Dexter, T. W. (R63); lot on N side of Wide West east of John Dailey's, lot NW corner of Bullion and Aurora (E64).
Deyo, J. A. (M61); (P61); (R62).
Dias, Crus (M61)
Dick, Lawrence cabin W side of Cottonwood (E64).
Dickenson, E. B. (R63); elected Esmeralda County Clerk on 9/2/63 and re-elected on 9/7/64 (N81).
Dickenson, J. (E62)
Dickenson, W. H. ranches and toll road from Sweetwater to Aurora (E64).
Dickson, Thos. J. (M61)
Dickson. W. H. (M61)
Dill, A. (M61).
Dimmock, J. (R63)
Dinneen, Patrick (R63)
Dixon, Louis (R63)
Dixon, William M. district attorney (G84).
Dodd, Charles H. (P61); tinsmith (R62); (R63); house 100' N of Wide West (E64), Lieutenant in the Esmeralda Rifles; (tax1864).
Dolan, Jamie miner (E64).
Dolan, Michael (R63)
Dolan, N works for Wide West Mining Co. (E64).

Doll, F. B. (R63)
Don, J. W. (R63)
Donahue, E. (M61); (R62), (R63).
Donahue, P. (M61).
Donelly, George (P61)
Donely, Charles cabin N side of Wide West (E64).
Donevan, M. E. (P61); (R62)
Doneway, E. (R62)
Doney, William (E64).
Donley, G. W. miner (R62)
Donnavan, M E. (E64)
Donnell, George H. First Lieutenant Hooker Light Infantry (G84).
Donnelly, C. B. (M61).
Donnelly, George (M61); (R62).
Donnelly, William (R62); NW corner of Del Monte and Bullion (E64).
Donnelly, William F. (P61); (R62).
Donnely, T. (P61)
Donney, J works for the Wide West Mining Co. (E64).
Donohue, E. (P61)
Donohue, Jno. (R63); (G84).
Donovan, E. (R63)
Donovan, Johnny killed Richard McGuire (G84).
Donovan, M. E. (M61)
Donovan, Thos. (M61)
Doran, Frank (R62)
Doran, Lewis elected Senator on 11/8/64 (N81).
Doran, Martin killed by James Downey (G84).
Doran, S. (R63)
Dorn, G. W. partner in Searing, Dorn, & Co. store on Wide West (T63); partner with Burt at Union Meat Market (?)(E64).
Doron., L. (P61)
Dorr, T. E. (R63); (E64)
Dorr, W. C. (R63)
Dorr, Y ranch W of Del Monte mill in Bodea [Bodie] Gulch (E64).
Doss, Geo. W. (R63)
Doubleday (E?) & Co. proprietors of restaurant in Exchange Hotel (E64); eating house (tax1864).
Douceance, Peter (R63)
Dougherty, Geo. (R63)
Douglass, G. (R62)

173

Douglass, Geo. (M61)
Douglass, Wm. works at Winter's Mill (E64).
Dovan, Martin house on Higgins lot on S side of Wide West (E64).
Dow, James G. (M62); (M61).
Dowd, J. H. (M61); (P61); (R62).
Dowd, William A. (R62); limekiln near tollgate on old stage road (E64).
Dowell, J. W. (P61)
Downey, James (R63), house on S side of Spring (E64); killed Doran (G84).
Doyle, C. (M61)
Doyle, John miner (R62); (M62).
Drake, Elias (P61); (E62); (R62); cabin on N side of Pine adjacent to Huber (E64).
Draper, Robert E. owner/editor of the Aurora Times, office E side of Silver (E64) (G84).
Drennan, Jas. (R63)
Duane, Thos. (M61)
Duddell, T. A. (R62)
Duddle, Thos. A. (M61)
Dudevich, M. (P61)
Dudleston, J. M. (M61)
Dumay, Angelina (R63)
Dumay, Chas. (R63); partner with Crofts (E64); liquors (tax1864).
Dunaway, E. (M61)
Duncan, E. G. (P61); (R62).
Duncan, Frank (P61)
Dunn, A. (R63)
Dunstars, Wm. (R63)
Durand, Frank (M61); (R63); (M62); SW corner of Juniper and Silver (E64), owned stamp mill.
Durfalz (Durfeldt?), S. S side of Juniper (E64).
Durgin, Preston lot and cabin on hill behind Monroe & Thatcher on Wide West St. (E64).
Durkin, A. (M61); (R62).
Dye, William miner in cabin on N side of Pine (E64).
Dyer, Benj. (P61); (R62)
Dyer, T. C. (R63)
Dyer, Thos. (R63)

E
Eagan, Wm. (R63)

Earl, A. C. (R63)
Early, A. C. (R63)
Edes, W. H. (R63)
Edgar, A. W. (M61); (P61); (R62).
Edgerly, Frank (R63)
Edler, W. (E64) N side of Spring (E64).
Edmonds, E. (M61)
Edwards, H. H. (M61); (R63); (M62).
Edwards, J. (R63)
Edwards, J. W. (R62)
Edwards, Justine (R63), wood house on W side of Cottonwood
Egan, Jno. H. (R63)
Eggers, George (R63)
Eichelroth, Dr. William (G84); house on lot on W side of Antelope (E64); on the Cotillion Party Committee (T63); physician (tax1864).
Eldridge (?), Edward (?)(M61).
Elgerly lot between Preble & Co. on S and Pioneer Bakery on N (E64).
Elliott, E. W. (or W. E.) (R63) & Co. (with G. W. Markely) brick store on E side of Court Street (E64); (tax1864).
Elliott, S. (M61)
Elmore, D. T. (M61)
Elsmer, M. R. (M62)
Elsner, M. R. (R63)
Enstenor, R. M. Cotillion Party Committee (T63).
Elstner, M. R. (E64).
Elsworth, Wm. (R63)
Emerson, Sylvester (R63)
Engelbrecht, Louis (M61); (P61); (R62).
Enley, C. (R62)
Ennor, W. H. groceries, meat, fruit in Hutchinson bldg W of Express Office (E64).
Erwin, George miner (E64).
Estell, A. H. (R63)
Euler, J. (R63)
Euner, Josh (R63)
Euner, W. H. (R63)
Evans, A. E. (R63)
Evans, Ariel (R63)
Evans, C. L. works for the Wide West Mining Co. (E64).
Evans, G. W. (M61); (P61); (R63); lot on W side of Antelope N of Barkers (E64).
Evans, R. H. (R63) Superintendent Wide West Mining Co.; (tax1864).

Residents of Aurora 1861-1864

Evans, W works for the Wide West Mining Company (E64).
Evatt, Daniel (R63)
Ewing, Thos. (R63)

F

Fagan, Charles house N side of Spring W of Bodea [Bodie] Stable (E64).
Fagan, M. (or N) saloonkeeper on E side of Antelope (E64).
Fagan, Mike member of Daly gang (G84).
Fairdhild, O. L. C. (M61).
Fall, Wm. H. H. (P61); Notary Public (R62).
Falley, R. C. miner (R62)
Farborough, G. W. (R62)
Farland M. (E64) cabin on hill N of Spring near City Brewery.
Farland, H. L. (M62); (M61).
Farnham, S. B. (M61)
Farnham, W. K. (R63)
Farnsworth, Dr. physician with office on Winnemucca, also teacher at the public school.
Farnum, Wm. (R63)
Farrell, [or spelled Farwell per (E64), and (M61)] Isaac Jr. stockbroker (R63); (M62).
Farrell, J. J. (R63)
Farron, Mike (R63)
Farrot, I. (P61); (R62)
Fassman, A. (E62); (M62)
Fasten, J. (M61)
Favon, A. J. works at Winter's Mill (E64).
Favon, John works at Winter's Mill (E64).
Favor, A. J. (R63)
Feast, William (M61); (R62); (M62); cabin NE corner of Silver and Del Monte St., lot on E side of Antelope (E64), elected Mono County Treasurer on 6/1/61 (N81), secretary Gibraltar G&SMCo., died in Aurora during 1864 (N81) (G84).
Feeney, Chas. (R63)
Fenender, C. P. (R62)
Fenires, S. (R63)
Feriel, Thomas at Bloomindale store corner Pine and Silver (E64).
Ferris, Andrew (R63)
Ferris, J. (M61).
Fey, Henry liquors at Hurdy Gurdy Dance house (E64).
Fill, John (M62)

Finie, J. C. (R63)
Finlayson, James (R63)
Finley, Henry (M61); (R63).
Finley, J. C. (R63)
Finn, Wm. (R63)
Finnigan, Daniel (R63)
Finnigan, Henry (R63); owner (with Henderson, P.) of Orleans Restaurant, E side of Antelope (E64).
Fisher, Fred'k (R63)
Fisher, John (R63); member IOOF, Esmeralda Lodge No. 6 (T63).
Fisher, W. S. (R63); (M62); house S side of Del Monte (E64).
Fitzgerald, Jas. (R63)
Fitzgerald, M. (R63)
Fitzgerald, Michael (R63)
Fitzgerald, Pat (M61).
Fitzpatrick, Owen cabin S of Last Chance Hill (E64).
Flaherty, Edward (R63)
Flannigan, Patrick (R63)
Fletcher, Geo. (R63)
Flood, Hugh (P61); (R62)
Flynn, James (R63); NE of Wide West in rear of John Bests house (E64).
Flynn, Jno. (R63)
Fogus, S. C. owns mill on south side of Spring (E64).
Ford, D. J. (R63)
Forest, [or Forrest (M62)] William (R62).
Forman, L. S. (R63)
Forsman, Hugh (R63) Superintendent Antelope Mines
Fosgate, C. O. W side of Antelope (E64).
Fossman, A. (R63)
Foster, E. A. (M61); (R62).
Foster, H. M. (P61)
Foster, J. (P61); miner (R62).
Foster, William (R62)
Fousman, H. (M62)
Fowler, B. C. (M61); (P61); (M62); (R63); cabin W side of Antelope (E64).
Fowler, Charles (E62)
Fowler, T. B. (R63)
Fox, J. blacksmith (R62); (M61).
Fox, J. S. (R62); (M61).
Frage, G. A. (R62)
Francis, Chas (R63)

175

An 1864 Directory and Guide to Nevada's Aurora

Francis, D. G. (R63); (M62); appointed Esmeralda County Sheriff 6/22/63, elected Sheriff on 9/2/63 and re-elected on 9/7/64 (N81), (G84).
Francis, E cabin E side of Cottonwood (E64).
Franklin, S. C. (M61).
Freidman, S. fruit and confectionary in Minard's saloon E side of Antelope (E64).
Freize, W. D. (P61); (R62)
French, C. H. (R62); (M61).
French, S. (R62)
Frenner, W. B. lot on S side of Pine with Schwartz's book and Garland's fruit stores (E64).
Freshett, M. (R63)
Frink, S. W. SE corner of Mono and Pine (E64).
Froit, J. L. (R63)

G
Gaboe, Miss brick house on SW side of Wide West (E64).
Gaff, A. (M61)
Gage, H. U. (P61)
Gage, Herman K. (R63); photographer on Pine Street who left Aurora for Truckee during the late 1860s.
Gaige, M. M. partner with Steiner at Sazerac Saloon (T63)
Galinsky, D. (R63)
Gallager, Mrs. wood house E side of Silver occupied by Kendall, Quint & Hardy (E64).
Gallagher, E. (M61); (P61); (E62).
Gallagher, Edward (M61); (P61); Dist. Recorder (R62); (R63); (M62).
Gallattan, J. (M61)
Gallick, Jacob (R63); clothing groceries and merchandise in "Aurora City Store" on S side of Pine (E64).
Galligan, B. (M61)
Galtry, [or spelled Galtrey in (M61)] John (P61); (R62).
Gamble, J. (M61).
Gamble, Peter (P61); (R62); (M61); brother of Alexander Gamble from San Francisco; mine speculator with Wide West Mining Co. who brick house on N end on Winnemucca in "middle of street" (E64).
Garden, Thos. (M61)

Gardiner, E. L. H. recorder for Esmeralda [mining] Dist. (R63).
Gardiner, J. N. (R63)
Gardiner, Pliney (G84)
Gardiner, T. W. (R63)
Gardner, J. N. (M62)
Gardner, L. (R62)
Gardner, L. M. (M61)
Gardner, W. S. (M61)
Garesche, Frances (P61); banker, agent for Wells Fargo (R62); banker in Wells Fargo Office on Pine (T63); house on S. side Spring opposite Bodea [Bodie] Stable (E64); banker (tax1864).
Garland, F. A. (R63); fruit store on S side of Pine (E64); retail dealer (tax1864).
Garland, W. D. (R63)
Garren, Thos. (P61)
Garrishay, F. (M61)
Garrison, Ephraim (R63)
Garrison, Isaac (M61)
Garrison, J. (R62)
Garrison, John W. (R62); (R63)
Garrison, Wm. (R63)
Garvand, (?) N. A. (M61)
Garvin, "Doc" Superintendent of Antelope Mine (G84).
Garvin, N. A. (P61); (R63); (M62).
Gassaud, Paul (R63); wood bldg on N side of Pine E of Wingate's brick bldg (E64).
Gavin, John (M61); (E62); miner (R62); lot on N side of Spring (E64).
Gaynard, Charles E side of Bullion (E64).
Gebhart, [spelled Gephards, N. L. in (M61)] Nathaniel died April 1862 at the age of 52 of gunshot wounds (G84); mentioned in a 4/13/62 letter by Samuel Clemens (Mark Twain).
Genely, P. B.(or T. B.) brick store on SW corner Silver and Aurora (E64).
Gennella (or Genella), Joseph real estate and mining stock broker with office at Pioneer Drug Store (T63); house S side of Aurora, lot N side of Wide West (E64).
George, I. (R62)
Gergiman, S. (R63)
German, M. (R63)
Gerum, Michael (R63)

176

Residents of Aurora 1861-1864

Gibbens (or Gibbins), John liquors and bar on S.side of Wide West at intersection with Aurora (E64).
Gibbens, [or spelled Gibbons in (M61)] S. restaurant in G. Booth's bldg on Pine (E64).
Gibbons, W. P. owned stamp mill in Esmeralda Gulch (M62).
Gibbs, J. H. (R62); (M62); S side of Pine (E64).
Giblin, Jno. (R63); (M62).
Gibson, John (P61)
Gibson, S. (M61); (R62); or Samuel (M62).
Gifhart, N. L. (R62)
Giggs, Wm. (R63)
Gilbert, Frank (R63) Dr.
Gilbert, G. I. (M62)
Gilbert, J. F. (P61); (E62); miner (R62).
Gilbert, M. (M61)
Gilbert, Minor (P61); (R62).
Gilbert, Robert (R63)
Gilbert, T. Y. or J. (M61)
Giliken, S. F. (R63)
Gillespie, Charles "rowdy" arrested during August, 1864 (G84).
Gillespie, John (R63)
Gillett, D. E. (P61)
Gillman, John member of Daly gang (G84).
Gilman, E. (M61)
Gilman, Joseph works at Winter's Mill (E64).
Gilmer, Ed (P61); (R62).
Git, Chin (Chinese) house on N side of Spring on Travis & Smith lot (E64).
Given, J. W. (M62)
Glascock, Jacob (R63)
Glasgow, J. (M61)
Glassby, J. K. (P61)
Glasson, James (P61); (R62).
Glenn, Hugh (R63)
Glenn, R. partner with Draper in Aurora Daily Times (N81).
Glessedy, M. (R63)
Goldman, Alexander (R63)
Goldner, N. (P61); (R62).
Goldstein, S. cigarstand in Bilinas Store on NE corner Pine and Silver (E64).
Gonzalez, D. (R63)
Goodman, D. (M62)
Goodman, M. (M61); lot on N side of Wide West Street (E64).

Gordon, F. M. (R63)
Gordon, John (R63)
Gore, James J. (P61); (R62).
Gorman, John (G84)
Gorman, Mrs. John (G84)
Gossland shot Gephart in 1862 (G84).
Goucher, J. W. (R63)
Gough, W. T. (R63); (E64); attorney with Allen in building formerly occupied by the Mono Co. Recorder on E side of Silver (T63).
Gowan, Robert (R63)
Grafton, Henry C. (M61); (R62); (R63).
Gragelwitz, E. (R63)
Graham, R. W. (R63)
Graham, Thos. (M61).
Grainy, Geo. works for the Wide West Mining Company (E64).
Grant, G. W. (R62)
Grant, J. N. (R62); (M61).
Grant, John house on N side of Pine (E64).
Graves blacksmith partner with Cooper on N side of Pine (E64).
Gray, David (R63)
Gray, Issac (M62)
Gray, J. H. (M61); (R62); (R63); (M62); three lots (E64); elected (but did not take seat) Territorial Representative on 9/2/63 (N81).
Great, F. (R62)
Greely, Thos. (R63); saloon on SW corner of Pine and Antelope (E64).
Green Ralph R. works for the Wide West Mining Company (E64).
Green, (Dr.?) Alfred A. (R63); Drug Store in Shier bldg S side of Pine (E64); on the Cotillion Party Committee (T63); apothecary (tax1864).
Green, B. F. (M61)
Green, Edmund (M61); (P61); (E62); owned Pioneer stamp mill, Aurora's first mill (M62); (R62); three or four lots and houses (E64); elected Mono County Commissioner on 6/1/61 (N81); superintendent of Wide West mine (G84).
Green, George Albert (R63); elected Esmeralda County Commissioner 9/2/63, elected, but later rejected, Assemblymen on 1/19/64, elected Esmeralda County Commissioner on 9/7/64 (N81).

177

An 1864 Directory and Guide to Nevada's Aurora

Green, Jacob (R63)
Green, John (M61)
Green, T. C. miner (R62)
Greenan, Peter (R63)
Greger, F. N side of Pine (E64).
Gregorivich, E. (P61); (R62)
Gregory, J. owns "Clayton's mill" (M62)
Gregory, L. B. (M62)
Gregory, T. L. (P61)
Gregovich, Ellis (M61).
Gregovich, Nick (M62); (M61); lot and improvements on N side of Pine E of Bradford's Store (E64).
Greigherwich, Nick (P61); (R62)
Greitzner, A stationery in Post Office bldg (E64).
Grenshaw, George H. (P61)
Grey, J. (M62)
Griffin, Clines (P61)
Griffin, O. (R62); (R63)
Griffith, O. (M61).
Griffith, Thomas (G84)
Grimes, J. C. (R63)
Gringley, T. L. (R62)
Grinnell, Stephen (R63)
Grist, Fr. (P61)
Gritzner, A. (R63); partner with Keeney who had "merchandise in PO bldg. (E64).
Groherty, Pat. (R63)
Gustan, Jas. (R63)
Gwin, C. adobe house S of Antelope (E64).
Gwin, D. J. (R63)
Gwinn, W. J. (R63)

H
Haas, A. (R63); of Haas & Finlayson; frame house on N side of Pine occupied by Bird, clothing store on SE corner of Pine and Winnemucca (E64).
Haas, G. W. (R63)
Hackett, James C. (M61)
Hackler, G. (M61)
Haffstrom, F. E. (P61); (M61).
Hafky, P. (or J., or Isaac) stock of goods in Martin's bldg on W. side of Antelope (E64); retail dealer (tax1864).
Hagen, Thomas (R63)
Hager, J. D. (R63)
Haggerty, Dan. (M61)
Halcey, Wm. (R63)

Hale, A. W. (R63)
Hale, Ira P. (M62); lot on W side of Silver, S of Brown & Weston (E64); elected County Superintendent of Schools on 9/7/64 (N81); (tax1864).
Haley, J. F. (R63)
Hall, A. (R62)
Hall, C. (M61)
Hall, J. (R63)
Hall, J. P. (R63)
Hall, Wm. H. (M62)
Ham, G. F. (M61)
Ham, W. A. (R63)
Hamilton, Daniel (M61); (P61); (R62); (R63).
Hamond, D. G. (M61)
Hancock, W. H. (R63)
Haniscern, L. (R63)
Hank, A. (M61); (P61); (R62).
Hanke, A. (R63)
Hannah, A. B. (R62)
Hank, E. A. (E64)
Hanson, Francis (M62)
Hanson, T. (R63)
Hapsman, T. miner (R62)
Harding, Isaac (M62)
Hardy, J. H. attorney with Kendall, Quint and Hardy (T63).
Harkness, M. K. (T63); partner with Runyon, lot on E side of Winnemucca, lot on W side of Silver, saloon in Wingate bldg E side of Silver (E64).
Harkness, M. R. (P61); (E62); on the Cotillion Party Committee (T63).
Harman, D. G. (P61); (R62).
Harness, James (M62).
Harnley lot W of McBride's (E64).
Harp, L. (R63)
Harrington, T. (R63)
Harris, Edwin (R63)
Harris, H. (M62)
Harris, J. (R63)
Harris, James (R63)
Harris, N. G. (P61); (M61); (R62)
Harrison, E. H. (M61); (P61); (R62); (R63); jeweler in Kennedy & Porter's saloon on E side of Antelope, lot S side of Wide West (E64).
Harriss, Jacob (R63)
Hart, J. M. (R63)

178

Residents of Aurora 1861-1864

Haskell, D. H. (P61); (E62); (R62); (R63); lot on S. side of Aurora St. occupied by Esmeralda Star, also cabin on hillside N side of Wide West & notes and accounts of toll road down "Bodea Gulch" (E64); elected Assemblymen on 11/8/64 (N81); (tax1864).
Haskell, Rachel wife of D. H. Haskell.
Haskill, Anna Daly gang "favorite" (G84)
Haslam, R. (M61).
Haslett, A. Y. (M61).
Haslett, Ben (M62); (may be same as Hazlett, B.J. below) laundry on N side of Aurora (E64).
Haslund, N. (?) C. (M61).
Haslund, N. L. (P61)
Hastings, D. W. (R63)
Hastney, S. (M61)
Hatch, John joined Sherman in publishing the Esmeralda Star in 11/18/63 (N81).
Hatwill, J. (M61);
Haun, Wm. (M61)
Hawkins, [Capt. per (M61)] John. miner (P61); (R62); (R63), appointed Esmeralda County Commissioner on 6/22/63, elected County Recorder on 9/2/63 but died (N81); on the Cotillion Party Committee (T63).
Hawkins, Cyril (R63); Deputy County Recorder (E64); appointed Esmeralda County Clerk on 6/22/63, elected County Clerk on 9/2/63, elected Assemblymen on 11/8/64, replaced John Hawkins as County Recorder on 1/8/64 (N81).
Hawley, A. T. (P61); (R62).
Hawley, B. F. (M61); (P61); miner (R62).
Hayden, R. attorney in partnership with Boring (T63).
Hayes, Jas. (R63)
Hayes, Jno. (R63)
Hayes, Jos. (R63)
Hayne, Thomas (R62)
Haynes, John (R63)
Hays, John (R63)
Haywood, H. (M61); (P61); (R62).
Hazlett, A. J. (R62)
Hazlett, B. J. (P61); market keeper (R62); lots in Aurora (M62); (may be same as Haslett, Ben above).
Heal, W. (P61); (R62).
Healy, Patrick (R63)
Heard, Frank (R63)

Heath, E. W. (M61); (P61); (R62); (M62).
Heath, F. (R63)
Heaton W. F. (M61); (P61); (R62).
Heeney, W. (R63)
Hefky, I. (M62)
Heil, Austin (E64)
Heldibron, Fred with Sigamond in butcher shop under Merchant Exchange Bldg. (E64).
Hemstreet, D. (M62)
Hen, Ah (Chinese), lot on S side of Spring W of Eltsner's lot (E64).
Henay, William (R63)
Henderson, D. M. (M61).
Henderson, John (R63)
Henly, W owns St Charles Hotel on SE corner of Silver and Aurora (E64).
Hennessy, D. (R63)
Henney, D. (R62)
Hennis, D. W. miner (R62)
Henry, J. (M61); (P61); (R62).
Henry, S. C. (M61)
Henry, Thomas (R63)
Herbert, J. B. (M61); (R62); owned Herbert House (M62).
Hergan, D. (R63)
Hern, Louis (M62)
Hess, George (R63)
Hess, Jacob (R63); elected Territorial Representative 9/2/63 (N81); Captain Hooker Light Infantry (G84).
Hewitt, Geo. (M61)
Hewitt, S. (R63)
Hibbons, J. (M61)
Hickey, P. J. (M61); miner (R62); (R63); (M62).
Hickman, E. L. (M61)
Hicks, E. R. one of the founders of the Esmeralda Mining District on August 25, 1860 (N81).
Higbie, Calvin. H. (spelled Higby, C. H. in P61 and E62; and Higley, C. H. in R62); (M61); (R63); cabin on S side of Spring (E64); partner with Samuel Clemens (Mark Twain) during the summer of 1862.
Higgins, E. (M61)
Higgins, Frank (R63); works for the Wide West Mining Company (E64).
Higgins, I. (M61)
Higgins, T. J. (R63)
Hill, A. G. (R63)

179

Hill, A. J. (R62)
Hill, G. H. (P61); (R62); (M62); (M61).
Hill, G. M. (R63)
Hill, H. A. (M61)
Hill, I. L. (M61); (P61); engineer (R62); on the Cotillion Party Committee (T63).
Hill, J. L. (R63)
Hill, W. W. (M61)
Hill, William H. (M61); (P61); (R62).
Hilliard, B. F. (R63)
Hilo, G. H. (M62)
Hirth, Frank (M62)
Hitchens, Samuel (R63)
Hiveley, Wm. S. (R63)
Hixon, Jacob B. (R63)
Hodgkin, E. (M61)
Hodgkins, M. W. (R63)
Hodnut, R. (M61); (P61); (E62).
Hoffmeister, H. (R63)
Hoge, P. H. (R63)
Hogue, [or spelled Hoge per (M61)] Thos. (P61)
Holland, J. (R63)
Holland, M. (R63)
Holmes, H. B. (R63)
Holmes, Thomas (R63)
Holton, A. (R63)
Homer, S. (M61)
Honeycutt, Wm. (R63)
Honeywell, N. C. (R63) [may be same as Hunniwell].
Honlow, J. E. (R63)
Honness, James deputy (G84).
Hood, M. W. (R63)
Hoop, Wm. (R63)
Hooper, J. (R63); of Hooper & Chase (R63)
Hoover, A. B. (M61); (M62).
Hopkins, L. B. (P61); (M61); miner (R62); (R63); Superintendent of the Real Del Monte Mine (G84); auctioneer (tax1864).
Horton, J. M. partner with Converse in Fashion Stable (T63).
Horton, M. (R63)
Houck, A. B. (R63)
Houseley on Towles & Co. lot (E64).
How, James (R63)
How, Mary (R63)
Howard, J. L. (R63) banking partner with Sanchez in Howard & Sanchez (T63); banker (tax1864).

Howard, Mrs. J. L.
Howard, Thomas (M61); (P61); miner (R62); (M62).
Howard, W. A. (R63); at Aurora Times Office (E64).
Howd, R. (R62)
Howe, James (R63); works for the Wide West Mining Company (E64).
Howell, R. D. (R63)
Howen, S. miner (R62)
Howland, L. (R63)
Howland, Robert Muir (M61); (P61); (R62); (R63); former Town Constable or City Marshall, partner with Samuel Clemens (G84); owned lot with Preble on SW corner of Pine and Silver (E64).
Hoye, [or spelled Hoy, O (M61)] Owen (R63); owner of Gem Saloon (E64).
Hoyt, B. F. (M61)
Hoyt, W. W. (R63)
Hubbard, H. M. (R62)
Hubbard, T. J. (R63)
Huber, C. gun shop on N side of Pine (E64).
Hucy, Mildred (M62)
Hudnot, R. miner (R62) (possibly same as Hodnut, R.)
Huey, Harris (R63)
Huey, John (R63)
Huey, O. M. (P61); (R62)
Huey, W. H. (M61).
Huey, William miner (R62)
Huff, Henry (M61).
Huff, J. W. (R63); of Mortimer & Huff colored barbers in shop in Sheir's bldg S side of Pine, house on lot on Del Monte and Mono (E64).
Huggan, And. (R63); at Pettit & Perry's office (E64).
Hughes, H. saloonkeeper (R62); (M61).
Hughes, J. (M61).
Hughes, James E. (R63)
Hughes, John G. (M61).
Hughes, T. H. (P61); (M61); (R62).
Hughes, W. S. (M61).
Hughes, Wm. (R63); (M62); house on E side of Winnemucca (E64); on the Cotillion Party Committee (T63).
Hughie, W. H. (P61)
Huie, Wm. lot on N side of Spring W of Winnemucca (E64).

Residents of Aurora 1861-1864

Hull, Austin (P61); (M61); (R63); (M62).
Humphrey, David (R63)
Hunniwell owned buildings on north side of Spring Street (E64); [may be same as Napolean Bonaparte Hunewill original settler of Bridgeport Valley, see also Honeywell, N. C.].
Hunstreet, D. L. (R63)
Hunt, A. (M61)
Hunt, Frank (M61)
Hunt, J. (M61)
Hunt, John (P61); (R62).
Hunt, S. M. (M61); (R62).
Hunter, Amelia (R63)
Hunter, John (R63); (M62).
Hunter, W. H. (P61)
Huntley, A. (R62)
Hurd, Frank (M61); (M62).
Hurd, R. (P61); (M61).
Hurley, Jas. (R63)
Hurley, Jas. (R63)
Hutchinson, [or spelled Hutchison in (M61)] J. F. (R63); on the Cotillion Party Committee (T63).
Hutchinson, Andrew (M61).
Hutchinson, F. (P61); (R62); Francis per (M62).
Hutchinson, Luna (R63)
Hutchinson, P. T. (E62)
Hyatt, A. (M61)

I

Ince, J. (R63)
Ingraham, P. (R62)
Ingram, Peter (E62); (R63).
Irving, [or spelled Irwin in (M61)] H. J. (P61); (R62).
Irving, D. H. (E62)
Irwin, Geo. (R63)
Isabell. David L. (P61)
Issac, Robert (M62)
Ives, John elected Senator on 11/8/64 (N81)

J

Jacks, Wm. (R63)
Jackson, J. (M61)
Jackson, J. B. (R63)
Jackson, J. G. (R62)
Jackson, James (P61); (R62); (R63).
Jackson, John (R63)

Jackson, Levi (R63)
Jacobs, Richard (R63)
Jacobs, Susanna (R63)
Jacoby, Andrew (R63)
James, Richard colored tripe cleaner in cabin on SE corner of Del Monte and Silver (E64).
James, Thomas lot on N side of Pine E of Elstners (E64).
Jameson, Jas. S. (R63); partner with Pebelie in Washington Baths (T63).
Jamieson, John (R63)
Japaud, Luke (R63)
Jaques, James (P61); lot on N side of Aurora W of Kelly & Vernon (E64).
Jeffrey, Albert (P61); (R62)
Jennings, J. (R62)
Jewett, A. P. (P61); (M61); (R62)] [spelled Jewitt in (R63)] carpenter partner with Mosher.
Johnson, Albert (R63)
Johnson, C. G. (M61)
Johnson, Christian (R63); works for the Wide West Mining Company (E64).
Johnson, E. H. (P61); (R62); (M62).
Johnson, Hovel (R63)
Johnson, J. (R62)
Johnson, J. R. (R63)
Johnson, J. W. (M61); (R63).
Johnson, Peter principal owner of Pride of Utah mine, proprietor of the Union Mill (12/27/62 *California Alta*).
Johnson, R. P. (R63); [may be same as Johnson, Peter] known as "Capt." and was connected with Wide West mine (11/19/62 *California Alta*).
Johnson, W. E. (M61); (M62).
Jolley, J. H. on the Cotillion Party Committee (T63).
Jones, D. H. (M62)
Jones, Daniel (R63)
Jones, David (R63)
Jones, E. (R63)
Jones, F. A. S. (M61)
Jones, H. C. (M61)
Jones, J. (M61)
Jones, J. C. (P61); (R62).
Jones, J. T. (R63)
Jones, James (P61); (R62).

181

An 1864 Directory and Guide to Nevada's Aurora

Jones, Samuel (P61); (R62); (R63); on the Cotillion Party Committee (T63).
Jones, Wm. (R63); (M62); works at Winter's Mill, wood bldg on W side of N Silver (E64).
Judd, W. E. (P61); Captain of Esmeralda Rifles (R62).
Judy, A. C. (R63)

K

Kaesch cabin S side of Aurora, liquors in S. B. Clements bldg SW corner of Antelope and Silver (E64).
Kale, John (R63)
Kanhahan, Robert (R63)
Karley, Augustus (P61)
Kauffman, Jonas (R63)
Kaufman, G. (M61); (M62); on the Cotillion Party Committee (T63); (tax1864).
Kavanah, Jas. (R63)
Kavanaugh, James (M61); (M62); (P61).
Kavanaugh, Thos. (R63)
Kearn, John (R63)
Kearney, Patrick (or R. M.) (R63); possibly same as R.M. Kearny & Williamson who owned clothing store in Miller bldg N side of Pine (T63); retain dealer (tax1864).
Kee, A. H. store in Bulpin bldg on W side of Antelope between Campbell and Hansen (E64).
Keefe, Martin (R63)
Keefer, Henry house on W side of N Silver (E64).
Keefer, John (R62)
Keefer, M. (M61)
Keefer. J. W. (M61); (P61); (R62).
Keenan, R. T. (R63)
Keenay, J. B. (R63)
Keener, H. (P61); (R62)
Keiser, C. A. (R62)
Keisley, A. (M61)
Keith, J. M. (P61); (M61).
Keith, J. W. (R63)
Keizer, George (M62)
Kellogg, Frank (P61); (E62); (R62); (R63); (M62); house on N side of Wide West east of S. Jones lot (E64).
Kellogg, Samuel (R63)
Kellogg, William R. (P61); (R62); (R63)

Kelly, A. B. (M61); (P61); (R62); lot on N side of Del Monte (E64).
Kelly, H. A. (R63)
Kelly, J. (M61)
Kelly, Jas. (R63)
Kelly, John (P61); (R62)
Kelly, L. L. (P61); (R62)
Kelly, Patrick (R63)
Kelly, S. L. (M61)
Kelly, T. A. (R63)
Kelly, Thomas (R62); (R63).
Kemp, M. (M61)
Kendall, C. W. (R63); attorney in Kendall, Quint & Hardy on Silver (T63); (tax1864).
Kendall, Germain (M62)
Kendall, John (P61); (R62).
Kendel, Phillip (R63)
Kendry, Jas. (R63)
Kennedy, A. (R63); (M61).
Kennedy, J. (R63)
Kennedy, Michael (R63)
Kennedy, Wm. (R63)
Kent, Alvin S. (P61); (R62)
Kent, T. H. (R63)
Keppler, Chas. (R63); (M61); (M62); of Keppler & Mack who owned wood store on SE corner Pine and Court, and two other lots in town (E64); retail dealer (tax1864).
Kern, John (P61)
Kerney, P. (M61)
Kerrick, James (P61); (R62).
Ketchum, R. W. (M61); (P61); (E62); (R62).
Kever, Henry (M62)
Keyser, C. A. (P61); (M61).
Kidd, A. K. (R63)
Kies, George O. at Times office on silver (E64); member IOOF (T63).
Kiesley, Augustus (M62)
Killay, Jno. (R63)
Kimball, H. S. (or O.) (R63); Kimball & Canfield two story brick clothing store E side of Antelope (E64); (tax1864).
Kincaid, Wm. F. (M61); (P61); ranchman (R62); (R63).
King, C. M. (M61); (P61); (R62); (M62).
King, C. W. N of Pine at head of Court (E64).
Kingsbury, E. E. (M61)
Kingsbury, Edward (R63)
Kingsman, William (R63)

182

Residents of Aurora 1861-1864

Kinnies, Robert S. (R63)
Kinsey, E. (M61).
Kinsman, Jas. (R63)
Kinstry, L. M. (M61)
Kirkoff, Wm. (R63)
Kirner, J. (R63)
Kirth, Cany N of Wide West E of Simmons property (E64).
Kirwin, P. (R63)
Koerner, Thomas (M61); (M62).
Kohler, Thomas (P61); (R62)
Krasser (or Kranser), G. lot on W side of Antelope (E64).
Krauss, Theo of Krauss & Reese at Pioneer Assay Office on Pine (T63); (tax1864).
Krauss, Thos. (R63)
Krenekler, G. W. (R63)
Kries, George at Aurora Times Office (E64).
Krim, Daniel (R63)
Kusby, A. (R62)
Kuster, E. W. (R63); Edward per (M62); (M61).
Kyle, J. J. (M61); (R63); builder per 11/19/62 *California Alta*.
Kyle, Mary (R63)

L

La Rue, J. D. [or J. H. per (P61)] (M61); Deputy Recorder (R62); (M62); one wood bldg known as Old Sazerac on N side of Pine (E64).
Ladd, H. (R63)
Ladd, H. C. (R63); house on NE corner of Aurora and Roman (E64).
Laher, (or spelled Laker?) T. H. (M61)
Lake, William (R63)
Lake, William B. (G84); on the Cotillion Party Committee (T63); furniture in Preble & Devoe brick bldg on Aurora St. (E64); (tax1864).
Lake, Mrs. William B. (G84)
Lake, Wm. H. (R63)
Lake, W. J. (R63)
Lall, A. (R63)
Lall, J. W. (R63)
Lamb, E. (M61)
Lambert, F. owned lot and bldg on W side of Antelope (E64).
Lambert, T. (R63)
Lamprey, H. L. (P61); (E62); (R62).

Lampry, H. S. (M61)
Landen, J. B. (R62)
Lander, Nathan (R63)
Lands, F. (R62)
Landsberger, L. (M61); (M62).
Lane, F. A. (M61)
Lane, P. (R63)
Lane, S. T. (M61)
Lane, Thomas A. (P61); (R62).
Lange, J. (R63)
Lannegan, O. (R63)
Lard, Otis (R63)
Larimer, J. (M61)
Larimer, Robert (P61); (R62).
Larkin, J works for the Wide West Mining Company (E64).
Larkin, John (R63); (E64) brick saloon on E side of Antelope (E64).
Larkum, John (P61)
Larrigan, M. (R63)
Lasbatter, R. H. (R63)
Lathrop, Horace (R63)
Laughlin, A. M. (M61)
Laughlin, James (R63)
Launce (Lounce?), Montet French laborer (E64).
Lawer, W. E. on the Cotillion Party Committee (T63).
Lawrence lot on W side of Silver N of Rev.Yagers (E64).
Lawrence, B. M. (P61); (R62).
Lawrence, D. M. (M61)
Lawrence, J. (P61)
Lawrence, James (R63)
Lawrence, John S. (R63)
Lawrence, Leonard (R63); (M62).
Lawrence, R. M. (M61); (P61); (R62); (R63).
Lawton, T. (R63); saloon in John Somer's brick bldg E side of Antelope (E64).
Leach, A. G. (P61)
Leach, O. G. (R63)
Leary, M. (R63)
Leaver, G. W. (R63)
Lee, Sam (M62)
Leech, H. W. (M61); (P61); 1st Sergeant in Esmeralda Rifles (E62); (R62); former Deputy Sheriff once candidate for City Marshall (T63); floor manager for the Cotillion Party Committee (T63).

183

Leech, H. W. (M62)
Leeman, H. C. (R63)
Leich, H. W. (R63)
Leman, C. (M61)
Lemsee, T. (R63)
Lenahon, T. (R62)
Lenman, M. (R63)
Lenord, R. H. (P61)
Lenovich, Peter cabin E side of Winnemucca (E64).
Leonard, H. (R63)
Levi, Ike (T63) of Levy & Co., see Levy below.
Levi, L (M62)
Levison, J. & Co. (R63); owners of Bee Hive Saloon in Bechtel's bldg N side of Pine (E64).
Levy, B. (R63)
Levy, D. S. (E62)
Levy, david (M61)
Levy, J. (K.?) (R63); on the Cotillion Party Committee (T63).
Levy, M. (R63)
Levy, Nathan (T63) of Levy & Co.
Lewis, A. (R63)
Lewis, B. G. (M62)
Lewis, B. T. (R62)
Lewis, D. L. miner (R62)
Lewis, H. (R63); (M62).
Lewis, L. (M61); (P61); (R62).
Libby, ?, G (?)(M61).
Libby, A. E. (R63)
Lifer, J. (R62)
Linchan, P. (M61).
Linekin, E S of Spring (E64).
Linn, James L. (R63)
Linn, W. P. (R63)
Linnahan, Pat. (R63)
Linton, C. B. (R63) & Co. retail dealer (tax1864).
Linton, Thos. (R63)
Litt, Chas. (R63)
Little, J. (R63)
Litz, James (R63)
Livermore, C. B. (R63); of Livermore & Bro's meat market on S side of Wide West (E64).
Livermore, J. H. (R63) of Livermore & Bro's meat market.

Livingston, Y. lot and wood bldg know as Barnum Restaurant on W side of Antelope (E64).
Lloyd, George shot and killed by John Daly on 10/24/63 (N81); (G84).
Lockwood, T. (E62)
Loggins, A works for the Wide West Mining Company (E64).
Loman, M. miner works for Wide West Mining Co. (E64).
Loneben, J. miner (R62)
Loney, G. (M61).
Loomas, R. (R63)
Loomis, E. T. (R63), elected, but later rejected, Assemblymen on 1/19/64 (N81).
Loomis, R. B. (P61); (M61); (R62); (R63); cabin on S side of Del Monte, W of Court (E64).
Lord, Dr. S. P. (M61); (P61); (R62).
Lord, E. G. (M61).
Lot, Jas. (R63)
Lott, L. B. (P61); (R62); brick house on NW corner of Roman and Aurora (E64).
Love, Benjamin laborer (E64).
Lovelace, J. (M61)
Lovem, W. (R63)
Low, J. H. (R63)
Lowe, J. P. (R63)
Ludey, J. D. miner (R62)
Ludwig, J. D. (P61); (M61).
Ludwig, Jno. (R63)
Luff, Benj. (M61).
Luken, E. (R63)
Lummerman, P. B. (P61); miner (R62)
Lusk, Hiram (P61); miner (R62)
Luter, W. H. (R63)
Lynch, ? stone and wood cabin N side of Spring (E64).
Lynch, B. (M61)
Lynch, Daniel (R63)
Lynch, J. (R63)
Lynch, James (R63); N side of Spring W of Coffee Foundry (E64).
Lynch, M. (R63); works for the Wide West Mining Company (E64).
Lynch, Robert (R63)
Lyon, Capt. cabin on E side of Cottonwood (E64).
Lyon, J. (M61)
Lyons, E. W. (R63)

Residents of Aurora 1861-1864

Lyons, J. (M61)
Lyons, John (R63)
Lyons, John W. (P61); (E62); (R62)
Lyons, Thomas (R63)

M
Machin, Thomas N. (4/27/1931 Reno Evening Gazette) Elected Lt Governor of California on Sept 2, 1863 while Aurora was still thought to be in California, and served in that capacity for two years starting on December 1, 1863.
Mack, Albert (R63); (M61); on the Cotillion Party Committee (T63).
Mack, Augustus (R63); on the Cotillion Party Committee (T63).
Mack, Elizabeth (M62)
Mack, J. (R63); works for the Wide West Mining Company (E64).
Mack, P. L. (M61)
Magester, J. (M61)
Magilton, ? (M61)
Magre?, Thomas shoemaker in Newman's bldg S side of Pine (E64).
Maguire, R. (R63)
Mahan, A. J. (M61)
Mahan, M. (R63)
Maher, M. H. (R63)
Mahoney house on S side of Spring St. (E64).
Mahony, Wm. (R63); (M62).
Mann, Augustus (R63)
Mann, Charles L. (P61)
Mann, Chris. (R63)
Manning, Michael (R63)
Manning, William S. (P61)
Manuel, Francis (R63)
Marchant, John bakery south of Fashion Stable on Esmeralda (E64); (tax1864).
Marden, Horace "Hoddie" *Walker Lake Bulletin,* Nov. 4, 1915-
"In April, 1863, three weary pilgrims, following an old white horse with all our worldly possessions on the same, after seventeen days of traveling, arrived in the town of Aurora in search of the Golden Fleece. R.K. Colcord, T.B. Severance and the writer. Our combines capital in coin of the realm would not have paid one week's board for one of the party. The writer remained in that vicinity, including what is now Bridgeport, Aurora and Bodie, engaged in rustling to support a family until '79. [sic, '89]"
Marker, J. D. (P61); (E62).
Markley, W. J. (R63); agent for Elliot & Co. (T63).
Marks, Charles (R63)
Marks, G. (M61)
Marks, Moses (R63); of Marks & Co.saloon in La Rue bldg on Pine (E64); retail dealer in liquors (tax1864).
Marsh, J. W. (R63)
Marshall, F. (M61)
Marshall, Frank (P61); (R62).
Marshall, Fred works at Winter's Mill (E64).
Marston, B. O. (P61); (M61); (R62).
Martin, B. W. (P61); (R62); (M61).
Martin, C. (R62); house on Chatterton's lot NW Juniper Silver known as Hurdy Gurdy House (E64).
Martin, J. H. (M61); (R62); (R63); lot on W side of Court (E64).
Martin, J. Henry (P61); (R63); lot on N side of Aurora E of Radervitch (E64).
Martin, John W. (M61); (P61); (R62); (R63); (M62).
Martin, Phillippi works at Gregory's Mill (E64).
Martin, S. (M61); two wooden saloons on two lots on W side of Antelope (E64); (tax1864).
Mason, B. S. M. D. (P61); (R63); elected Senator 1/19/64 but later rejected (N81); physician (tax1864).
Mason, Thad (M61)
Massett, M. (R63)
Masterman, Edward (R63)
Masters, J. D. (R63)
Masterson, James member of Daly gang hung at Aurora on 2/9/64 (N81).
Mastny, Dr. Ma. dentist in Pioneer bakery (T63).
Matthews, E. J. (P61); (M61); (E62); (M62); mining agent (R62); (R63); mining claim broker on Pine (T63); wood bldg on lot on W side of Silver (E64).
Matthews, Fred. (R63)
Matthews, Maria (R63)

185

An 1864 Directory and Guide to Nevada's Aurora

Maun, B. S. (M62)
May, A. D. (M61)
May, H, (M61)
May, Hiram G. (E62); (R62); (M62); lot of E side of Winnemucca (E64); on the Cotillion Party Committee (T63).
Mayan, T. C. (R63)
Mayer, T. H. M.D. (R63)
Mayhugh, [or spelled Mayhew in (M61)] John S. (P61); miner (R62); (R63); (M62); cabin on E side of N Winnemucca (E64); elected, but later rejected, Assemblymen on 1/19/64 (N81), elected Assemblymen on 11/8/64 (N81); Foreman of Grand Jury, March 1864 (N81).
Mayon, C. R. (R63)
Mayon, Dr. T. (or Y) H. M. D. (R63); brick residence on S side of Aurora (was later used as Fried Walker's residence in the 1930-40s), office with Dr Mitchell on Parker's lot W side Antelope, three acres W side of Court N of Pine with Dr. Mitchell (E64).
McAdams, John (R63)
McAldon, J. (R62)
McArdle, James J. (R63)
McArthur, John (R63)
McBride, Charles (P61); carpenter (R62).
McBride, Wm. (P61); (R62); lot E of old Mono Co. jail (E64); elected Esmeralda County Surveyor on 9/2/63, re-elected on 9/7/64 (N81).
McCabe, John (R63); works for the Wide West Mining Company (E64).
McCarland, D. (R62)
McCarthy, C. (P61)
McCarthy, C. B. (M61)
McCarthy, W. (R63)
McCarty, (or Mccarthy) Luke (R63); laundry on E side of Silver next to San Francisco House (E64).
McCarty, Ann tent on E side of Silver (E64).
McClellan, R. A. on the Cotillion Party Committee (T63).
McClintock, J. E. boarding house on E side of Silver (E64).
McClinton, J. Giles (P61); miner (R62); (M61); (R63); city editor of Esmeralda Daily Union (N81); elected, but later rejected, State Assemblymen on 1/19/64

(N81). For more information, see Wedertz's *Bodie 1859-1900*, p. 119.
McCloskey, Hugh (P61); on C.D. Wingate's lot on S side of Spring (E64).
McCollins, T. (R63)
McCormack, B. F. (R63)
McCormack, J. M. (R63)
McCormack, Joseph (R63)
McCormack, W. P. (R63)
McCormick, B. F. (P61); (R62); (M61).
McCormick, F. (R63)
McCormick, W. (R63)
McCormick, W. P. (M61); (R62).
McCoy, O lot on S side of Spring W of Ah Hen's lot (E64).
McCree, John (R63)
McCulley, J. (R63)
McCullough, R. B. (M61); (P61); (R62).
McCully, J. (P61); (R62)
McDermot, C. F. (R63)
McDermot, Michael (R63)
McDermot, Patrick (R63)
McDonald, A. R. (R63)
McDonald, Allen (R63); lives at Stehler's Esmeralda Brewery (E64).
McDonald, C. P. (M61); (P61); (E62); (R62).
McDonald, George (R63)
McDonald, J. (M61)
McDonald, John (P61); (R62).
McDonald, M. (M61)
McDougal, John (R63)
McDowell, John (alias "Three-Fingered Jack") member of Daly gang hung at Aurora on 2/9/64 (N81).
McFarland, B. L. (R63); lot on N side of Pine W of Bradly lot (E64).
McFarland, Geo. M. (M61)
McFarland, John (R63)
McFarland, Thomas H. (R63)
McFay, J. (M61)
McFeely, John (R63)
McGee, A. L. (R63)
McGee, A. T. (M62)
McGee, Daniel (R63)
McGee, Taylor (R63)
McGinnis, John (R63)
McGowan, J. (R63)
McGrath, Edward (P61); (R62); (R63); (G84).

Residents of Aurora 1861-1864

McGrear, Robert (R63)
McGrorty, P. (R63); works for the Wide West Mining Company (E64).
McGuire, James (R63)
McGuire, R. M. (P61); (R62); a Richard McGuire was killed in Aurora April 1864 (G84).
McIntosh, Jas. (M61)
McKay, H. (R63)
McKay, M. (R63); works for the Wide West Mining Company (E64).
McKee, D. A. (R63); (tax1864).
McKeel, Arthur M. (M62); elected to the Territorial House of Representatives on 9/3/62 (N81).
McKeel, M. (R62)
McKeel, Robert miner (E64).
McKendly, Mrs. (E64) see Morris, Joe.
McKenna, Barney (R63)
McKenna, Charles (R63)
McKenny, W. B. (R63)
McKey, David copying in clerk's office (E64).
McKinney, John T. (M61); miner (R62); (R63).
McKinney, W. P. (M61); (P61); (E62); miner (R62).
McKinstry, Judge E. W. on the Cotillion Party Committee (T63); (tax1864).
McKintry killed in Aurora 4/63 (G84).
McLane, Ed (P61)
McLane, George (R63)
McLane, J. (R63)
McLaughlin, Alexander (R63); (M62); frame house on N side of Spring (E64).
McLaughlin, P. (R63)
McLaughlin, T. miner (R62); Thomas (M61); (R63); (M62); killed by McGrath in February 1863 (G84).
McMabeian, owned Del Monte Exchange Saloon in basement of courthouse (E64).
McMahan P. J., & Co. (E64); owned Del Monte Exchange Saloon (G84); on the Cotillion Party Committee (T63).
McMahon, F. M. (M61).
McMann, J. W. (P61); (R62).
McMann, John (M62)
McMannis, Patrick (R63)
McManus, T. D. (R63)

McNamee, J. (or McName, D.) owner of San Francisco Saloon on Parker's or Barker's lot on W side of Antelope (E64).
McNaughton, James (M61).
McNaughton, M. (R63)
Mcnaughton, M. M. (M61)
McNear, George (P61); (R62); or spelled McNeir in (M61).
McNorton, M. (P61); (E62); (R62)
McNue, Charles (R63).
McNulty, W. (M61)
McQuade, George deputy (G84)
McQuade, John (R63);
McQuillan, Robert (R63)
McShaffery, Charles (R63)
McShaffrey, Charles (M61); (P61); (R62).
McWeylaas, Phillip (R63)
McWilliams, J. (M61); (R63).
McWilliams, James (P61); miner (R62).
Mead, F. K. (M61); (R63).
Mead, G. L. (M61); (R63); (M62).
Mead, Hack gunfighter (G84).
Meagher, Jas. C. (P61); (R62).
Medley, P. H. (R63)
Meek, Edward E. (P61); (R62); (R63).
Meiner, C works for the Wide West Mining Company (E64).
Melahan, D. (R63); works for the Wide West Mining Company (E64).
Mellner, W. (R63)
Melovich, M. (M62)
Menafee, Thomas (R63)
Meredith, Capt Wm. C. (E62); (R63)
Meredith, J. M. (R63)
Mernoe, W. J. (R63)
Merrill, Enoch (R63)
Merrill, Thomas (R63)
Merriss, G. S. (R63)
Merritt, J. (R63)
Merse, A. C. (R63)
Mervin, W. L. (R62)
Mesan, Jas. (P61)
Mesick, Richard. S. Attorney (R63); partner with Van Voorhies (T63); elected District Prosecuting Attorney on 9/2/63 but resigned 1/22/64 (N81) (G84); on the Cotillion Party Committee (T63).
Metzner, J. on the Cotillion Party Committee (T63).

187

Meyer, T. F. (R62) [may be same as Meyer, T. F.]
Meyers, J. S. (P61)
Meyes, T. F. (P61) [may be same as Meyer, T. F.]
Michels, [or spelled Michaels in (M61)] William (P61).
Middlesworth, D. (M62)
Middlesworth, E. (M61)
Middlewort, D. C. (P61); (R62).
Middleworth, J. K. [or I. K. in (M61)] (P61); (R62).
Miles, J. (M62)
Miles, James (M61)
Mileurich, L. (P61)
Millard, George (R63)
Miller, Chas. laborer (E64); (M61).
Miller, D. J. (M61); (P61); (R62).
Miller, Edward (P61); (R62); (M62).
Miller, H. G. (R63)
Miller, J. (M61); miner (R62); (R63).
Miller, J. C. (R63); (M62).
Miller, J. W. (P61); (R62).
Miller, Jacob (P61); (R63); cabin on E side of Silver, below Del Monte (E64).
Miller, John (R63)
Miller, Mary E. (M62)
Miller, Robert (R63)
Miller, W. (M61)
Miller, W. W. (P61); (R62); cabin N of Spring (E64).
Miller, William N. (R62); (R63); proprietor of American Hotel on N side of Pine (T63); brickyard on S. side of Spring (E64), member of Morrison, Miller & Haley.
Milligan, William (P61); miner (R62).
Millis, S. R. (M61)
Mills, C. W. (R63)
Mills, E. A. (M61)
Mills, Samuel (E64)
Millsap, R. F. (M61)
Minard (Manard), Hiram saloon on E side of Antelope (E64).
Minear. W. L. (M61); blacksmith with Morrison (E64).
Miner, H. (R63)
Miner, Thos. (M61)
Mintura, J. (P61)
Mitchell, A. H. M.D. (R63); (P61); (E62); (R62); President of the Esmeralda Mining District, and the Antelope and Real Del Monte Mining Companies, elected in the fall of 1863 to the California Assembly (G84); shared office and owned property with Dr Mayon (E64)
Mitchell, Dr. E. F. (M61); (R62); (tax1864).
Mitchell, I. (?) H. (M61).
Mitchell, John (R63)
Mitchell, P. proprietor along with White of Merchants Exchange Hotel (T63).
Mitchell, W. (R62)
Mitchell. E. H. (M61)
Moehr, L. T. (M62)
Moffat, W. S. (M61)
Moffatt, S. P. [or B. per (M61)] (R62); District Recorder (R63); (E64); (tax1864).
Molena, Manuel (R63)
Molinivick, L. (R62)
Molyneux (or Molineux) dealer in hardware R62), William (R63) part of Molyneux & Co. two story brick store N side of Pine (E64).
Monie, Len (P61)
Monroe, Col. U. P. (M62); brick "Monroe House" hotel on N side of Wide West (E64); on the Cotillion Party Committee (T63); hotel (tax1864).
Montarg, Alex (R63)
Montarg, Joseph (R63)
Moody, James L. (M62)
Moonen, Center (M62)
Mooney, James S. (M61); (P61); (R63).
Moore, D. J. (R63)
Moore, J works for the Wide West Mining Company (E64).
Moore, J. A. C. (R63)
Moore, J. C. (M61)
Moore, James (P61); (R62)
Moore, John F. appointed Esmeralda County Commissioner on 6/22/63 (N81).
Moore, John T. (R62); (R63); served as Justice of the Peace and as coroner (G84).
Moore, M. (R63)
Moore, Michael (R63)
Moore, R. (M61).
Moore, Robert (P61); (R62)
Moore, S. (M61).
Moore, W. L. (M61); (R62); (M62).
Moore, W. S. (M62)
Moore, William (R63)

Residents of Aurora 1861-1864

Moorehead, J. (R63)
Moorman,T. J. (R63)
Moran, Thomas (R63)
Morand, John (R63)
More, William L. (P61)
Morehouse, J. J. (R63)
Morgan, Daniel (M61); (P61); (E62); (E62).
Morgan, E. (M61); (E62); miner (R62).
Morgan, E. W. (P61); miner (R62)
Morgan, Ed (P61); (E62); (M62).
Morgan, Eliot (E62)
Morgan, L. F. (M61)
Morine, Francis (R63)
Morken, J. D. (R62)
Moron, B. S. (R62)
Morrill, C. (R63)
Morrill, J. K. (R63)
Morrill. W. H. (M61); (P61).
Morris, George (P61)
Morris, James (R63)
Morris, Joe & Mrs McKendly lot N side of Juniper (E64).
Morris, N. (R63)
Morris, Samuel (M62)
Morrison, H. (M61)
Morrison, J. M. (R62); (R63).
Morrison, John (R63)
Morrison, L. B. (R63)
Morrison, Robert H. (M61); (P61); "fifer" (E62; (R62).
Morrow, W. K. (E64)
Morse, A. C. attorney and Notary Public, office in A. M. Wingate bldg W side of Silver; on the Cotillion Party Committee (T63).
Morse, L. (M61); (R62).
Morse, S. C. (M62)
Morten (or Morton), A. G. (R63); barkeeper at Lawton's saloon (E64).
Mortimer, John (M62); colored barber with Huff in Shier's Bldg S side of Pine, also lot on N side of Wide West and lot Del Monte and Mono (E64).
Morton, George S. (M61); (P61); (R62); (M62); brick mason per 11/19/62 *California Alta*.
Morton, W. miner (R62)
Moses, J. C. (E62)

Moses, Phillip P. (P61); (M62); mill owner (R62); (R63); stamp mill on S side of Spring (E64).
Moses, Samuel A. (P61); (E62); (R62); (R63)
Moses, W. S. (R63)
Mosher, Daniel (R63); painter and partner with Jewett (T63).
Moulton, C, M. (R62)
Moutrie, J. A. County Judge (R62); appointed Mono County Judge on 6/1/61 (N81).
Mowbray, John (P61)
Mowbry, J. (M61)
Mower, A. H. (R63)
Muloy, James (R63)
Mumford, S. (R63)
Munckton, Daniel (R63)
Munroe, M. E. (R63)
Munson, P. C. (P61); (E62); (R62); (R63)
Murdock, H. M. (R63); cabin W side of Court (E64).
Murner, J. C. (R62)
Murphy, A. miner (E64).
Murphy, John L. (M62)
Murphy, Micheal A. miner (E64); (R63); moved to Aurora in April 1863 (N81), Attorney General of Nevada 1879-1882.
Murphy, Mrs. Micheal maiden name was "Matilda (or Martha) J. Myers" (N81).
Murphy, T. J. (R63)
Murphy, T. Y. miner (E64).
Murphy, Timothy (R63)
Murray, G. (M61)
Murray, James (P61); (R62).
Murray, P. (R63)
Murray, Tho,as, miner (E64).
Murta, Charles (R63)
Murtha, Patrick (R63)
Musser, J. C. (P61); (M61).
Myer, J. M. [or Myers, J. M. per (P61)] druggist (R62).
Myers, J. L. (M61)
Myers, J. S. (M61)
Mygatt, Henry (R63)
Mynea, W. L. (P61)
Myson, Joseph (R63)

N
Need, F. K. (P61)

189

Neely, A. L. (R63)
Neidy, John (M61); (R63); (M62); brick bldg on N side of Pine (E64); lived in Aurora from 1860 till his death in 1890 making him the longest resident of Aurora.
Neily, J. M. (P61); (R62).
Neison, J. (R62)
Nevis, R. L. (P61); (R62)
Newfield, A (M61)
Newman, A. (M61); (P61); (R62).
Newman, Edward (R63); works for the Wide West Mining Company (E64).
Newman, Jos. (R63)
Newman, Merchant (R63); clothing store on S side of Pine, E of Well Fargo (E64).
Newman, Samuel (R63)
Newman, Thomas (P61); (R62); (M62); City Laundry on E side of Winnemucca (E64).
Newton, Alex (M62)
Newton, Charles (P61)
Newton, L. H. (P61); miner (R62).
Newton, R. (M61)
Newton, S. H. (M61)
Nicholls, D. C. (R63)
Nichols, W. (R63)
Nicholson, B. (P61); (R62)
Nicholson, F. H. (R63)
Nicholson, James (P61)
Nielson, Christian (M62).
Niles, C. A. (M61).
Niles, H. W. (E62); (M62).
Niles, Mrs. Torben two wood bldgs on S side of Spring (E64).
Niver, J. D. (R62); (E62).
Nolan, T. J. (M61)
Nolen, J. C. (M61)
Norman, Mrs. D. French Laundry on E side of Esmeralda (E64).
Norris, George S. (P61); (R62); (M62).
Northrop, C. E. (R63)
Northrope, A. S. (E64) lot on E side of Antelope W of Esmeralda.
Norton, Valintine (M61); (M62).
Nowell, N. B. (R63)
Nowlan, (or Nowland?), Jas. M. (R63); slaughter-yard on N side of Spring, butcher shop on W side of Antelope (aka Nowlan & Barlow) (E64).
Nowlen, J. C. (R62)
Noyes, J. (R62)

Nugent, Thos (R63)
Nutter, Barney (R63)
Nye, Capt. John (R63)
Nye, Peter house on N side of Juniper, W of Court (E64).

O
O'Brien, James laborer (E64); (R63).
O'Brien, Thos. (R63)
O'Connell, C. O. (M61)
O'Conner, Cornelius (R63)
O'Conner, T. (R63)
O'Connor, Daniel (R63)
O'Donnell, C. (R63)
O'Hara, Uncle Billy African American "capitalist" of Aurora. For more information, see Wedertz's *Bodie 1859-1900*, pp. 124-125.
O'Neil, A. (M61)
O'Neil, C. (M61)
O'Rourke, W. (R63)
O'Sullivan, J. P. house on Antelope and Sage (E64).
Ober, C. W. (R63)
Ogilvie, L. C. (R63); (or Ogilby, L. C. per P61 & R62)
Oglesby, L. C. (M62); (M61).
Oliver, J. C. miner (R62); (R63)
Oman, Jno. (R63)
Ondero, Joe (R63)
Openheimer, Julius (R63); (tax1864).
Oppenhammer, C. on the Cotillion Party Committee (T63).
Oppenheimer, P. B. [spelled Oppenheim in (M61)]; (P61); (M62); mining agent (R62); lot on E side of Silver (E64).
Orlom, D. miner (R62)
Orr, Henry (M62)
Osborn, A. A. (R63)
Owens, William (R63)

P
Packer, J. J. (R63)
Page, Anne liquors in Thomas Greely Saloon on Pine (E64).
Page, John (M62)
Paige, B. G. (R62)
Palmer, George S. appointed District Attorney 1/22/64 (N81).
Palmer, J. M. (M61); (M62).

Residents of Aurora 1861-1864

Palmer, James (R63)
Palmer, John A. (R63); cabin E side of cottonwood, first lot S of Capt Lyon prop. (E64); former Town Constable or City Marshall, Captain of Hooker Light Infantry, head of vigilantes during February 1864 (G84).
Palmer, T. J. (R63)
Pamrevether, Geo. (R63)
Pander, D. C. (R62)
Panmore, Thomas (P61)
Pardoe, F. (R63) owned San Francisco House a brick hotel on NW corner Aurora Silver (E64).
Park, A. D. (M61)
Parker, B. G. (M62); two wood bldgs. on lot on W. side of Antelope, slaughterhouse behind Miller's brickyard S side of Spring (E64).
Parker, E. G. (R63)
Parker, F. G. (R63)
Parker, G. W. (R62); (R63); wood bldg E side of Antelope occupied by Cohn, wood bldg occupied by Chinaman, also lot with Chamberlin on N side of Spring (E64).
Parker, J. H. (P61); (R63).
Parker, J. P. (M61)
Parker, J. S. (R63)
Parker, T. H. (M61); (M62).
Parker, W. (E64) lot on E side of Antelope.
Parker, Wash member of Daly gang (G84).
Parks, J. (M61)
Parks, J. C. elected Councilman on 9/7/64 (N81).
Parlan, J. (M61)
Parlin, [or Parlan per (M61)] H. T. (P61); (R62); (M62); miner (R63); (G84); killed John E. Campbell on 6/6/64 (N81).
Parling, John T. (P61)
Parris, G. W. owns lot (E64).
Parrish, Edward (R63)
Parry, John of Petit & Parry (E64).
Parsons, C. N. & Co. brick soda factory on S side of Wide West (E64).
Patchell, J. (R62); (M61).
Patchin, C. H. (M61); attorney-at-law (R62); (M62); (R63).
Patrick, T. F. (M61); (P61); miner (R62).

Patten (Patton per (T63) J. E. (R63); lot on E side of Silver opposite Armory Hall (E64); on the Cotillion Party Committee (T63).
Patten, S. J. (R62)
Patter, S. D. (M62)
Patterson works for the Wide West Mining Company (E64).
Patterson, A. H. (P61); (R62); (M61).
Patterson, H. (M61)
Patterson, J. H. (R63)
Patterson, R. S. (R62); (R63)
Patton, John (M62)
Paul, G. W. (R63)
Paul, H. C. (R63)
Paulding, Wm. (M61); (P61).
Paultgnis, G. A. (R63)
Pawling, T. M. attorney-at-law (R62); partner with Phelps (R63); attorneys in wood bldg on Wingate's lot W side of Silver (E64). Also partner with Sims (T63).
Paxton, Alex (R63)
Payne, Geo. C. (R63)
Payne, Sarah (R63)
Peake, Henry (R63)
Pearson, H. H. (R63) partner with Robinson in Union Stable?
Pebelie, John L. partner with Jameson in Washington Baths (T63).
Peck, Addison S. (R63); elected Esmeralda County Judge (N81).
Peck, Levi P. (R63); clerk (T63).
Peck, O (M61); (P61); (R62)
Peeler, B. (R63)
Peelin, Hans (M62)
Pelling, J. (M61)
Pendergrast, J. M. (P61); (R62); brick house on N side of Wide West (E64).
Pendergrast, Mrs. (M62)
Pendicord, John cabin N of and next to Last Chance Tunnel (E64).
Penfield, G. V. N. (M61)
Pennie, J. C. (R63)
Pennie, Wm. (R63)
Pennyweather, George (P61); (R62)
Percival, S. J. (R62)
Pereau, Joseph H. (R63)
Perens, Robert (R62)
Perkins, Geo. (M61); (R63).
Perkins, J. B. storehouse on lot on W side on N Winnemucca (E64).

191

An 1864 Directory and Guide to Nevada's Aurora

Perkins, Jno. W. (R63)
Perkins, John (P61); miner (R62); (R63); (M62).
Perkins, T. H. (R62)
Perry, S. B.[or P. per (M61)] (P61); blacksmith (R62); (R63).
Perry, W. (M61)
Perry, Wm. (R63)
Persglove cabin on W side of Esmeralda (E64).
Peterson, E. miner (E64).
Petit, A. P. carpenter and builder (R63); of Petit & Perry, contractors and builders Petitt (E64)
Petitt, R. H. (M61); (P61); (R62).
Pettigrew, J. saloon at corner of Pine and Antelope (E64).
Peyton, H. (R63)
Phalen, James (R63); works for the Wide West Mining Company (E64).
Phalen, John (R63); works for the Wide West Mining Co. (E64).
Phazen, William (M62)
Phelan, Jno. (R63)
Phelan, Thomas Jefferson (M61); (P61); miner (R62).
Phelps, R. E. (M61); attorney-at-law (R62); of Phelps & Pawling, law office (R63); (M62); elected Mono County District Attorney on 6/1/61 (N81), (G84).
Phenix, E. (R63)
Philips, W. (?) C. (M61)
Phillips, Horatio G. (M61); (P61); (E62); (R62); mining partner with Samuel Clemens; owned lot on north side of Spring St (M62)
Phillips, William (P61); (M62).
Piatt, O. R. miner (E64); (M62).
Pickle, F. works at Winter's Mill (E64).
Pickle, John works at Winter's Mill (E64).
Pierce, J. B. (R62)
Pierce, J. M. (M61); (P61); (R62).
Pierce, William (M61)
Pierson, Chas. (M61)
Pine, Daniel. H. (P61); (M61); (E62); Mono County Post Master (R62); (R63); Town Constable or City Marshall (G84); on the Cotillion Party Committee (T63).
Piper, R. (R63)
Pisson, T. (M61)

Pitman, James H. (R63); cabin E side of Silver (E64).
Pixley, G. (M62)
Pixley, H. G. (R62)
Plank, D. K. (M61); (R62).
Platt, M. miner (M61); (R62).
Platt, S. (R63)
Plauf, F. saloon in Somers bldg W of Bradford's Store (E64).
Plazer, P. (M61)
Pleasant, M. C. (R62)
Plummer, C. A. (R63)
Pollard, J. P. (R63)
Pollo, A cabin W side of Winnemucca S of Mathews (E64).
Pool, E. B. (M61)
Poole, E. B. (R63)
Poole, E. P. (R62)
Poole, W. P. (P61); (E62); (M62).
Poole, William (R63)
Pooler, William (R63)
Poorman, E. lot on W side of Silver (E64).
Pope, A. miner (E64).
Pornie, D. D. miner (R62)
Porter, B. T. (P61); (R62); (or B. F. in R63); owned Porter's Saloon on Antelope (T63); on the Cotillion Party Committee (T63); liquors (tax1864).
Porter, G. W. (M61)
Porter, S. (R63)
Porter, Z. (P61)
Portor, B. F. (M61)
Potter, S. D. (P61); (R62)
Powell, A. (M61)
Powell, J. W. (P61); (R62)
Powers works for the Wide West Mining Company (E64).
Powers, M. (R63)
Powers, Patrick (R63)
Powers, R. (M61)
Powers, Robert (P61)
Pratten, R. (R62)
Preble, E. (R63) of Preble & Devoe lots on W side of Silver, NE corner Silver Antelope, SE corner Pine Silver, and owner of Preble & Co. brickyard up Cottonwood Gulch S of Barbien's brickyard (E64).
Preston, R. (M61); (R62).
Price, A. M. (R63)
Price, E. (R63); (M62).

Residents of Aurora 1861-1864

Price, J. (M61)
Price, J. B. (M61)
Price, J. P. (R63)
Price, Jacob (P61)
Price, W. owner of Last Chance Saloon on Antelope (E64); billiards, liquors (tax1864).
Prience (or Prince), Charles (or Prence per T63); Pioneer bakery on E side of Silver (E64).
Prince, H. A. miner (E64).
Prince, J. T. (M61); (P61); (R62); (R63).
Proper, E. A. (P61)
Pruitt, Edward (R63)
Pugh, Dr. John W. (M61); (P61); member First Legislative Assembly of Nevada Territory (R62); (R63); physician (tax1864).
Pulprit, William (E62)
Purceull. S. J. (P61)
Purlin H. S. (E62)
Pye, Alexander (R63)
Pye, M. (R63)

Q
Quail, William (P61)
Quebec, Jas. (R63)
Quentin, Gus (M62)
Querner, F. (R62)
Quesenbury, John (R63)
Quigley, Thos. (R63); works for the Wide West Mining Company (E64).
Quinn, Charles (M62)
Quint, Geo. W. (R63)
Quint, Leander (R63); attorney with Kendall, Quint, & Hardy on Silver (T63).
Quinton, Augustus "Confederate sympathizer" (G84).
Quisenbury, M. (M61)

R
Radcliff, C. M. (M61)
Raderford, D. lot on S side of Del Monte (E64).
Radervitch (or spelled Radovitch) Peter owns Tremont Hotel on NE corner Aurora and Antelope, plus other lots (E64).
Raellmaker, Jno. (R63)
Rafs, R. (M61)
Ragan, R. C. (M61)
Rahents, Eli (R62)
Ramsdell, J. (M61)

Randall, P. W. elected Esmeralda County Commissioner 9/2/63 but resigned 1/22/64 (N81).
Randolf, Dr. (R63)
Randolph, E. (M61); (M62); blacksmith shop N side of Pine (E64).
Raney, William E. (P61); (R62)
Rapson, Mathew lot E side of Silver S of Simpsons (E64).
Rashwell, Thomas (M62)
Rathwell, Thomas (R62)
Rawling, P. M. (R63)
Raymond, G. (M61)
Raymond, J. E. (R62)
Raynoud, G. (P61)
Readmaker, John furniture repair shop in house on Medley and Balls prop, house at intersection Silver and Esmeralda (E64).
Ready, P. (R63) see Reddy, Patrick
Rearden, D. shoe shop in Williams & Stewartson bldg on W side of Antelope (E64).
Redding, Wm. (R63)
Reddy, Patrick later became a famous lawer. See McGrath's *Gunfighters,* p. 121.
Reed, ? works for the Wide West Mining Company (E64).
Reed, C. W. (M61)
Reed, Henry (R63)
Reed, M. (R63)
Reed, Mathew (R63)
Reed, P. (M61); (R62).
Reed, W. LaRogue photographer in 2nd floor of Bradford's Store on Pine (E64); (tax1864)
Rees, Thos. B. (R63)
Reese, H. W. partner with Krauss at Pioneer Assay Office (T63).
Reese, N. W of Reese & Frund, owners of barber shop Lambert's lot on W side of Antelope (E64).
Reese, Thos. (R63)
Regan, A. (R62)
Reilley, C. (R63)
Reily, T. N side of Spring opposite Hoems Brickyard (E64).
Reins (or Reims) Dr. J. W. (spelled Renis in R63) physician with office at Collins Drug Store (T63); (tax1864).
Reisnecker, H. (R63)
Reno, Louis (R63)

193

Reynolds works for the Wide West Mining Company (E64).
Reynolds, J. H. (M61); (R62).
Reynolds, L. (P61); (R63).
Reynolds, W. B. (M61); (R63).
Reynolds, William (P61); (R62).
Rhoade, A. J. cabin on NW corner of Juniper and Antelope (E64).
Rhoades, Eben R. (R63); of Rhoades & Co. which owned a brick hardware store on South side of Pine, also lot on W side of Roman south of Winchester's prop (E64); elected Mono County Treasurer on 9/2/63 and re-elected on 9/7/64, also elected Mono and Esmeralda Co Treasurer on 9/2/63 (N81).
Rhoades, H. (R63)
Rhoades, H. J. (R63)
Rhodes, H. A. (M61); (P61); (E62); (R62).
Rice, A. J. (R63)
Rice, A. S. (R63)
Rice, A. T. wood house on E side of Silver (E64).
Rice, Elvina (R63)
Rice, L. (R63); elected Representative on 9/7/64 (N81).
Richards, H. (M61)
Richards, Henry (M62).
Richardson, Joseph H. (M61); (P61); (R63); (M62); owned six or seven lots and buildings (E64); Broker and Notary Public (T63); elected Esmeralda County Assessor on 9/7/64 (N81); (tax1864); conveyancer (tax1864).
Richarson, S. C. (M62)
Ridgely, M. G. (R62)
Ridgely, M. W. (M61)
Ridgerly, Charles improvements on N side of Spring opposite Esmeralda Brick Yard (E64).
Rife, S. B. (P61); (R63); (M62).
Riggins, T. (M61)
Riley, George (R63)
Ripp, S. B. (R62)
Rippeden, Isaac (R63)
Rison, W. R. authorized agent for the Aurora Times (T63); tobaccomist (spp?) (tax1864).

Rittengers, S. T. wood house S side of Wide West adjacent and west of U.T. Monroe (E64).
Robert, L. B. (R63)
Roberts, E. (M62)
Robertson, M. E. (E62)
Robinette, James (P61); merchant (R62)
Robinsen, Martin miner (E64).
Robinson, A. (M61)
Robinson, Bob on the Cotillion Party Committee (T63).
Robinson, Charles J. (or P.) (R63); proprietor (?) of Union Stable N side of Pine (E64); on the Cotillion Party Committee (T63); (tax1864).
Robinson, E. P. (M62)
Robinson, Mark (R63); proprietor (?) of Union Stable N side of Pine (E64); on the Cotillion Party Committee (T63).
Robinson, Martin miner (E64).
Robinson, Moses (M62); (tax1864).
Robinson, N. (R63)
Rockwell, Frank (R63)
Roddea (or Roccea?), Joseph boardinghouse (E64).
Rodebank, J. W. (P61); merchant (R62); (M62).
Rodenbaugh, A. (M61)
Rodgers, W. (R63)
Roe, Morris (R63)
Roger, Nathon lot E side of Silver (E64).
Rogers, A. K. (R63)
Rogers, Amos (P61)
Rolan, Geo. (R63)
Roman, R. (R62)
Ron, J. S. (P61); (R62)
Rook, Amos (R63)
Rook, Elroy (R62)
Rooney, M. (R63); works for the Wide West Mining Company (E64).
Rose, Jas. (R63)
Ross two lots (E64)
Ross, John L. (R63)
Ross, John S. (M61); elected to the Territorial House of Representatives on 9/3/62 (N81).
Ross, S. E. (R63)
Rothe, C. W. (R63)
Rucker, J. M. (R63)
Rule, J. W. (P61); (R62)

Residents of Aurora 1861-1864

Runkell, Richard (R63)
Runyon, W. S. (T63); partner with Harkness, lot on E side of Winnemucca, lot on W side of Silver, saloon in Wingate bldg E side of Silver (E64).
Rush, P. C. (M61)
Rush, Patrick (R63)
Russell, F. H. (R63)
Russell, H. A. (R63)
Russell, J. H. (R62)
Russell, John P. (M62)
Russell, Wm. (R63)
Rutherford, C. (R63)
Rutherford, C. M. (P61); (R62).
Rutherford, J. (R63); lot S side of Wide West (E64)
Rutherford, J. C. (M61); (P61); (R62); (M62).
Ryan, James (R63); (M61).
Ryan, M. E. (R63)
Ryan, P. (M61); (R63)
Ryerman, J. W. (R63)

S
Sachman, Davis (M62)
Sale, Luke (R63)
Salisbury (or Salsbury), J. H. of (?)
Saulsbury & McKinsley store in Preble & Devoes bldg (E64); on the Cotillion Party Committee (T63).
Sampson, E. S. (R63)
Sanchez, Laura wife of Raymon Sanchez.
Sanchez, Ramon B. (R63); bank partner with J. Howard (T63); brick residence S side of Aurora (E64); mayor of Aurora in 1864 (G84); on the Cotillion Party Committee (T63); banker (tax1864).
Sanders, H. S. (M61); (P61); druggist (R62); (M62).
Sanders, Jessie (P61)
Sanderson, W. G. (M61)
Savage, M. (R63)
Saxe, E. A. (R63)
Saxton, Rev J. B. elected Esmeralda County Superintendent of Schools on 9/2/63 (N81); pastor First Baptist Church and chief editor of Esmeralda Daily Union (N81).
Scawperry, George (R63)
Schaefer, Adam (R63)
Schaeffer, Martin (R63)

Schaffer works for the Wide West Mining Company (E64).
Schibler, Randolph two log cabins W of Winnemucca between Humphries and Baptist Church (E64).
Schier (or Scheier), G. (R63); (M62); brick clothing store on Antelope and other property (E64).
Schoonmaker, Frank (M61); (R63); owned Bank Exchange saloon (G84); partner with Runyon billiard room (tax1864).
Schram, Mrs. B. superintendent of St Charles Hotel (T63).
Schultry, J. S. (R63)
Schultz, A. (R63)
Schultz, George T. (R63); house on SW corner of Juniper and Court (E64).
Schwartz, M. book store in Shiers bldg on Pine (E64).
Schweininger, Joseph (M62); lot on south side of Spring between Elstner's and Garishe's property (E64).
Schwob, Adolphe (R63); stockbroker, commission office on N side of Pine, lot on S side of Del Monte (E64); retail dealer (tax1864).
Schwob, Annette (R63)
Scott, N. F. (M61); (R62); first elected Sheriff of Mono County on 6/1/61 (N81); killed by Indians in Owens Valley on 4/6/62 and buried at Aurora (G84).
Seale lot S side of Juniper, between Smith and Ross property (E64).
Searing, Wm S. grocery store on Wide West (T63); of Searing & Dorn & Co. (E64).
Sears, Ellen "Nellie" (G84)
Sears, H. D. (R63)
Seawell, Wm. M. (R63); attorney with office on Pine (T63); owned four lots and houses (E64); (tax1864).
Seeley, O. (M61)
Seely, O. (P61); (R62).
Selsor, A. J. (R63); works for the Wide West Mining Co. (E64).
Sephleurtz, Stephen (R63)
Sever boarding house on N side of Spring (E64).
Severance, T. B. (see Marden, Horace)
Seymour, Y. S. works at Winter's Mill (E64).

195

Shafer, A. (M62)
Shaff, J. A. (M61)
Shaffery, C. M. lot at intersection of Silver and Cottonwood (E64).
Shafrey, Charles (M62)
Shakespear, C. (R63)
Shanley, J. (R62)
Shannon, Giles L. (M61); (P61); (R62); (R63); house on W side of antelope, S of Del Monte (E64).
Shansworth, Antone (G84)
Shappee, James (R63)
Sharp, J. W. (R62); (M61).
Shaw, G. H. (R63)
Shaw, T. (M61)
Shaw, Thomas (M62)
Shed, J. T. (M61)
Sheehan, John H. in house on Issacs lot (E64).
Sheffer, A (R63)
Sheffrer, Levi (R62)
Shelden, S. G. (P61); (R62).
Sheldon, Adela (R63)
Sheldon, Byron (P61)
Sheldon, M. (R62); (M62); houses on SE corner Antelope and Del Monte (E64).
Sheldon, Maria (R63)
Sheldon, Myron (M61); (R63); house on SE corner Antelope and Del Monte (E64).
Sheldon, S. G. (M61)
Sheridan, P. (R63)
Sheridan, Park (R63)
Sherman, Issac (R63)
Sherman, Major Edwin A. (R63), lot at intersection of Esmeralda and Antelope used as China Washhouse (E64); also owner/editor of the Esmeralda Star (N81).
Sherry, J. M. (M61)
Shibler, Rudolph (R63); (M61).
Shields, T. J. (R63); works for the Wide West Mining Company (E64).
Shier, G. many lots and buildings in town (E64).
Shiller, R. (P61); (R62)
Shimmen, W. E. (R63); (M62).
Shimmer, E. R. (R63)
Shimmins, T. W. (M61)
Shimmins, W. E. (M61)
Shimnenek, E. lot on N side of Wide West (E64).

Shordlow, W. M. (P61); (R62).
Show, Frank miner (E64). Shults, B. (R62)
Shults, C. W. (P61); (R62).
Shultz, George cabin on C. Millers lot SW corner of Juniper and Court (E64).
Shultz, Jacob S. (P61); (M61); lot on E side of Court (E64), elected Mono County Commissioner on 6/1/61 (N81).
Sibley works for the Wide West Mining Co. (E64).
Sides, E. H. (R63)
Siegmand, W. M. (or spelled Sigmund) butcher in Somers bldg N of Merchants Exchange (E64); butcher (tax1864).
Sike, Peter (R63)
Sill, Dr. H. C. M. D. (R63); physician with house on W side of County Jail and office on Pine (E64).
Silliman, Sam. (M61)
Simmons, H. F. (M61)
Simmons, O. (R62)
Simpkin, W. A. (M61)
Simpson, A. C. (R63)
Simpson, E. H, (R63)
Simpson, G. (R63)
Simpson, J. (W?) (R63); stone cabin E side of Silver (E64).
Simpson, J. J. (R63)
Sims, Col. C. (R63); attorney with Pawling (T63).
Sims, Geo. E. (M61)
Sing, Tee (Chinaman) on Sam Davis lot NE corner Pine and Winnemucca (E64).
Sinnott, James, (R63); works for the Wide West Mining Company (E64).
Sinsnig, Don (P61)
Skinner, Chas. (R63)
Skinner, Chas. W. (P61); (R62); (M61).
Skinner, S. (P61)
Skinner, William. E. (P61); (R62)
Skyram, W. (E62)
Skyrme, Wm. (M62)
Slade, Rev. H. D. Methodist Church.
Sloper, A. T. (P61); conveyancer (R62); (R63)
Slossen, John J. [or spelled Slasson in (M61) or spelled Slassen in (M62)] (P61); (R62).
Slossum, Capt. cabin on estate of E. Poorman on W side of Silver (E64).
Smith, A. W. (R63)

Residents of Aurora 1861-1864

Smith, C. (M61); (R62)
Smith, C. B. (M61)
Smith, C. E. miner (R62)
Smith, Chas. (M61)
Smith, Fisher C. M. D. physician with office on Pine, two doors down from Dr. Green's Drug store (T63); physician (tax1864).
Smith, Fredrerick (R63)
Smith, G. B. (M62)
Smith, George W. (R63); (M61); lot north of Somers and slaughter house on S side of Spring (E64).
Smith, H. (R62); on the Cotillion Party Committee (T63).
Smith, H. B. works at Winter's Mill (E64).
Smith, H. D. (?)(M61)
Smith, Harry (T63)
Smith, Henry (R63); (M62).
Smith, J. E. (R63)
Smith, J. E. Jr. (R63)
Smith, J. H. (or N.) (R63); elected Mono County Assessor on 6/1/61, elected Assessor again on 9/2/63 (N81); lot on S side of Juniper (E64).
Smith, J. N. & Co. County Assessor, lot on S side of Juniper (E64).
Smith, J. W. (P61); (E62); (R62).
Smith, Jacob (R63)
Smith, James (R63)
Smith, James L. (M61)
Smith, Jerome (R63); brick cabin on hill east of Cottonwood (E64).
Smith, L. (M61); (P61).
Smith, Louis C. (R63)
Smith, M. (M61)
Smith, M. M. (M61); (P61); (R62).
Smith, Mrs. Mary three houses and lots (E64); a Daly gang "favorite" (G84).
Smith, S. B. (M61)
Smith, S. C. (M61)
Smith, Sam. (M61)
Smith, Thomas (R63)
Smith, W. J. (P61)
Smith, W. L. (M61)
Smith, W. R. (M61)
Snow, J. (R63)
Snow, J. J. (R62); (M61).
Snyder, B. F. (M61); (P61); (R62); (R63).
Snyder, G. O. (M61)
Snyder, J. N. (R63)

Snyder, Maria (R63)
Snyder, Mrs. alias Sage Hen, house on SW corner Mono and Del Monte (E64).
Snyder, O. N. miner (R62) (E62)
Somer, John brick bldg E side of Antelope (E64).
Sommers, Jessie brick bldg N of Pine, W of Bradford's store, also brick bldg W side of Winnemucca N of Merchants Exchange (E64).
Sommers, John brick house residence on hillside south of Spring (E64).
Spaulding, A. (R62)
Spaulding, Adam (P61); (R62).
Spaulding, John (M61); (P61); (E62); (M62); (R62); (Spalding per R63); lot NE corner of Pine and Roman, lot on N side of Pine W of Elstners (E64).
Spaulding, John (R62)
Spawling, A. (M61)
Spayth, A. M. (R63)
Spencer, Edward (R63); lot SW corner Sage and Silver (E64).
Spencer, W. H. (M62)
Spiller, Frank (R63)
Spinney, Wm. (M61)
Spinny, R. (P61)
Spino, Samuel (M61)
Sprague, J. W. (M61); (R63); (M62); lot on N side of Wide West (E64).
Sprague, Joseph (R63)
Spraig, J. (P61); (R62)
Spray, Jesse D. (M61); (R63); (M62); house N side of Wide West E of Pendergrass (E64).
Spring, William (R62)
Springer, Alfred (M62)
Springer, H. M. (R63); lot N side of Spring W of Nowlan prop (E64).
Springer, J. S. (R63)
Staehler, F. (M62); owns Esmeralda Brewery (E64); see add in 11/18/63 *Esmeralda Star*; brewer (tax1864).
Stafford, M. (R62)
Staniford, G. M. (M61)
Stanley, W. L. (R63)
Stanley, W. S. (M61)
Stanley, William (P61)
Stanten, F. G. cabin on S side of Del Monte (E64).

197

Starchman, F. (M61)
Stark, John or James cabin on W side of N Antelope (E64); on the Cotillion Party Committee (T63).
Starkey, I. G. "colored" on lot on S side of Juniper (E64).
Starkweather, A. (M61)
Statts, B (M61)
Statts, J. W. (M61); (R62).
Statz, B. (R63)
Statz, Bernard N side of Wide West between Hall and Goodman (E64).
Stavan, Jno. (R63)
Stearns, L. O. (E62); attorney-at-law (R62)
Steel, Thomas (R63)
Steele, W. (M61)
Steiner, N. (R63); of Steiner & Gaige's Sazerac saloon in Wingate's bldg (E64); floor manager for the Cotillion Party Committee, partner with Gaige in Sazerac saloon (T63); (tax1864).
Steiner, V. house on Blanchard NW corner Pine and Roman (E64).
Sterns, L. O. (M61); (R63).
Sterrett, T. C. house on S side of Spring west of Mrs. Niles (E64).
Stevens, R. (R63)
Stevenson, R. R. (M61)
Steward, H. (R63)
Stewart, Alex (R63)
Stewart, J. G. (M61)
Stewart, J. Q. (R63)
Stewart, M. Y. (M61); (P61); (E62); house NE corner Antelope and Juniper (E64); on the Cotillion Part committee (T63); (tax1864).
Stewart, W. (R63)
Stewart, W. C. (M61)
Stewartson, R. R. (P61); (R63); cabin on W side of Mono between Brady and Adams property, of partner with Warner as owners of Antelope Restaurant on W side of Antelope (E64).
Stich, P. (M61)
Stilts, Ed S. (P61); (R62).
Stilwell, James (R63)
Stitt, E. S. (M61)
Stivich, John (M62)
Stonecliff, George, M. (P61); (R62).
Stonelipp, B. (R62)

Stonely, William S. (P61); (R62).
Stratton, George W. miner (E64); (R63).
Stuart, J. G. (P61); carpenter (R62); (R63).
Stuart, N. S. (R62)
Stuart, W. G. constable (R63)
Studley, John works at Winter's Mill (E64).
Stutts, P. (P61)
Su & Op (Chinamen?) S side of Pine (E64).
Suckett, A. W. (M62)
Sullivan, C. (M61)
Sullivan, E. (R63)
Sullivan, Florence (R63)
Sullivan, J. (R63)
Sullivan, J. H. (R63); wood house S side of Wide West (E64).
Sullivan, Thomas (R63)
Summer, William B. (P61)
Summers, Jessie (or John) N. (R62); (M62).
Sumnegan, Chas. (R63)
Surdum, [or spelled Surdam in (M61)] R. G. (R63).
Swart, L. O.[or A. per (M61)] (R62)
Sweedy, M. (R63)
Swenson, C. A. (M61)
Swift, S. H. (R63)
Swinson, C. (P61)
Syke, Peter (R63)

T
Tabor, J. D. (M61)
Tade house on S side of Wide West (E64).
Talbott, [or spelled Talbot per (M61)] C. (P61); (R62).
Talcot, E. P. (M61)
Tannawick, P. (R62)
Tanneyhill, [or spelled Tannihill in (M61)] G. J. (P61); (R62).
Tanneyhill, [or spelled Tannihill in (M61)] William (R62).
Taunsend, W. R. (P61)
Taylor, Cornelius (R63)
Taylor, E. O. (M61); (M62); two lots on S side of Wide West, one known as Willard House (E64).
Taylor, E. S. (R62); (M62).
Taylor, F. B. deputy (G84).
Taylor, F. J. miner (R62)
Taylor, J. R. (P61); (E62); (R62).
Taylor, L. (M61)
Taylor, L. R. (P61); (R62)

Residents of Aurora 1861-1864

Taylor, M. J. (R63)
Taylor, Mart (P61)
Taylor, S. B. (R63)
Taylor, T. (P61); (R62).
Taylor, T. J. (R63)
Taylor, Thomas (M61); (P61).
Taylor, W. K. (R63)
Teall, William E. (M61); (P61); member First Legislative Assembly Nevada Territory (R62).
Teas, W. M. (M61)
Tecton, T. W. (R62)
Teel, H. J. (P61); saloon-keeper (R62); (R63); (M61); (M62); elected Mono County Sheriff 9/2/63, then appointed Deputy Sheriff of Esmeralda Co. (N81); Captain of the Esmeralda Rangers (E62); of Teel & Wand's frame house with saloon on E side of Antelope (E64); on the Cotillion Party Committee (T63).
Teel, J. W. (R63)
Teene, Louis (P61)
Tehhe, Elser (R63)
Teitjehn, F. W. (M61)
Temple, William (R63)
Tenant, Jno. H. (R63)
Tennwich, P. (P61)
Thatcher, A. M. (P61); (R62); (R63).
Thayer, J. (M61)
Thayer, John (M61); (R63)
Thayer, W. (M61)
Thayer, William (P61); (R63)
Thom, Jame (P61)
Thomas, G. M. (R62)
Thomas, James (R63)
Thomas, William (R63)
Thompson, A. (M61)
Thompson, Andrew (M62)
Thompson, C. D. (P61); (M61); (R62).
Thompson, D. B. (M61)
Thompson, Geo. (R63)
Thompson, J. H. (P61)
Thompson, R. E. (R63)
Thorn, J. D. (M61); (P61); (R62).
Tildew, J. W. (M62)
Till, J. (M61)
Till, John (P61); (R63); lot on S side of Aurora, W of J.R. Jones Prop between Court and Bullion (E64).

Tillman, A. (R63); of (?)Tillman & Bros., house on Brinns lot SW corner of Pine and Winnemucca (E64).
Tilson, J. W. (M62)
Tilton, J. W. (M61); lots in town (E64).
Tilton, L. (R63)
Tilton, S. S. (P61); (R62); (R63)
Tinkham, H. A. (R62)
Tinkham, L. B. (M61); (R62).
Tolles, James R. (M62)
Tompkins, C. H. (R63)
Toombs, Jerry (P61); (R62)
Toomy, Jeremiah (M62)
Toukin, Elisa (R63)
Toukin, William (R63)
Toumey, D. D. (M61)
Toumey, Dan. (M61)
Toumey, Jer. (M61)
Tourney, Patrick (R63)
Townsend, W. R. (E62)
Tracy, Jno. (R63)
Traidall, M. F. (P61); (R62)
Trask, J. W. (R63)
Travers, Samuel (P61); (R62)
Travis, D. C. of (?) Travis & Crocker or Travis & Smith (E64).
Trenovich (spp?), N. (P61); (M61).
Trotter, Robert (M61); (R63).
Tryon, N. lot on N side of Spring W of Travis & Smith (E64).
Tswttes (spp?), Robert (P61)
Tucker, J. (P61)
Tucker, Samuel (M61)
Tucker, Stephen G. (M61); (P61); (M62); miner (R62); (R63); (E64) adobe house W side of Silver.
Tuma, Jerry lot on N side of Del Monte north of Mary Smith (E64).
Tuoney, Daniel (P61); (M62).
Turey, M. miner (R62)
Turner, F. (R63)
Turner, George County Judge (G84).
Turner, J. R. (R63)
Turner, Judge George assigned Judge of the Second District including Aurora, held dual court with Baldwin (N81), (G84).
Turner, S. (M61)
Tuttle, L. (M61); County Surveyor (R62).
Twing, Daniel H. (M62); mining partner with Samuel Clemens (G84).

199

An 1864 Directory and Guide to Nevada's Aurora

Tyler, Asa (P61)
Tyler, David (P61); (R62); (M61).
Tyler, H. (R62)
Tyler, Judge J. W. Justice of the Peace (R62); (M61); (M62); (R63); (G84); owned three or four lots and buildings (E64); lawyer (tax1864).
Tyler, William (R63)
Tyrell (N81) (G84)
Tyron, N. lot on E side of Winnemucca N of Mays prop., harness shop on E side of Winnemucca (E64).
Tysing Chinaman in Towels house on W side of Esmeralda (E64).

U

Uhlenger, [spelled Uhlmeyer in (M61)] Fred'k (R63); S side of Del Monte (E64).
Umbuster, M. (R63)
Underwood, J. C. (R63)
Underwood. H. A. (R63)
Uniac, Miss Emily liquors on E side of Antelope on Somers lot or in Orleans Rest. (E64).
Urn (spp?) J. C. (M61)

V

Valentine, E. H. (M61); (R62).
Valentine, Ed B. (P61); (R62).
Valer, A. saloon in Sommers bldg on N side of Pine (E64).
Van Dyke D. M. (R62)
Van Fliet (R63)
Van Horn, W. (M61)
Van Luren, Jno. (R63)
Van Luren, S. (R63)
Van Read, L. [likely same as Van Reed] mining (R62); (P61).
Van Reed, L. [likely same as Van Read] (M61); house on W side of Silver used as Mono Co. Recorder's Office (E64).
Van Slyke, W. M. P. (R62)
Van Tyne, John (E64)
Van Voorhies, William M. attorney (R63); attorney for Real Del Monte Company (G84); partner with Mesick (T63); on the Cotillion Party Committee (T63); (tax1864).
Van Wyck, Mrs. Sidney M. wife of Sidney Van Wyck.

Van Wyck, Sidney M. partner with Winchester in "Van Wyck & Winchester" (R63); (M61); assay office on Silver (E64); on the Cotillion Party Committee (T63).
Vance, S. (M61)
Vance, S. B. friend of Daly (G84).
Vanderdecker, Geo. (R63)
Vandusen, L. (M61)
Vanrankin, Benjamen miners cabin S side of Last Chance (E64).
Varmattoe, Geo P. (R63)
Vaughn, W. W. (M62)
Vaughn, W. W. N side of Wide West, west of B.S. Masons lot (E64).
Venny, P. (R62)
Vernon, John (G84)
Vernon, William (P61); (R62)
Vibbard, Col. Phillip G. (P61); miner (R62); (M62).
Vidu, D. R. (R63)
Viler, A. (R63)
Vinder, Otto liquors and cigars in Madame Clara's Saloon on Pine (E64).
Vinet, Peter (M62)
Vining, R. (M61)
Vitchenhausen, A (R63)

W

Wadell, Andrew cabin N side of Wide West (E64).
Wagener, Ted B. (M62)
Wagner, H. B. (M61); (P61); (E62); miner (R62).
Wahl, Joseph (M61); (M62).
Waitt, A. K. (R63)
Waitt, A. R. (R63)
Walker, E. (M61)
Walker, L. (R63)
Walker, W. G. (P61); miner (R62); (M61).
Wall, J. (R62)
Wallace, C. (R63)
Wallace, George T. (P61); (R62)
Wallace, James (E64)
Wallace, Jno. (R63)
Wallace, Milton (M61)
Walsh, R. (M61)
Walters, George (R63)
Walters, Jas. (R63)
Wand, P. H. (M61)
Wanel, P. H. (R63)

200

Residents of Aurora 1861-1864

Ward, E. (R63)
Ward, E. L. (R63)
Ward, J. E. (M61)
Ward, J. T. (R62)
Ward, Thos. (R63)
Ward, [see Wood, W. L.] W. L. (P61)
Wardell, Andrew (M62)
Wardell, J. T. (R63)
Wardell, Sol. (M61); (P61); (R62); (R63); (M62).
Warfield, (Major?) Samuel R. (P61); (M61); (R63); (M62); lot SW corner Court and Pine (E64).
Warin, S. W. (R63)
Warner, Ackley (R63)
Warner, Norton stone cabin N side of Del Monte, E of Court adjacent to Rich James prop on east (E64).
Warner, S. (M61); (P61); (R62).
Warrington, S. R. (R63)
Washburn, William (M62)
Waterman, C. R. (P61); (R62); of Waterman & Davis who owned lot on SE corner of Spring and
Waterman, W. F. (P61); (R62).
Waters, G. M. (E62); (R63); (M61).
Waters, R. (R63)
Watkins, W. F. (R62); (G84).
Watkins, Wm. T. (M61); (M62); (R63); miner with houses on Pine and NW corner Winnemucca and Del Monte (E64).
Watson, James (R62)
Watson, Robert (M61); (P61); (R63); cigar stand in saloon on S. Martin's lot on W side of Antelope (E64).
Watson, W. A. (R63)
Wau, P. H. (P61); miner (R62)
Way, W. G. (M61)
Wayman, Edward (R63)
Weaterall, William elected Senator on 1/19/64 but later rejected (N81).
Weber, M. (R63)
Webster, A. (M61)
Webster, James L. (M62)
Webster, Jos. (P61)
Weed, G. (?) O. (M61)
Welbourne, [or Welbourn per (M61)] L. C. (R63)
Weldsig, Evans (M62)

Wellington, D. elected Assemblymen on 11/8/64 (N81).
Wellington, G. E. (R63)
Wellington, Geo. (R63)
Wells, J. R. (P61); (R62)
Wells, S. (M61)
Weneger works for the Wide West Mining Co. (E64).
Wertby, G. (R62)
West, J. J. (R63)
Westfall, C. M. (M61); (P61); (R62).
Westlake, G. (M61)
Westlake, George C. (M62); cabin on lot in N Winnemucca (E64).
Westlick, Geo. (P61)
Weston, G. S. (R63)
Weston, M. W. (R63); works for the Wide West Mining Company (E64); (tax1864).
Wetherell, W. (M61)
Wethergreen, F. (R63)
Wethergreen, T. (R63)
Wetherill, Wm. (R63)
Wheaton, Charles E. H. killed by William Lake on 9/27/64 (G84).
Wheeler, A. D. (R63)
Wheeler, H. C. (P61); (R62); lot on E side of Silver (E64); (M62); (M61).
Wheeler, Lewis (R63)
Wheeler, N. (or H) C. four lots in town (E64).
Wheelock, [or possibly spelled Whilock in (M61)] R. P. (P61); (R62).
Whisper, J. (M61)
White, B. R. (R63)
White, C. (M61)
White, C. H. (R63)
White, Frederick (R63)
White, George (R63)
White, H. K. (R63); lot E side of Winnemucca, N of Mary Smith prop (E64); proprietor along with P. Mitchell of Merchants Exchange Hotel and on the Cotillion Party Committee (T63); (tax1864).
White, Henry (R63)
White, J. F. (M61)
White, J. R. (M61)
White, J. S. (R63)
White, John (R63); (M62).
White, Phillip house at mouth of Last Chance Tunnel (E64).

201

An 1864 Directory and Guide to Nevada's Aurora

White, Robert (R63)
White, W. (R63)
White, William (M62)
Whitehead, C. C. (M61)
Whitehead, James miner (E64).
Whiteside, Thomas in rear of Monroe House on side of hill (E64).
Whitman, G. W. (M61)
Whitman, P. N. (R63)
Whitney, E. (P61)
Whitney, G. E. (E62)
Whitney, George A. (P61); (E62); (R62); lot on W side of Winnemucca between Coddington and Denton (E64); elected Esmeralda County Commissioner 9/2/63 (N81); on the Cotillion Party Committee (T63); (tax1864).
Whitney, James (E62)
Whitney, W. (R63)
Whitney, W. C. (R63)
Wieswanger, Dan lime kiln near toll gate (E64).
Wilborne, S. lot on S side of Aurora between A. Hanke and A. McKills prop (E64).
Wilbourn, T. J. (M61)
Wilcox, Charles (R63)
Wilcox, T. J. [or J. J. per (M62)]; (M61); (P61); (R62); (R63); (E64) lot on W side of Silver N of Bannister's lot.
Wilder, E wood cabin west side of Silver (E64).
Wilder, E. wood cabin on lot on W side of Silver (E64).
Wildes, Frank lot S side of Wide West (E64).
Wilds, A. E. (P61); (R62); (R63)
Wilds, B. F. (M61); (P61); (E62); ranchman (R62); (M62).
Wiley, Moses (R63); owns Nine Mile Ranch (E64).
Wilkining, F lot N side of Pine west of Grank (E64).
Willhip, H. (R62)
Williams, A. B. (M61); (R63); (M62); carpenter of Williams & Waters in carpenter shop east side of Silver, cabin on lot E side of Silver (E64).
Williams, B. D. (R63)
Williams, Charles (R63)

Williams, David miner (E64); (R63).
Williams, E. (R63); wood bldg E side of Antelope south of Cases prop. (E64).
Williams, Elizabeth Daly Gang "favorite" (G84).
Williams, Frank gunfighter (G84).
Williams, H. P. (M61)
Williams, Henry (R63); (M62).
Williams, J. (R63); cigars in Exchange Saloon (E64); (tax1864).
Williams, O. J. lot on SE corner Mono and Del Monte (E64).
Williams, Thomas H. (P61); (R62); miner in cabin on lot north of Wide West and west of Nevada Tunnel Co. (E64).
Williamson, J. (M61)
Williamson, Jon. W. partner with Kearney (T63).
Williamson, Wm. (M61)
Wilson, Dr. William A. (P61); (M61); (R63); physician with office on Pine next door to Wells Fargo (E64).
Wilson, George A. (P61); (M61); (R62); (R63).
Wilson, John (R63); (M62).
Wilson, M. (R62); (R63).
Wilson, R. (M61)
Wilson, Richard M. Mono County Clerk (R62); (R63), (G84), elected Mono County Clerk on 6/1/61 (N81),
Wilson, Robert miner (E64).
Wilson, Samuel (R63)
Wilson, Thomas (R63)
Winchester, William Jr. Mining Stock Broker in partnership with Wm. L. Higgins of San Francisco (T63); lived in wood bldg west side of Roman also partner with Krauss in an assay office on Silver (E64).
Wind, Chas. (P61)
Wingate, A. M. merchant (R63); (M61); owned many lots and buildings including Wingate Hall on Pine, and Hoems Brickyard (E64).
Wingate, C. D. (M61); (P61); merchant (R62); (R63); owned many lots and buildings including Pioneer lumber yard on S side of Spring (E64); appointed Esmeralda County Commissioner on 6/22/63 (N81).
Winnegar, Lewis (R63)

Residents of Aurora 1861-1864

Winnemucca (E64); on the Cotillion Party Committee (T63).
Winston, E. L. (M61); (P61); (R62).
Winston, Mrs. (M62)
Winther, Charles (R63)
Wisw, A. B. (M61)
Witham, William (R63)
Wolverton, Levi (P61)
Wood, C. F. superintendent of the Real Del Monte Mine, on the Cotillion Party Committee (T63).
Wood, James T. (P61); (R63)
Wood, Louis (M61); (P61); (R63); (M62).
Wood, W. L. [see Ward, W. L.] (M61)
Woodbarn, James (P61); (R62); (M62).
Woodburn, P. (E62)
Woodbury, E. A. (R63)
Woodcliff, Thomas (R63); drug store in Sam Davis' bldg on west side of Antelope (E64).
Woodriff, Eliza "Lizzie" house on Aurora Street (G84)
Woodruff, John (M61); (R62); (M62).
Woods, S. H. (R63)
Worfield, D. B. miner (R62)
Worland, Charles R. elected Mono County Commissioner on 6/1/61 (N81).
Worthington, S. G. (M61)
Wright, Bill (M62)
Wright, Edward (R63)
Wright, J. A. (M61)
Wright, L. J. (R63)
Wright, S. B. (M61)
Wright, S. C. (R63)
Wright, Thomas (P61); (R62); (R63); cabin south side of Pine east of Gibbs lot (E64).
Wright, W. S. (R63)
Wyatt(e), William. J. (R63); north side of Pine east of Meades house, US Tunnel & Mining Co. (E64).
Wyseng, J. H. (R63); works for the Wide West Mining Company (E64).

Y
Yager, C. (M61); (R63).
Yager, W. L. (R63)
Yankers, George (R63)
Yarbrough, G. W. (P61)
Yeagar, [spelled Yeager in (G84) and (E64)] Reverend C. (R62).
Yeigh, John works at Winters Mill (E64).
Yeisher, Daniel (R63)
Young John G. cabin on hill west of J. Gary, N of Spring (E64).
Young, Henry (P61); (R62); (R63).
Young, M. P. (R63); works at Winters Mill, adobe house NE corner Cottonwood and Antelope (E64).
Young, S. (M61)
Young, Thos. A. (M61)
Youngs, Samuel Col. (P61); (M62); (E62); member First Legislative Assembly Nevada Territory (R62); miner (R63); owned cabin on Sage St. (E64); appointed (but declined) Esmeralda County Commissioner on 6/22/63, also appointed Esmeralda County Commissioner again on 4/11/64, elected Esmeralda County Commissioner on 9/7/64 (N81).

Z
Zealner, I (?) (M61)
Zevenirtz [or spelled Zenovich in (E64) and (M61)], Peter (R63); lot and cabin E. side of Winnemucca, SW corner Court Aurora (E64).
Zill, T. (R62)
Zimmer, Fred (P61)
Zine, W. O. N. (R63)

NOTES

Aurora's Bullion Production

The total bullion estimate of $2-3 million found on page 156 is based on the following accounts from the 1860s which discuss bullion shipments during the two years Aurora's important mines and mills were operating:

For 1863, only $625,000 in bullion was shipped by Wells, Fargo & Co. according to the January 16, 1864, issue of the *Mining and Scientific Press*.

During the last three months of 1863 and the first three months of 1864, only about a half a million dollars in bullion was shipped from Aurora by Wells, Fargo & Co. according to the Esmeralda County Grand Jury report of December 31, 1864, reprinted in the *History of Nevada, 1881*.

For 1864, only about a million dollars in bullion was shipped from all of Esmeralda County (including Aurora) according to J. Ross Browne's 1867 *Report on the Mineral Resources of States and Territories West of the Rocky Mtns*.

The McKeough Family in Aurora

The McKeoughs were well-known citizens in Aurora during the late 1800s and early 1900s. John and Julia McKeough owned a house on Spring Street and had a son named Walter in 1884. John died in 1904 and is buried in Aurora's cemetery. Walter was one of Aurora's last residents when he left the ghost town in 1939. He died in 1942 and is buried at Hawthorne, Nevada. Kenneth L. McKeough, Walter and Pauline's son, was born in Aurora in 1908.

BIBLIOGRAPHY

Books and Articles

Ackley, Mary Ellen. *Crossing the Plains and Early Days in California.* San Francisco, 1928.

Angel, Myron. *History of Nevada with Illustrations and Biographical Sketches of its Prominent Men and Pioneers.* Oakland, 1881.

Brewer, William H. *Up and Down California in 1860-1864.* New Haven, 1930.

Browne, J. Ross. "A Trip to Bodie Bluff and the Dead Sea of the West." *Harpers New Monthly Magazine,* 1865.

Davis, Sam. *History of Nevada.* Reno, 1913.

DeGroot, Henry. "Mining the Pacific Coast," *Overland Monthly,* 1871.

Esmeralda County Tax Roll for the Fiscal Year Ending May 1, 1864. Nevada Historical Society, Reno.

Guhm, Susan. "Doc and the Professor," Yosemite Association, Winter 1989.

Kelly, J. Wells. *First Directory of Nevada Territory.* San Francisco, 1862.

Kelly, J. Wells. *Second Directory of Nevada Territory.* San Francisco, 1863.

Kinchloe, Jessica. *"The Best the Market Affords": Food Consumption at the Merchants' Exchange Hotel, Aurora, Nevada.* MA University of Nevada, Reno, 2001.

King, Clarence. *Mountaineering in the Sierra Nevada.* Boston, 1872.

King, Joseph L. *History of the San Francisco Stock and Exchange Board.* San Francisco, 1910.

McGrath, Roger D. *Gunfighters, Highwaymen and Vigilantes.* Berkeley, 1984.

Murbarger, Nell. *Ghosts of the Glory Trail.* Reno, 1983.

Phillips, Michael J. "Mark Twain's Partner." *Saturday Evening Post,* 11 September 1920.

Shaw, Clifford Alpheus. "Mark Twain's Aurora Cabins," *Nevada Historical Society Quarterly,* 2003.

Shinn, Charles Howard. *The Story of the Mine.* New York, 1896.

Smith, Grant H. *The History of the Comstock Load 1850-1920.* Reno, 1943.

Stewart, Robert E. *Aurora Nevada's Ghost City of the Dawn.* Las Vegas, 2004.

———. *The Journal and Letters of Col. Samuel Youngs.* Carson City, 2009.

Torrence, C. W. *History of Masonry in Nevada.* Reno, 1944.

Twain, Mark. *Roughing It.* Hartford, 1872.

Wedertz, Frank S. *Bodie 1859-1900.* Bishop, California, 1969.

Manuscripts

Aurora Time Capsule. Nevada State Archives, Carson City.

"Origin of the 1st Baptist Church of Aurora, Esmeralda County, N. T. Nevada," March 4, 1864, American Baptist Historical Society, Atlanta, Georgia.

Bibliography

'Nevada's Plymouth Rock," Ruth Cornwall Woodman Papers, Special Collections and University Archives, University of Oregon, Eugene.

The Residents of Aurora 1861-1864 section is keyed to the following sources:

(M61) "A Correct list of the names of the voters polled at Aurora Mono Co State of California June 1st 1861," Mono County Museum Archives, Bridgeport, California.

(P61) List of voters polled at Aurora, August 31, 1861, courtesy of Robert E. Stewart.

(R62) Kelly, J. Wells. *First Directory of Nevada Territory.*

(R63) Kelly, J. Wells. *Second Directory of Nevada Territory.*

(E62) Esmeralda Rifle roster as of May 15, 1862, courtesy of Robert E. Stewart.

(M62) Mono County Tax Roll for the fiscal year ending March 2, 1863. Mono County Museum Archives, Bridgeport, California.

(T63) *Aurora Daily Times* (3 December, 1863). Mono County Museum Archives, Bridgeport, California.

(E64) Esmeralda County Tax Assessor's Roll for the fiscal year ending May 1, 1864. Nevada Historical Society, Reno.

(N81) Angel, Myron. *History of Nevada with Illustrations and Biographical Sketches of its Prominent Men and Pioneers.*

(G84) McGrath, Roger D. *Gunfighters, Highwaymen and Vigilantes.*

(tax1864) List of Aurora citizens and companies who paid federal income taxes in 1864.

An 1864 Directory and Guide to Nevada's Aurora

Aurora Newspaper List 1860-1864

ANNOTATED LIST OF NEWSPAPER ARTICLES ABOUT AURORA FROM 1860 THROUGH 1864

Note- Each date is keyed to a list of newspaper names starting on page 223. For example, the symbol "CA" after 9/14/60 refers to the San Francisco *Alta California*. Although the list includes just about all of the articles written about Aurora from California newspapers, it does not include many editions of Aurora's newspapers. See page 123 for the publication dates for Aurora's newspapers. The following editions of Californian newspapers are available for viewing on microfilm at the Californian State Library; Aurora's newspapers are available for viewing on microfilm at the Nevada State Library and Archives.

1860

9/14/60 CA- First mention of Esmeralda Dist. "Cory, Craly [sic] & Hicks" visit San Francisco.
9/21/60 CA Letter from Washoe, new silver wave at Esmeralda.
9/22/60 DE "Silver from Mono" Short note on value of ore sent from Esmeralda by George O. Snyder.
9/23/60 CA Trip through Walker's River Tributaries, Masonic, Indians
9/29/60 MD "Braly" Corey and Hicks discover Esmeralda Dist.
9/29/60 DE "Latest from the Mono Mines" from the Columbia Times of Sept 27th- mentions new strikes 30 miles east of Mono [i.e. Esmeralda].
10/4/60 DE about Esmeralda discovery in a letter written from Monoville on Sept 23rd.
10/7/60 CA about "Boda" [Bodie] and Mono Lake.
10/8/60 CA "The Mono Mines" by MONO about new Esmeralda Dist.
10/8/60 CA "Notes on a Trip Through Western Utah" about Monoville.
10/11/60 DE Short note "From Mono Mines" from Sonora Age of 10/6: excitement about "Esmeralda silver mines." Also says water from Walker River reached Monoville.
10/13/60 DE letter from "Camp Esmeralda, U.T. Oct 8th" possibly the first letter from Aurora, about 200 miners.
10/25/60 DE Short note "From Mono" from the Visalia Delta of 10/20 mentions rich silver leads at Esmeralda.
10/31/60 SD about specimens of Esmeralda ore arriving in Sacramento.
11/3/60 MS short Wide West mine report
11/3/60 MG Cleaver returns fro Esmeralda to Mariposa
11/6/60 SD from TE, two towns Esmeralda Aurora laid out by Clayton.
11/6/60 SD reprint of 11/3/60 TE article?
11/7/60 CA "The Mono Mines" New town called Aurora. Project afoot to bring water from West Walker River. Wide West mine ore $5100 to the ton.
11/10/60 DE Correspondent from Marysville Appeal from Esmeralda on 10/21 who has been on scene since the discovery says: 2 towns surveyed, canvas store, saloon, butcher shop, and stone Recorders office
11/10/60 UD complete reprint of 11/3/60 TE article.
11/13/60 MG From TE similar to 11/15/60 CA
11/15/60 CA From TE, Esmeralda and Aurora laid out, how lots were sold

209

11/15/60 DE Short note from the Placerville Democrat of 11/14 says: Nye's train from Esmeralda arrived here [Placerville] with ore from major Esmeralda leads and was shipped to San Francisco for smeltering.
11/15/60 DE short article about 2 new mining companies and who are the trustees including Alex gamble.
11/21/60 DE From Placerville Central Californian- only 10-12 left at Monoville, rich leads at Esmeralda.
11/22/60 SD "from *Silver Age*"- town, ledges, Mono road.
11/30/60 MS from Nevada Journal- ore, tunnels
12/4/60 DE Rich specimens from Wide West mine at Esmeralda assayed at $17,844 per ton.
12/10/60 DE The Nevada Transcript gives an account of the discovery and history of Esmeralda mostly furnished by John S. Mayhugh. Miners from Esmeralda have moved to the new town of Aurora. Many gentlemen from San Francisco have visited Esmeralda in the past few weeks.
12/12/60 DE A correspondent from the Tuolumne Courier writing from Esmeralda on 11/21 says: 2 towns here with 7-8 bldgs in one and 60 bldgs in the other. 200 people there.
12/12/60 WD county
12/14/60 MS rich ores
12/15/60 HM "as reported in TC, 11/21.."…"Two Towns here.." 200 pop, 60 bldgs
12/18/60 DE "The Esmeralda Mining Region" from the Nevada Transcript gives the history of discovery.
12/24/60 DE Letter from Washoe about Esmeralda.
12/27/60 DE "Washoe and Esmeralda Mines" Letter dated Dec 15th says 300 people there

1861

1/9/61 DE "The Mines of Western Utah" discusses Washoe, etc, and Esmeralda.
1/10/61 CA 400 men at Esmeralda Dist, 60-70 tents and huts,
1/13/61 CA rich specimens from Esmeralda
1/17/61 CA Short notice about incorporation of Wide West mine.
1/19/61 WD route from Visalia to Esmeralda and Coso
1/21/61 SD rush to Aurora
1/24/61 CA about Esmeralda
1/26/61 DE discusses roads to Esmeralda.
1/26/61 LA short article on need to improve road to Coso & Mono & Esmeralda from correspondence from Clayton.
2/1/61 DE Discusses incorporated mining companies by month. Alexander Gamble is a trustee in the Real del Monte, Antelope, and Consolidated Silver Hill, and Wide West.
2/2/61 WD Clayton map, diggings in CA
2/5/61 MG letter from Aurora dated 1/20/61- camp description, population 300-400, cold & snowing, citizens resolution on lots
2/6/61 DE "An Esmeralda Pack Train" of 55 mules led by Col Wingate (an old resident of Sacramento) & Brothers [i.e. CD Wingate] encamped at the Piazza at Sacramento on their way to Esmeralda. They intend to establish a trading post there.
2/10/61 CA 300 people in Aurora. Also breakdown on structures, businesses,
2/15/61 MS short article quoting Sacramento Bee.
2/16/61 LA short article on goods from LA to Coso & Esmeralda
3/6/61 DE 60 companies with $17 million in capital at Esmeralda. Mentions Alex Gamble.
3/8/61 DE Long article (one of the longest ever written) - "The Esmeralda Mining District" from correspondent letter dated 2/26: 800 population, 130 buildings with a dozen of lumber and the rest earth

Aurora Newspaper List 1860-1864

stone and logs, how town lots surveyed by Clayton were disposed, where lumber is located, abundant pinyon pine, roads,

3/8/61 CA "Letter from Esmeralda" dated 2/20/61- big article about life in Aurora. Pop-8-900, cost of living, Washoe and Esmeralda compared, how claims are recorder,

3/9/61 SD "Letter from Esmeralda District" dated 2/26/61- long article on influx of people to Aurora, businesses, roads, mines, business, 150 bldgs.

3/21/61 DE from letter dated 3/12/61- town, mines.

3/22/61 CA "Our Esmeralda Correspondence" dated 3/9/61- Long article all about Aurora, mining, ledges, population now 1200-1300.

3/23/61 DE Letter from Esmeralda dated 3/16- population 1300, values of claims, mines, mills, names of claims and Aurora Esmeralda Mono names.

3/30/61 MS Joshua Claytons map

3/30/61 MS Washoe and Esmeralda

4/?/61 GV Correspondent from Grass Valley writes from Aurora on 3/31/61- 500 ledges, 13,000 claims, 1,600 companies; town laid out by Clayton in Oct 1860; population 600; 200 houses/cabins/ includes list of businesses; prices of goods/lumber.

4/4/61 NT population was 200 over winter, 800 now. "unaccountable faith" in mines

4/6/61 LA short art on Esmeralda mines

4/6/61 MS mines, town, Esmeralda & Monoville deserted, weekly stage, Post Office established (article taken from Downeville's *Mt Messenger*)

4/8/61 SD objection by Tuolumne Co to Mono Co creation

4/14/61 CA about the new town, cost of provisions, Claytons toll rd,

4/25/61 DE From letter from Esmeralda to a friend in San Francisco dated 4/9: 1000 population, hotel called the Aurora House, 4 stores, etc.

4/27/61 WD letter from Aurora dated 4/11/61- Aurora has as many lots as Sacramento, county organization, 800-1200 population.

5/6/61 MS about Aurora; nearby Esmeralda Camp is "dead"

5/11/61 WD from letter by ORLANDO dated 4/13/61- county proposed, mines, Aurora.

5/15/61 DE letter from Aurora by D.S.L. dated 5/11/61- politics, loyalty to the Union.

5/18/61 WD "Mono Correspondence" by ORLANDO dated 5/2/61-,politics, county organized

5/22/61 CA short article- County of Mono, population about 600.

5/25/61 MS town, location, mines

5/30/61 WD from "POSEY" dated 5/13/61- mines

5/30/61 WD from "SELKIRK" dated 5/1/61- mines, 600 pop, 250 canvass bldgs,

6/1/61 DE "Letter from the Esmeralda Mines" from "DSL" an occasional correspondent dated 5/28: first mill showed up in town, huge 36' long American flag ordered and 98 foot pole erected.

6/1/61 MS present population 600

6/6/61 WD from "ORLANDO" dated 5/21/61- Visalians numerous in Aurora, elections, patriotism

6/8/61 MS short paragraph about Esmeralda Dist

6/8/61 DE from "D.S.L." dated 6/4/61- Union Mtg held, liberty pole erected, election held last Saturday, politics.

6/9/61 CA letter dated 6/9/61- about Union Mtg, election of Mono Co officers, New County judge.

6/14/61 NC letter dated 4/30/61- mines, The "New Esmeralda" is a lively little camp 4 miles east of Aurora.

6/14/61 DE Letter from Esmeralda Mines" from our own correspondent dated 6/10: 1200 in Aurora, 700 in Monoville, and 200-300 scattered around county. Green Culver & Jackson have first mill to start the 12th, "a local government at last" including names of officers.

6/16/61 CA from 5/21 Contra Costa Gazette- list of businesses, boulder removal, Visalia ladies,

6/21/61 SD letter dated 6/11/61- 200 bldg, population 800, 500 ledges, mentions possibility of shallow deposits, district laws

An 1864 Directory and Guide to Nevada's Aurora

6/22/61 MS San Francisco Bulletin's Correspondent from Aurora writes about ledges, also mentions correspondence in Napa Reporter.
6/25/61 SD letter dated 6/17/61 from Aurora by "D."- weather, rumor gold may be "confined to surface", wild cat claims, ledges, mills, growth of town, no bldgs yet made of brick.
6/25/61 CA from correspondent from the SD- people, town, mills
6/26/61 DE letter from Aurora dated 6/17/61- flag staff ceremony, 1400 population, politics, mining techniques, mills.
6/28/61 CA letter dated 6/20/61- "General Disappointment" about current slump, early "swindles," about ore, blind leads, mines, 'Bodey" [Bodie] district, to other nearby new mining districts.
6/29/61 MS letter dated 6/4/61- 1,300 population, list of businesses, mills, labor costs, Monoville.
6/29/61 MS Mono County population is 2,500, 1,400 in Aurora, 700 in Monoville, boulders on ground,
7/2/61 MG "Mono Correspondence" written by MARTEL dated 6/14/61- about mines, prices.
7/2/61 SD "Letter from Mono" by "D."- about mines, Monoville, population 600-700, travel routes to Aurora, work and wages.
7/6/61 MS "correspondent from Mariposa Gazette writes about mines.
7/6/61 DE "From the Esmeralda and Mono Mines" letter dated 6/28/61- geography of east sierras, describes following mining districts: Wright, Cornell, New Esmeralda, Van Horn, and White Mt Mining Dists. Also describes cattle at Smith/Mason valleys, Walker Lake described.
7/11/61 SD Union Mtg, politics
7/18/61 WD
7/19/61 DE "Explorations on the Eastern Slope of the Sierra Nevada" from our own correspondent from Vining's Creek dated July 9th- good description of Coso Mines, Mono Lake, Owens River and Valley, Owen's lake, Indians, and story of Farnsworth murder.
7/20/61 MS mining, mill,
7/20/61 TE "a correspondent of the Mariposa Gazette, writing from Aurora under recent date, says:" population 1200, "boulder companies," prices, lack of flour.
7/20/61 SA from Aurora dated 7/15/61- times are dull, politics
7/20/61 SA by CARL, about "Times are Dull" politics,
7/22/61 Marysville Express-
7/23/61 SD correspondent of the Union writing from Aurora on 7/18/61- ledges, waiting for mills
7/24/61 DE from the 7/18/61 WD- projected road to Mono/Esmeralda via Sonora pass
7/25/61 WD from Aurora 7/9/61 by POSEY- 4th July, plans to build mills on Mono Lake islands, one mill operating, competition between Esmeralda and Washoe.
8/1/61 DE correspondent from Aurora from the 7/22/61 *Marysville Express*- new placer diggings
8/1/61 WD one mill a failure; new strike at sink of Walkers River
8/3/61 MS mines, Wide West mine, ore
8/10/61 MS "correspondent from Marysville Express writes.." (presumably in 7/22/61 edition)
8/17/61 MS from TE- mines east of Aurora a humbug (possibly related to 8/1/61 article)
8/19/61 MS mines, ledges, mills, 1500 population, elections, bldgs of brick and stone.
8/27/61 SD politics
9/14/61 MS from the TC- about Monoville; and from the *Placerville Republican* about Aurora.
9/16/61 DE taken from a letter from Aurora dated 9/8/61 in *Placerville Democrat*: 3 mills in operation, Fleishman & Kaufman's new brick store will be finished soon.
9/21/61 CC
9/23/61 DE 12 mills "ready on the ground," two of which are owned by Clayton.
9/26/61 DE from 9/21/61 *Columbia Courier*- breakdown of businesses, prices, Indian problems.
10/11/61 DE from Aurora 10/4/61 by W.S.L.- mills, money, building,
10/16/61 MS about town and mines
10/18/61 from *Grass Valley National* from a letter by JSM from Aurora dated 10/2: 2 brick blds, lawyers Richardson and Chase have opened law offices, population 1,200, 84 ladies and 14 children,

Aurora Newspaper List 1860-1864

Masons and Odd Fellows organized, and 125 in the Temperance Society, 4 mills in operation, and surrounding "dreary, never-ending, scorched plains and bald and naked summits—the earth brown and burnt, as though a thousand years of scorching summer suns had never been succeeded by a single spring shower."

10/20/61 SD politics, Col Sam Youngs
10/21/61 CA correspondent from 9/21 *Columbia Courier* gives statistics of town.." list of business, prices, mentions 10 brickyards.
10/21/61 DE from 10/17 *Silver Age*: 4 mills operating, 5 new brick bldgs.
10/22/61 DE "Number I" "from our own correspondent'- history of Aurora to spring of 1861.
10/24/61 DE "Number II" "from our own correspondent" -description of leads,
10/25/61 DE from *Silver Age*- 300 buildings, 1000 population
10/28/61 DE from *Silver Age*- fences required for lots.
10/28/61 DE "Number III" "from our own correspondent"-about mills, cost of mining, 1500 population, mail, mills on Walker river, wealth is in many leads, Big Meadows, Monoville, competition with Washoe- "Esmeralda has had to contend with the power of several newspapers in Nevada Territory."
11/1/61 DE correspondent writes from Aurora on 10/21/61 in the *Silver Age*- lists brick buildings completed, mills, leads, miners building cabins, more quartz mining than anywhere else,
11/9/61 MS Moses mill
11/18/61 DE correspondent of the Grass Valley *National* writing from Aurora 10/2/61- town, buildings, business, prices, 4 mills operating.
12/4/61 NC from letter from Aurora 11/27- 14 mills only 3 running, Juniata, Wide West mine,
12/12/61 SA
12/18/61 DE from 12/12 *Silver Age*- soda deposit found by Teall [sic] & Harris used in extracting silver, coal from Bodie, average yielded of rock is $47.50, 8 mills operating, production of mills.
12/21/61 MS from our correspondent in Aurora 12/13/61- town, 5 mills operating.
12/28/61 MS many leave for holidays, new discoveries daily.
12/28/61 MA from the *Silver Age*- tunnel companies, union mill,
12/30/61 CA "Mining Enterprises in Esmeralda" Capt Johnson of Aurora informs the *Silver Age* about various mining companies' progress.

1862

1/1/62 SD mining corps formed in 1861- mentions Real De Monte, Antelope, Wide West, Bullion,
1/2/62 DE letter from Aurora 12/25/61- climate, fuel wood, coal, lumber, mills,
1/8/62 DE from Aurora 12/29/61 by C.H.D.- mines and mills described.
1/11/62 MS now has 10-12 brick bldgs, mines, mills in operation is 7,production
1/11/62 DE 300 bldgs, 1200 population, 4 mills reducing 40-50 tons daily, $25 to crush rock, prices, 14,000 ledges, 2,000 companies, 250,000 feet of mining ground.
2/1/62 DE major floods in Aurora, much damage, mills and their production.
2/12/62 DE from Aurora 1/30/62 by C.H.D.- major storm in Aurora, damage described, Union mill,
2/22/62 DE from *Silver Age* of 2/16- lists the mills in operation.
2/22/62 CA Letter from Esmeralda dated 2/22/62 by QUARTZ. storms, floods, mines, mills,
2/22/62 MA from 2/16 *Silver Age*- mills in operation,
3/1/62 MS from Aurora dated 2/16/62 by ARGUS.- some brick bldgs, Pinyon, Mines
3/16/62 MS Map of Esmeralda by Brady completed
3/21/62 DE "Claim of Nevada for a slice of California"- letter from Gov Nye to CA legislature.
3/26/62 DE from Aurora 3/18/62 by C.H.D.- Indian wars in Owens valley described.
3/28/62 DE from Aurora 3/15/62 by C.H.D.- weather, prices, Clayton's process, Union mill,
4/2/62 DE H.W. Bagley from Aurora describes Indian troubles

An 1864 Directory and Guide to Nevada's Aurora

4/2/62 DE by G.H.M.- Owens river & lake, Digger Indians, Coso mines, prices and route from LA to Aurora,
4/2/62 DE Correspondent from the Tuolumne Courier from Aurora on 3/10 discusses shooting.
4/5/62 MD- Indian troubles; Clayton and trouble with mills; Wide West mine lead yields $40/ton; coal found.
4/9/62 MS H.W. Bagley writing from Aurora on 3/15- Moses mill started-20 tons/day
4/9/62 MS from 3/15/62 letter in *Silver Age*- ledges.
4/13/62 Letter from Samuel Clemens (Mark Twain) residing in Aurora
4/16/62 CA from 4/11 *Silver Age*- mines, no flour
4/16/62 DE from *Silver Age* and TE- lack of food, Esmeralda Rifles formed Capt Teel, Clayton, Humboldt, Piutes & wood.
4/18/62 MD- from Aurora Times- list of mines, including Wide West mine and Del Monte, and what they are doing
4/22/62 SD Letter from Esmeralda dated 4/13/62 by Vox Populi- Gebhart shot, Owens River Indian war
4/24/62 Letter from Samuel Clemens (Mark Twain) residing in Aurora
4/25/62 DE from TE and *Silver Age*- about Indian war, and from Mr. Bagley 6 mills running day and night,
4/28/62 Letter from Samuel Clemens (Mark Twain) residing in Aurora
4/30/62 DE from Bagley in Aurora- 5 mills in operation, Indian trouble
5/4/62 Letter from Samuel Clemens (Mark Twain) residing in Aurora
5/6/62 DE from Aurora 4/28/62- "Another Indian War Ended," prices, 4 mills in operation, Gebhart shot, business dull, Monoville active.
5/8/62 MS from Bagley in the *Silver Age*- Clayton process, Gebhart shot, 6 mills running day & night, 6 days/wk.
5/11/62 Letter from Samuel Clemens (Mark Twain) residing in Aurora
5/13/62 DE letter from Aurora dated 5/5/62- mines claims, mills do not save metals.
5/17/62 Letter from Samuel Clemens (Mark Twain) residing in Aurora
5/17/62 ES first ES, printed in Molineux bldg
5/21/62 DE "From the Esmeralda Region" from an occasional correspondent "DSL" dated 5/14/62- mining operations, Indian troubles in Owens Valley, printing press has arrived, Grand Jury in session, no amusements, and one complaint- the "wretched postal and express facilities."
5/22/62 SD from letter from Aurora dated 5/10/62- all about Owens Valley Indian War.
5/26/62 CA from 5/17/62 ES- Indians,
5/29/62 DE from Aurora 5/25/62- food scarce, water running in streets
5/30/62 DE "East Walker Mines" from Sierra [Silver] Age of 5/24.
5/31/62 ES Wide West mine
6/2/62 Letter from Samuel Clemens (Mark Twain) residing in Aurora
6/3/62 CA from Sonora *Courier* by Z. B. Tinkum- mills, lumber
6/5/62 DE "Starvation in Esmeralda" "Men too Weak to Work"
6/5/62 DE from Aurora 5/31/62 by NEMO- mines, Wide West mine in 55 & 75', other veins.
6/6/62 SB letter from Aurora 5/30- want of flour and other necessaries.
6/9/62 Letter from Samuel Clemens (Mark Twain) residing in Aurora
6/9/62 DE from 5/31 ES- Indians in Owens Valley.
6/11/62 DE flour arrives but still short.
6/12/62 HM recent letter from Esmeralda about Wide West mine, Esmeralda lead.
6/14/62 HM from ES- about various leads
6/21/62 MS from ES- veins, coal found
6/22/62 Letter from Samuel Clemens (Mark Twain) residing in Aurora
6/23/62 DE from Stockton Independent- coal discovered, Pioneer Mill and Clayton's mills discussed,
6/23/62 CA from ES- Coal found

Aurora Newspaper List 1860-1864

6/23/62 CA From 6/16 ES- mines, Pride of Utah mine, Gibbons mill going
6/25/62 Letter from Samuel Clemens (Mark Twain) residing in Aurora
6/24/62 DE from Esmeralda Star- coal discovered and the "Cumberland Coal Mining Dist" formed and Father Yager was appointed Secretary.
6/25/62 SD from 6/21 ES- mines, mining companies.
7/2/62 DE from 6/21 ES- Owens route open, beef comes this way, Indians
7/2/62 MS Mines
7/2/62 SB from Aurora 6/23/62 by VENI, VIDI.- describes trip to Aurora, describes mines.
7/8/62 MS Mines, Wide West mine, Pride of Utah, Johnson
7/9/62 Letter from Samuel Clemens (Mark Twain) residing in Aurora
7/12/62 DE by "W. S. H" (?)- coal recently discovered may be finest on the coast, Van Horn district is 8 or 9 miles from Aurora accessed by a good wagon road.
7/12/62 SB from Aurora 7/3/62 by VENI, VIDI.- Wide West mine, cement mine, politics
7/21/62 SB from Aurora 7/13/62 by VENI, VIDI.- 4th of July celebration described in detail, Wide West mine, coal mines, Cambridge dist., mines on E Walker, Wide West mine down 60 feet and found it "rich beyond anything yet tried in the district."
7/22/62 SD from 7/20 TE from a correspondent (likely Samuel Clemens) from Aurora on 7/13/62- Johnson's ledge, Pride of Utah mine, Wide West mine,
7/22/62 DE letter from Aurora dated 7/13/62- warfare between Wide West mine and Pride of Utah mine; also brick making, and news from Owens River area.
7/23/62 Letter from Samuel Clemens (Mark Twain) residing in Aurora
7/26/62 NC from ES- 2000 population, 681 occupied dwellings, business breakdown, 10 mills.
7/30/62 Letter from Samuel Clemens (Mark Twain) residing in Aurora
7/31/62 MS Wide West mine
8/1/62 CA from *Silver Age*- "Affairs at Aurora- correspondent from the Carson Age [likely Samuel Clemens] writes thus from Aurora under date of 25th [July]" about town.
8/1/62 SB from Aurora 7/28/62 by VENI, VIDI.- politics, cement mine, Teels Marsh mined for salt
8/1/62 CA "Wealth of Esmeralda" about Wide West Pride of Utah mines
8/3/62 CA "Wealth of Esmeralda"- Wide West mine, Pride of Utah mine,
8/4/62 DE from ES- pop 2000, breakdown of business,
8/7/62 Letter from Samuel Clemens (Mark Twain) residing in Aurora.
8/11/62 DE from the *Esmeralda Star* [same as 8/11/62 DE]- population is 2,000, list of businesses.
8/13/62 DE from 8/10 *Silver Age*- Aurora in NV per Kidder & Ives Survey, no more 2 elections & legislatures.
8/14/62 MS from ES- mines.
8/14/62 DE from *Silver Age* of 8/10: "The Eastern Boundary Question—Aurora Claimed to be in Nevada Territory" established by Kidder and Ives.
8/15/62 Letter from Samuel Clemens (Mark Twain) residing in Aurora
8/20/62 DE Chorpenning dies
8/20/62 CA Chorpenning dead, rich rock from Rio del Monte
8/20/62 SB from Aurora 8/13/62 by VENI, VIDI.- Dr Chorpenning funeral, beauty of area, arrival of stage.
8/25/62 CA Letter from Esmeralda by QUARTZ LEDGE- boundary line, arrest of a "Secesh,' Pooler who shot Corpenning in jail.
9/6/62 SB from Aurora 9/3/62 by VENI, VIDI.- politics
9/7/62 CA "A Trip to Esmeralda" letter dated 8/28/62 from Aurora by J.M.O. Arrives from San Francisco, visits Wide West mine which is the "richest mine in the world."
9/9/62 Letter from Samuel Clemens (Mark Twain) residing in Aurora
9/10/62 CA letter from Aurora 8/25/62 by J.STOUT.- Van Horn Dist, Walker River Dist
9/11/62 MS gold worth $12 per oz, telegraph, mines, also Wide West mine stock bids $450

An 1864 Directory and Guide to Nevada's Aurora

9/16/62 CA from Aurora 9/10/62 by Z.B.- mines.
9/18/62 SB from Aurora 9/15/62 by VENI, VIDI.- snow, strangers in camp.
9/23/62 SD from Aurora 9/19/62 by Col Samuel Youngs (his first correspondence to the SD)- Sherman shot, Wide West mine & Johnson case in court.
9/23/62 SD another correspondent from Aurora- Sherman
9/23/62 DE from 9/19/62 *Silver Age*- Walker River timber and ranches described.
10/7/62 MS Esmeralda stock quotes
10/9/62 MS Wide West mine stock quote
10/10/62 SB from Aurora 10/7/62 by VENI, VIDI- politics, telegraph, Wide West mine, coal mines discovered.
10/27/62 CA from Aurora 10/19/62 by H.S.- Johnson, Wide West mine, Pride of Utah mine, stocks mentioned, Middle Hill, Silver Hill, relocating claims, Esmeralda Rifles.
10/29/62 CA "Affairs in Aurora" 9 mills in district, 200 miners, $4/day, economics of milling discussed, other info about Aurora.
11/7/62 CA letter from Aurora 10/17/62 by A.J.- discusses various mines, Wide West mine is building a mill.
11/10/62 CA letter from Aurora 11/1/62 by Z- 150 families, population 1800-2000, mines, Wide West mine erecting mill,
11/12/62 DE letter from Aurora 11/7/62 by E.F.G.- 300 bldgs, view from Mt Brawley, mines, no pines left on hills, people of town, bad water.
11/14/62 CA letter from Aurora 11/6/62 by PIONEER- many of new buildings, richest mining area discovered, problems with mills.
11/16/62 CA Wide West mine suit settled, Wide West mine stockholders receive 400 ft of Johnson etc.
11/17/62 SD letter from Aurora 11/10/62 Wide West mine
11/18/62 CA letter from Aurora 11/11/62 by PIONEER- story of prospectors flocking to Aurora, Wide West mine mining.
11/19/62 CA 2 articles both from ES of the 15th- "Wide West mine New Mill" and Wide West mine and Johnson settles legal cases.
12/6/62 MS Wide West mine stock is quoted at $405 per share, improved $20 during the week.
12/11/63 CA "Letter from Esmeralda" from "LILY-DALE (Resident Alta Correspondent) dated 11/30/62- About winter, history of Bodie Mines, Wide West mine, Magdalena Ledge, Crittenden ledge.
12/14/62 CA from Aurora 12/8/62 by PIONEER- mills, new discoveries, Ball of Esmeralda Rangers, Mining Matters, Boundary Question.
12/20/62 SD ES- Alturas ledge, Johnson lode
12/20/62 MS notice that Zenobia claims Johnson ledge.
12/27/62 CA from the ES of 12/20/62- detailed tour of Wide West mine, Pride of Utah, and Johnson.
12/29/62 MS Esmeralda stock quotes
12/31/62 DE letter from Aurora dated 12/22/62 by SAHAB about "Feet," and the "Wide West"- humorous letter about "feet"; milk comes from Nine Mile ranch, and "we want a mint."

1863

1/1/63 SD list of Mining corporations formed in 1862
1/1/63 CA from Aurora 12/20/62 by KESEPH- improvements in town, mines, Festival of the Pilgrims, firemen.
1/1/63 CA survey of Wagon RD Big Oak Flat to Aurora
1/3/63 MA from Aurora 12/28/62 by CHOYNO- pop- 1200, freedom 6,000 claims, prices.
1/5/63? MS Wide West stock $265 to 290, "new stock consolidated with Johnson Co."
1/5/63 SD

Aurora Newspaper List 1860-1864

1/6/63 from letter dated 12/28 from Aurora in the MA- 6000 claims and Wide West mine Antelope and Esmeralda take the lead.
1/6/63 DE complete list of San Francisco mining companies with may from Esmeralda and the Van Horn Mining Dist.
1/8/63 DE 8 mills operating in Feb, yield of rock, East walker River dist,
1/12/63 MS about mines, Wide West mine, mills
1/13/63 DE "A Stock Exchange of Supposed 'Experts' at Esmeralda" Esmeralda Stock Exchange Board formed.
1/13/63 CA FROM aurora 1/1/63 by XYZ- "above all ranks the Wide West mine," mills
1/15/63 DE from Aurora 1/7/63 by PIONEER- about mills, Dimes injunction, and how Esmeralda is becoming the 'foremost' mining district.
1/16/63 CA by J. W. Tucker- "A pioneer Mining Shark," response to 1/15/63 DE, Wide West mine, Dimes injunction.
1/17/63 DE short article about quartz from Wide West mine crushed at San Francisco at $1200 per ton.
1/19/63 MS Dimes and Wide West mine injunction
1/19/63 MS "Esmeralda stocks appear to be attracting much more attention" Wide West mine stock $415 to 350, "Wide West mine rapidly advancing to the rank of first class mine" and new Aurora Stock Exchange
1/21/63 CA from Aurora 1/12/63 by X.Y.Z.- mines, Wide West mine, Esmeralda Rifles.
1/22/63 DE "The Winter of Our Discontent" from an Occasional Correspondent "SAHAB" letter dated 1/13: 6 hills of Aurora described, news from Bodie, money worth 10% per month on the best collateral.
1/25/63 CA from Aurora 1/18/63 by KESEPH- Esmeralda stocks going up, reason for rise in stocks (Nevada Incorporation bill), J. W. Tucker "has more feet than any other man," also 'Mail Matters.'
1/26/63 MS recently established stock exchange board
1/26/63 MS .stock quotes, lots of interest, Wide West mine injunction with Dimes,
1/28/63 DE letter from "D." dated 1/17. Misc items.
2/1/63 CA "Our Letter From Aurora" dated 1/27 by "PIONEER" Wide West mine is "Ophir" of the district. Wide West mine mill is nearly complete.
2/2/63 MS considerable interest in stocks, heavy trading in Wide West mine causing decline.
2/3/63 CA "The Brodie [sic] Dist"
2/3/63 CA from Aurora [no date] by X.Y.Z.-"Everyone is daft," coated gentry, Nabobs, Wide West mine, get fat rich, old miners, new arrivals,
2/3/63 DE from Aurora on 1/24/63 by SAHAB- Sherman duel, Bamboo strike, Dimes injunction, 6000 claims- too many to name.
2/7/63 DE letter from SAHAB at Aurora dated 1/31: "The Feet 'Still Marching On'" Feet mania is on the increase. "More Room for Lawyers" "fine time for lawyers."
2/9/63 MS "Esmeralda Correspondence" dated 1/30/63 – feature article about mines, Johnson lead
2/11/63 CA from Aurora 2/3/63 by KESEPH- mines
2/12/63 DE About the "The Esmeralda Rifles" from the Sacramento Union of 2/5: 55 members built an armory for $3400 and $3000 in uniforms at their own expense.
2/14/63 DE letter from Esmeralda by SAHAB dated 2/8: "The Greatest Strike Yet" new discovery at the "New Esmeralda" 2 ½ miles from town.
2/16/63 MS 2 post offices, Bodie,
2/17/63 DE from Aurora 2/11/63 by D.- about mines, mills, and Bodie.
2/23/63 MS stock list
2/21/63 CA Letter from "Doctor" dated Feb 12- Last Chance Hill is in its glory, 10 mills running.
2/28/63 CA Items from Esmeralda mines per 2/21 ES
3/2/63 MS Aurora stock list
3/3/63 CA Clemons Gold and Silver Mining Co, and Annapolitan Mining Co. incorporated
3/8/63 CA from Aurora 2/28/63 by J.P.R.- politics, Wide West mine, Pond mine.

An 1864 Directory and Guide to Nevada's Aurora

3/9/63 MS Stock quotes, Wide West mine up to $500 per share briefly.
3/12/63 CA from Aurora 3/3/63 by DOCTOR- coal, mining, silver mines Walker River
3/14/63 CA "First Impressions of Esmeralda" from Aurora 3/5/63 by PHOENIX, JR.- Boundary question, arrival of stage, mail, dog fighting, mines, written in a humorous tone.
3/16/63 MS stock quotes-Wide West mine$380-385,Dashaway Co formed
3/18/63 CA "Phoenix Jr.'s Impressions of Esmeralda- (No. 2)" from Aurora 3/11/63 by PHOENIX, JR.- evil rum causes death, weather, mines not as good as Washoe.
3/19/63 SD Wide West mine
3/21/63 CA from Aurora 2/12/63 by DOCTOR- 10 mills running, jobs available
3/21/63 SD Wide West mine
3/23/63 MS complete list of mining co with office in San Francisco, "from 3/14 ES... about mines, also miners wanted, $4.50 wages"
3/28/63 CA from Aurora 3/27/63 by BRITON.- mines, Wide West mine.
4/1/63 CA from Aurora 3/24/63 by TRAVELLER.- Boundary, mines,
4/1/63 CA from Sacramento 3/31/63- "The Eastern Boundary" about survey
4/4/63 DE from Aurora on 3/28/63 by INDEX- mills, mines, want of a place to stay, Esmeralda Rifles.
4/9/63 MS Moses mill
4/10/63 CA from 4/4 ES, about mines
4/13/63 MS Esmeralda stock list
4/16/63 CA from Aurora 3/9/63 by TRAVELER.- "Will they never stop coming here?" Bodie, mines, Wide West mine mill, big influx of people.
4/17/63 DE from Aurora 4/13/63 by INDEX- 'rush for feet," influx of people, mills and mining, new Wide West mine mill has started, litigation, town improving, politics.
4/18/63 MD Discusses status of mines and some mills by name.
4/20/63 MS mines, mills including Wide West mine, Report of Stock sales, Wide West mine stock $377 to 300, big decline in Wide West mine stock caused by assessment of $50 per share.
4/20/63 SD from Aurora 4/12/63 by ?- mania for tunnels, Aurora Water Co's new tunnel
4/24/63 DE from an occasional correspondent "G" letter dated 4/15: influx of strangers is astonishing with 3000 in town.
4/24/63 DE from an occasional correspondent "INDEX" letter dated 4/15: misc info on mines, rush still continues- the "Concord coaches rattle in every evening," and all goes "merry as a marriage bell."
4/24/63 SD from ES- NV too fast in claiming Esmeralda is in NV
4/27/63 MS Esmeralda stock quotes
4/29/63 CA from Aurora 4/24 by J.S.M.- Every hotel and lodging house full, good town description, town lots now sell for $2,500 to $3,000, mines.
4/30/63 SD Stanford tunnel
5/1/63 DE from Aurora 4/22/63 by INDEX- bad weather, litigation, stock price manipulation, mines.
5/4/63 DE from Aurora 4/20/63 by L'ARGENT- rapid rise in population, no housing, bad weather, Indian difficulties, mines, Sheriff Scott burial.
5/4/63 MS Report of Esmeralda Stock sales, "Wide West mine not yet recovered from unexpected assessment, Wide West mine $375
5/5/63 DE from Aurora 4/27/63 by INDEX- Wide West mine assessment of $150,000, other mines, "crowded streets & saloons" like 'palmy days of 49-50,' many San Francisco in town
5/8/63 CA Leroy Vining shots himself, mumps in town.
5/9/63 DE from a correspondent in Aurora's letter dated 5/4: over 3,000 in town, 14 stores, 26 saloons, 3 hotels, 16 lawyers, etc, etc. and "Lord only knows how many brokers and jayhawkers—your correspondent could not count them." There are more traitors and rebels than 17 horses could draw."
5/9/63 MF Leroy Vining dies in Aurora.
5/11/63 MS Esmeralda stock quotes

218

Aurora Newspaper List 1860-1864

5/13/63 CA from Aurora 5/7 by J.S.M.- Wide West mine mill," why the stock is not worth $1000. .", "mines are now exciting considerable interest."
5/16/63 CA from Aurora 5/12/63 by J.S.M.- Wide West mine mill, general description of area.
5/18/63 MS Wide West mine stock sales, Wide West mine $350 to 300
5/20/63 CA Eastern slope description
5/21/63 DE from Aurora 5/17/63 by SAHAB- now a city full of people from every section, homicide, jumping of lots, mines, Wide West mine is the mother of the district,
5/21/63 DE from the Stockton Independent: road contemplated from Sonora to Aurora, population 4,000
5/25/63 CA from Aurora 5/18/63 by BULLY FOR U.- people, mines, Wide West mine, "what a country what a people" hints of problems
5/26/63 DE letter from Esmeralda dated 5/21 by "A FORTY NINER" (?) "Flush Times of a Mining Town" describes the many tunnels, discusses "where is the bullion?"
5/26/63 CA from Aurora 5/20/63 by J.S.M.- making brick, mines, Wide West mine," don't come unless you are prepared"
5/28/63 DE letter from SAHAB dated 5/24: "Sunday in the Silver Mines," claims on Last Chance Hill described,
5/29/63 CA from Aurora 5/16/63 by P.J.R.- decline of stocks, Wide West mine problems, at Del Monte mine "no shaft below 150 ft", very few leaving, population doubled in last 2 months.
5/30/63 CA "Traveler Redivivus [reborn]" by TRAVELER author humorously rambles about why he has not written in a while but little about Aurora.
6/1/63 MS Report of Esmeralda Stock sales, Wide West mine $320 to 300
6/3/63 DE from Aurora 5/31/63 by ARGUS- mines and mills, election for District Recorder, immigration unabated, abundance of roughs.
6/6/63 DE letter from SAHAB dated 6/2: "Election Day," election for District Recorder- Moffatt won. Silver Hill described.
6/10/63 CA all about telegraph arriving at Aurora.
6/15/63 CA from Aurora 6/16/63 by TRAVELER- telegraph, the mines, stock problems, "jay hawkers"
6/15/63 MS Report of Esmeralda Stock sales, Wide West mine $190 to 208
6/16/63 CA "Letter from Esmeralda" by "J.M.C. dated June 4th- 12 mills in operation, Wide West mine is enveloped in some sort of "mystery"?
6/18/63 DE from Aurora 6/14/63 by SAHAB- telegraph. Middle Hill, mines, mills,
6/21/63 CA from Aurora 6/5/63 by J.G.W.- mines
7/9/63 DE letter dated 7/3 from TRAVELER: building is going on in earnest, the Sonora Pass road should open this year—long overdue.
7/12/63 CA from Aurora 7/3/63 by TRAVELER- problems with mines, stock, why Wide West mine failed
7/17/63 DE Esmeralda Star of 7/11 says: sacristy of money, wildcat speculation.
7/20/63 MS Stock problems, Wide West mine, reasons for decline.
7/29/63 SD "The Daily Union" funeral of Mrs. Glen and her three children.
7/31/63 DE from Aurora 7/24/63 by VOYAGEUR- new hotel, mines, Wide West mine is only a second class mine, mills charge $25/ton is a problem
8/5/63 CA from Aurora 7/30/63 by NIMJA- all about Del Monte mine.
8/6/63 SD from Aurora 8/1/63- about climate, citizen's health, town.
8/12/63 CA from Aurora 8/7/63 by J.S.M.- Gold at $26, Wide West mine, population 4000, 47 brick bldg since 4/1, Baptist Church, Bodie District.
8/13/63 SD from Aurora 8/7/63 - politics, bullion credited to Washoe
8/17/63 DE from Aurora 8/12/63 by INDEX- mines, stock, Wide West mine is not a second class stock "more capitol has come to area than anywhere" Aurora is crowded.
8/21/63 CA 10 mills running," last chance hill in its glory"
8/22/63 DE from ES of 8/18-bloodshed at Esmeralda, violence on increase

219

An 1864 Directory and Guide to Nevada's Aurora

8/24/63 MS tunnels, ledges, Coffee's Foundry nearly complete.
8/26/63 CA from Aurora 8/18/63 by VERITAS- drawbacks of mines (lengthy discussion), shipment of bullion in August, litigation, Del Monte.
8/27/63 DE from Aurora 8/20/63 by INDEX- we have a dearth of good mills, population decreased in last few months.
8/29/63 SD Del Monte
8/29/63 DE letter dated 8/27 from INDEX: town's anger over the Pond injunction,
8/31/63 MS Del Monte,
9/4/63 CA from Aurora 8/31/63 by J.S.M.- buildings, 3500 population, brickyards, "Health of Aurora" with list of people shot in Aurora, Wide West mine tunnel and mill, Del Monte mill description.
9/7/63 MS Del Monte mine and mill
9/10/63 SD from Aurora 9/5/63 - politics, 300 men out of work cause of injunction
9/13/63 CA from Aurora 9/6/63 by TENNESSEE: Litigation.
9/16/63 VE theory on dull times (from Aurora Times)
9/19/63 DE from 9/15 AT- Survey nears Aurora, problems of converting to NV.
9/25/63 SD Del Monte, Wide West mine
9/25/63 DE the Aurora Times of 9/17 says: Real del Monte and Pond are back to work not because it was settled but because of the boundary survey.
9/26/63 DE from Aurora 9/24/63 by INDEX- boundary settled, miners go back to work, Bodie
9/28/63 MS suffering from law suits, new mills going up.
9/30/63 ST by "L. L." letter 9/19/63- Sonora Rd survey completed, town impression, mills, mines, fuel water, new county seat. Bodie mill is owned by JW Tucker, jeweler from San Francisco
9/30/63 CA from Aurora 9/24/63 by NIMJA.- survey completed, "Anomalous State of Affairs", Pond and Del Monte companies,
10/2/63 CA Letter from Esmeralda by JWE. Mining prospects, water proposed to go to Aurora from Twin Lakes.
10/4/63 CA "Our Letter from Esmeralda" dated 9/28 by DOCTOR. Mines, discusses new brick buildings and courthouse.
10/5/63 MS Esmeralda stock quotes
10/6/63 DE from 9/28 AT- shootings, reign of terror
10/6/63 CA from Aurora 9/27/63 by X.X.X.- citizens leaving, mines, Reign of Terror
10/7/63 DE Aurora Times says: about the mines and mills going back to work again.
10/7/63 CA "Our Letter from Esmeralda" by ? About new brick bldgs- hotel, Courthouse, etc. Wide West is a "fifth rate claim"
10/8/63 SD Duel at Aurora.
10/12/63 SD Duel at Aurora.
10/14/63 DE from Aurora 10/10/63 by S.- About Wide West mine, Del Monte best claim in Dist, new Durand mill coming.
10/15/63 CA "A Mining Decision" (Del Monte vs. Pond) from CA Supreme court
10/15/63 CA legal aspects of new NV/CA boundary line near Aurora
10/15/63 CA duel, Esmeralda court now in session
10/15/63 AF Eichelroth-Draper Duel, new Merchants Exchange hotel opens, Judge Turner opens court in Aurora, Esmeralda rangers return to Aurora,
10/21/63 SD Armory hall used for many things. Judge Turner, Grand Jury report.
10/25/63 AF by MONO- Judge Turner swears in lawyers at Armory Hall, Sonora/Mono Wagon Rd. Also info by JSM- population 3500, 700 houses, 47 which are brick, description of business and mills in Aurora (see 4/29/63 CA for JSM's earlier business/population breakdown)
10/28/63 CA from Aurora 10/21/63 by LAGRANGE- mines, Wide West mine and Del Monte mine.
10/30/63 GH from AT- crime wave.
10/30/63 SD "Aurora Matters."

Aurora Newspaper List 1860-1864

10/31/63 CA from Aurora 10/20/63 by NIMJA- humorous retrospective on history of mines, the present and future of the mines.
10/25/63 AF by MONO
11/2/63 MS mines and mills
11/5/63 AF by "C." Saw mills, Big Meadows [Bridgeport] stamp mills, water, hotels,
11/30/63 MS reasons for decline, Wide West mine
12/3/63 DE The "Lake Water Company" will develop a 36 mile long water ditch starting 1000 feet above Aurora from the Walker River. It has already been completed to Monoville.
12/11/63 CA from Aurora 11/30/63 by LILY-DALE- History of the Bodie mines, Wide West mine, other mines.
12/13/63 TE politics

1864

1/8/64 VD Aurora Items
1/9/64 VD Esmeralda Items
1/16/64 MS bullion shipments from Aurora by month in 1863
1/26/64 SD politics, Del Monte
1/30/64 MS drop in Del Monte stock not due to poor ore
2/3/64 VD W.R. Johnson murdered in Aurora
2/4/64 CA Esmeralda Items from Aurora Daily Times of Jan 30- About Bodie and Excelsior Districts, and the Durand Company and their new mill.
2/6/64 VD more on W.R. Johnson murdered in Aurora
2/6/64 MS mines
2/6/64 MS Esmeralda Correspondence- letter from Frank Warddell- mines, mills
2/10/64 SD Daly gang
2/10/64 SB about Daly gang.
2/11/64 EU Report of Mono Cp Sups (Bridgeport)
2/12/64 DE from Sacramento Union on the "Aurora Men of Blood" Daly was worth between $12 & 15k.
2/12/64 VD Daly gang hanged
2/13/64 MS Esmeralda Correspondence dated /23/64 about the "Climate and Mines" by "An Observer"
2/13/64 MS "Mining Gossip" (about Real Del Monte) by Frank Warddell
2/15/64 SB Letter from Aurora Daly gang from letter by William B. Lake
2/15/64 VD Daly gang
2/15/64 CA Letter from Aurora by OBSERVER dated 2/9/64- Daly gang, Del Monte speculation
2/15/64 SD Daly gang
2/16/64 VD Gov Nye returns from Aurora after hanging
2/20/64 CA Real Del Monte stockholders Mtg (similar to 2/20/64 MS)
2/20/64 MS Real Del Monte stockholders Mtg
2/24/64 DE from ES of 17th Feb- lengthy article about "Reign of Roughs," murders.
2/25/64 EU John Daly's Ghost
2/27/64 DE Wide West mine litigation between Garrison and Tucker
3/1/64 SD Del Monte
3/1/64 DE Tucker arrested on criminal charges. Wide West mine and Gamble mentioned,
3/4/64 DE Real Del Monte steam engine breaks- is it a humbug?
3/5/64 MS lengthy article about Pocket/Chamber Mines by J E Clayton, and Wide West mine Co financial summary.
3/5/64 MS "Romance of the Wide West" mine

221

An 1864 Directory and Guide to Nevada's Aurora

3/8/64 CA Real Del Monte's poor management
3/9/64 SD Real Del Monte
3/10/64 SD court case, bullion shipped, mills
3/11/64 CA Letter from Esmeralda Nev Territory from MOUNTAINEER dated 3/22/64- Esmeralda stocks, about failure Real del Monte.
3/12/64 MS report on Real del Monte stockholders mtg in San Francisco. Good financial breakdown
3/13/64 MS "The Del Monte Again" by A STOCKHOLDER
3/25/64 DE "End of Tucker-Wide West case" mentions Alex Gamble.
3/25/64 MS about Wide West mine and Garrison and Tucker litigation.
3/26/64 MS about Wide West mine and the end of the Garrison and Tucker litigation.
3/28/64 CA Esmeralda Stocks, mines by MOUNTAINEER
3/31/64 EU Report of the Grand Jury about courthouse, bullion shipped, lynching.
4/2/64 NT from ES of Feb 17- "Lynch Law" in Aurora, Daly gang history
4/13/64 CA Letter dated 4/6/64 from J.P.R. about Del Monte, Wide West mine, Bodie.
4/13/64 DE from Aurora Times of April 6th- about stamp mills and bullion production
4/18/64 EU Exchange dining room
4/22/64 EU Bullion rings, stocks, Bodie diggings
4/22/64 SD Bodie
4/26/64 DE from the AT of 4/21- "Ups and Downs of the Real Del Monte"
5/5/64 EU Union Foundry
5/7/64 EU new armory at Aurora.
5/13/64 stocks are down
5/26/64 Wide West mine
5/27/64 DE Long article Injunction against Real del Monte, mentions Alex Gamble.
5/28/64 MS "Esmeralda" about mines.
6/11/64 CA "Our Letter from the Esmeralda Mines" by "Lily Dale" dated June 1, population 2080, describes town- two military companies, Fire Dept, Masonic and Odd Fellows, 13-piece brass band, two churches, one public school. Describes election, mines, Bullion in May shipped was $118,000.
6/11/64 SD Aurora troublemakers jailed.
6/13/64 SD mines
6/13/64 DE from AT- stock bubble has exploded, "on the 31st of May there was assayed at one office $130,539 of bullion."
7/11/64 SD 4th July celebration described
7/12/64 DE mentions/describes "disaster" at Wide West mine and its effect on business
7/15/64 ST "About the Walker Country" by DOGBERRY. Humorous/sarcastic article about Bridgeport area and Aurora.
7/17/64 SD mines
7/20/64 DE letter from "AURORA" dated 7/12: "Mining Prospects at Esmeralda" are good.
7/23/64 DE mentions Atkins vs. Gamble lawsuit
7/28/64 SD politics
8/1/64 ST (Daily Independent) Description of "Aurora and its Surrounding Hills" by DOGBERRY. About Aurora's mines and mills.
8/9/64 EU Wide West mine decline described in detail.
8/10/64 EU response to 8/9/64 EU article on Wide West mine
8/11/64 EU more discussion on Wide West mine
8/15/64 EU Bridgeport described.
8/24/64 EU Young America mine back to work causes celebration.
8/27/64 EU Mr. Dudlestons School.
9/5/64 EU J Ross Browne lecture, dancing at Armory hall
9/22/64 SD Durand mill burns

Aurora Newspaper List 1860-1864

9/28/64 EU Wheaton homicide in front of Wide West mine saloon
10/4/64 EU "Benefit to the Wizard," misc
10/5/64 CA homicides in Aurora
10/21/64 EU Detailed account of "Great Union Demonstration" and parade. Also Owens road will soon be completed.
10/22/64 EU completion of Sonora and Mono Road.
10/24/64 EU Union Mtg at Preble & Devoe's hall, Cardinell's Dancing Academy, Baptist church singing.
11/3/64 SD miners going to Montgomery dist
11/5/64 EU Union Rally at Cardinell's Hall.
11/30/64 MS about failure if mines by J. B. Saxton including Wide West mine- "Great swindle or great fizzle?"
12/7/64 EU I mines, dull times, Cardinells Dancing school.
12/12/64 EU Carder shooting, ice skating across from Fogus mill
12/19/64 DE Carson City Post says: about survey line.
12/28/64 EU Festival at Wingate's hall, Cardinell's Ball.

NEWSPAPER KEY

Aurora
    AT *Aurora Daily Times* (published 5/63-4/64, and 7/64-11/64); *Aurora Weekly Times* (published 4/63-5/63, and 4/64-7/64)
    ES *Esmeralda Star*- weekly or semiweekly 5/17/62-3/64
    EU *Esmeralda Daily Union*- 3/21/64-fall 64.

Bishop
    IR *Inyo Register*

Carson City
    NA *Nevada Appeal*
    SA *Silver Age*

Grass Valley
    GV *National*

Los Angeles
    LA *Star*

Mariposa
    MF *Free Press*
    MG *Gazette*

Marysville
    MA *Daily Appeal*

Nevada City
    NC *Transcript*

223

An 1864 Directory and Guide to Nevada's Aurora

New York
    NT *New York Times*

Placerville
    PR *Republican*
    MD *Mountain Democrat*

Sacramento
    SB *Daily Bee*
    SD *Daily Union*

San Francisco
    CA *Daily Alta California or Alta California*
    DE *Daily Evening Bulletin*
    HM *Herald and Mirror, or Daily Herald and Mirror*
    MC *Daily Morning Call*
    MS *Mining and Scientific Press*

Sonora
    AF *American Flag*
    TC *Tuolumne Courier*
    UD *Union Democrat*
    CC *Columbia Courier*

Stockton
    ST *Weekly (or Daily) Independent*

Visalia
    WD *Weekly Delta*

Virginia City and Gold Hill
    GH *Gold Hill News*
    TE *Territorial Enterprise*
    EB *Evening Bulletin*
    VD *Virginia Daily Union*

DIRECTORY INDEX

Armories, 14
Assay Offices, 20
Attorneys and Brokers, 20
Bakeries, 23
Bankers, 23
Barber Shops, 23
Baths, 23
Blacksmith Shops, 24
Boardinghouses, 75
Breweries, 26
Brickyards, 27
Brothels, 28
Builders, 31
Camp Nobel, 29
Carpenters, 31
Cemetery, 32
Chinese, 34
Churches, 35
Courthouse, 38
Dance Halls, 45
Dentist, 47
Drug Store, 48
Esmeralda Camp, 48

Esmeralda Mining Dist., 49
Fire Companies, 51
Flag Staff, 52
Fraternal Organizations, 54
Fuel Wood Companies, 55
Gas Companies, 139
Government Officials, 57
Hotels, 75
Jail, 77
Laundries, 78
Lumber Yards, 78
Meat Markets, 80
Militia Companies, 15
Mines, 81
Mining Companies, 81
Newspapers, 85
Paiute Indians, 86
Parks and Recreation, 90
Photographer, 92
Physicians, 94
Post Office, 95
Race Track, 98
Residences, 99

An 1864 Directory and Guide to Nevada's Aurora

Restaurants, 103
Roads, 105
Saloons & Liquor Stores, 111
Schools, 116
Sewer System, 119
Shoe Shops, 119
Slaughterhouses, 120
Societies, 120
Soda Factory, 122
Stables, 122
Stage Lines, 123
Stage Stops, 124
Stamp Mills, 126
Stores, 131
Surveyors, 137
Telegraph Office, 138
Undertakers, 139
Water Companies, 139
Wide West Mine, 142
Wingate Hall, 151

About the Author:

Clifford Alpheus Shaw is a forester who retired from the U. S. Forest Service at the Bridgeport Ranger District, Humboldt-Toiyabe National Forest. He has served as an archaeological volunteer for the Forest Service at Bridgeport for seven summers. He now lives in Georgia.

3094289

Made in the USA